Standing For Something More

The Excommunication of Lyndon Lamborn

LYNDON LAMBORN

authorHOUSE®

AuthorHouse™
1663 Liberty Drive, Suite 200
Bloomington, IN 47403
www.authorhouse.com
Phone: 1-800-839-8640

First published by AuthorHouse   3/18/2009

ISBN: 978-1-4389-4743-3 (sc)
ISBN: 978-1-4389-4744-0 (hc)

Printed in the United States of America
Bloomington, Indiana

This book is printed on acid-free paper.

To Loraine

FOREWORD

I never had any intention to write a book about my exit from Mormonism until early 2008 when several close friends and family members urged me on. Their reasoning was difficult to refute: If nothing else, think of the keepsake you will leave your descendants, they said. Think of the people who might benefit from hearing your story and some of the lessons you have learned. So, I relented and accepted the challenge.

Just so things are crystal clear for the reader; I would like to dispel some potential misconceptions about this book. First of all, I have no ill feelings toward any church member, I have not been offended and left the church due to hurt feelings. There is only one valid reason to renounce a religion: one becomes convinced it is not true. No other reason is valid or rational. If I thought there was a reasonable chance that the beliefs and teaching of the Church of Jesus Christ of Latter-Day Saints (LDS church) were true, I would be a member in good standing today. Nothing could keep me away. Often my writing is blunt and to the point. This should not be interpreted as 'grinding an axe,' or venting of malice, it is just my writing style.

I have had many close friends who are still members come to the conclusion that I believe that Mormonism is evil by design. I do not. The good accomplished by religious organizations is laudable, but it does not make them true. Many freely associate good with truth, but the two are mutually independent. Indeed, truth has no need for inspiration, and inspiration does not necessarily lead to truth. The opinion of Ed Bliss matches my own. He said[1] (bold portions added):

> Whenever I am asked my opinion about Mormonism I am reminded of the response of Circuit Judge N.S. Sweat, Jr., of Corinth, Mississippi, when during a prohibition campaign he was asked where he stood on the whiskey question. He said:

[1] *The New Expositor*, No 6, July 2008

If when you say whiskey you mean the devil's brew, the poison scourge, the bloody monster that defiles innocence, dethrones reason, destroys the home, creates misery and poverty, yea, literally takes the bread from the mouths of little children, if you mean the evil drink that topples the Christian man and woman from the pinnacle of righteous, gracious living into the bottomless pit of degradation and despair, and shame and helplessness, and hopelessness, then certainly I am against it.

But if when you say whiskey you mean the oil of conversation, the philosophic wine, the ale that puts a song in their hearts and laughter on their lips, and the warm glow of contentment in their eyes; if you mean Christmas cheer; if you mean the stimulating drink that puts the spring into the old gentleman's step on a frosty, crispy morning; if you mean the drink that enables a man to magnify his joy, and his happiness, and to forget, if only for a little while, life's great tragedies, and heartaches, and sorrows; if you mean that drink, the sale of which pours into our treasuries untold millions of dollars, which are used to provide tender care for our little crippled children, our blind, our deaf, our dumb, our pitiful aged and infirm, to build highways and hospitals and schools, then certainly I am for it. This is my stand. I will not retreat from it. I will not compromise."

That's sort of how I feel about Mormonism. If when you say Mormonism you mean the religion that asks its members to be honest, true, chaste, benevolent, and to do good to all men; the church that frowns on the use of tobacco, and teaches boys to be trustworthy, loyal, helpful, friendly, courteous, kind, obedient, cheerful, thrifty, brave, clean, and reverent; if you mean the organization that maintains the world's most famous choir, and teaches that man is that he might have joy; if you mean the religion that tells people to embrace everything that is virtuous, lovely, or of good report or praiseworthy, and claims the privilege of worshiping God according to the dictates of their own conscience, allowing all men the same privilege, let them worship how, where, or what they may, then certainly I am for it.

But if when you say Mormonism you mean the church that teaches that a dark skin is a sign of God's displeasure **and is a measure of personal righteousness**; if you mean the church that bans the reading of any religious material not approved by church leaders **and denies public access to its archives**; if you mean the church that has an estimated net worth of 50 billion dollars, but keeps its finances secret from its members and from the public; if you mean the idea that it is a sin to drink a cup of tea; if you mean the church that believes polygamy was once God's plan, but is now a sin, but is God's plan for the hereafter; if you mean the belief that an Egyptian funeral document was written by Abraham although he had been dead for 2,000 years when it was written... if you mean the church that teaches its members to obey without question everything their leaders ask..., **encourages young and old to stand and profess publicly to know the unknowable, sends uninformed young men and women into the world to proselyte; has leaders who censure truth-telling historians,** then certainly I am against it. This is my stand. I will not retreat from it. I will not compromise.

I have had many people tell me "but look at all the GOOD the church does!" For me, it is NOT about judging if religion is good or bad or even more good than bad; it is about the tactics of premeditated misrepresentation of events in order to persuade people to become or stay Mormons. It is about the attempts of the whiskey makers to mislead the buyers to the point of insinuating or outright propagandizing that other whiskeys are harmful, while our special whiskey will vastly improve your life, and God told us to tell you that.

Like Watergate, the most damning part of this story is the cover-up. It is about exposing the cover-up, the small wording changes to <u>The Book of Mormon</u>, selective storytelling, and all the continuing contrivances that can mislead good and honest people and control their lives. It is about closing church archives, the expulsion and censoring (and attempted censoring) of the truth-tellers[2], something I experienced first hand. For the objective researcher, it is the process of exposing the hidden facts that creates such an intense mistrust of the corporate church. It is a measure

---

[2] Grant Palmer, J. Leonard Arrington, Sterling McMurrin, John Heinerman, and the 'September Six' are among these truth-tellers.

of LDS corporate success that virtually all local leaders I have known have no idea of any of the major deceptions that permeate the church.

I will now paraphrase a metaphor used by others that matches my feelings. Mormonism was like a raft to me that was useful to get across the river, but now my path goes through the forest, and the raft is no longer needed or practical, so it is abandoned. There may be some who read this book, be them Mormon, Christian, or affiliates of other faiths who have crossed the river and are ready to step off the raft. I know it is frightening, but believe me, the ground is firm and while the journey is not easy, the rewards are great. This book is dedicated to you. Breaking out of mind-controlling and oppressive belief systems is something that many have experienced and that many more will experience in our generation, as the information age promotes skepticism of long-revered myths.

While this book documents the journey of one soul, it is intended to shine a light upon the scepter and machinations of religious fervor for all to see. This book is about giving people the opportunity to make informed and unencumbered choices and help them break out of manipulative circumstances, whether they be religious, societal, personal/familial, or business related. My hope is that this book and my life work would inspire responsibility, humanity, cooperation, ownership, scholarship, and leave the world a better place, where it is easier for humans to embrace reason and spurn delusion.

- Lyndon Lamborn December 2008

PREFACE

There are many facts and events that contradict the core tenets of organized religions. A few of these facts are mentioned in context of effective storytelling. However, the purpose of this book is not about documenting the historical facts and events. There are many excellent books available to the interested reader which establish pertinent historical events and scientific data. A boatload of books with copious references and iron-clad evidence is no match for a human emotional battleship. This book examines the battleship rather than adding another text of historical facts to the boat. The "Search for Truth" discussion, which summarizes many of the key historical and doctrinal issues at the top level, is attached as Appendix E. It provides a recommended reading list for those interested. A very fair treatise of all the major issues from both points of view is also available at www.Mormonthink.com and is highly recommended for the objective researcher.

The reader will notice that the story is told in first person, and the analysis and discussion of human nature and psychology is often told in the third person. This is by intent. The story telling is in my own words and is most effectively told in the first person. The analysis and discussion chapters, which alternate with the storytelling, are usually best communicated using a third person narrative. The alternating tense is also intended to be an aid for the reader to readily differentiate the storytelling from the analysis.

The beliefs of the LDS church are described in some detail in the first few chapters. It is important to note that these are the beliefs and doctrines of the church, not the beliefs of the author.

ACKNOWLEDGEMENT

I would like to thank my brother Dr. Vernon Lamborn for his invaluable contributions and suggestions. Likewise, I would like to thank my good friend Wayne Iverson for consulting with me on this book, and his boundless courage as he faces his own mortality. I would also like to thank many friends who also contributed to the editing of this book, too numerous to list. I would also like to thank Bob McCue in particular for his advice in helping me prepare for my lectures at the local evangelical congregation and his spot-on written musings which have helped me a great deal. I have quoted Bob several times, and assert that plagiarism is the greatest compliment. I also very much enjoyed the discussions I have had with Steven Hassan regarding cult mind control, which have also given me some valuable insights. I also appreciated the opportunity to address a local Evangelical congregation, and having the lectures posted on YouTube, which was made possible by my friend and co-worker Richard Weisenburger. A very special thanks to my friend Lawn Griffiths, formerly the spiritual living editor for the East Valley Tribune, not only for agreeing to tell my story, but also for his wisdom and tireless championing of humanity in adverse circumstances.

TABLE OF CONTENTS

CHAPTER 1
HOW DID I GET HERE?

In comes ideology and out goes common sense. This is my experience of life. - Doris Lessing

Philosophy is questions that may never be answered. Religion is answers that may never be questioned. - Anon

July 23 2007   Inca Trail, Peru

I was with my brother Lee and some friends hiking the Inca Trail to Machu Picchu. It was the first day of the trek, and we had stopped for lunch. Our guide, being very cordial, was asking the group, whom were all US citizens, about our home states. Lee said he lived in Salt Lake City, Utah. The next question was not a big surprise. Are you a Mormon? Lee responded in the affirmative, and since our guide knew we were brothers, he then turned to me and asked the same question. As I sat there in that tent in Peru, the experiences of the last two years of my life and my startling discoveries flashed through my mind. I looked around at the faces, the question hanging in the air; I realized that no matter where I went on the face of the earth the question would continue to come up. Are you a Mormon? There is no way to avoid it. To make matters worse, I had served as a membership clerk for the church. There was no middle ground on whether one was a member or a non-member in my mind, it was either 'yes' or a 'no'. I knew at that moment that I never wanted to answer that question in the affirmative ever again in my life. It was a defining moment. The 'yes' answer, for me, brought with it too much wasted emotion, too much frustration, too much revulsion, too much embarrassment, and too many worn-out follow-up questions that become exhausting to answer (How many wives do you have? You have never tasted beer or smoked a cigarette?). What I needed was a clean break with no residual ties to the Church of Jesus Christ of Latter-Day Saints (LDS Church).

How did I get here? What events transpired to land me in this predicament? Did I ask for this?

Leaving the church was not going to be easy. If she were to find out, my mother would be devastated. My wife and son were sure to endure pain as a result of my departure. Since I was a prominent and outspoken member of the congregation, my departure from the LDS church might include a 'disciplinary council'. A disciplinary council is a panel of fifteen men, most of whom I know personally, given the responsibility of judging what, if any, action should be taken to protect the church and help me see 'the error of my ways'. This process, if required, was going to be torture.

As with any story, the place to begin is at the beginning. Before I get into my discovery phase and exodus from Mormonism, it is worthwhile to review my mental chemistry and the basics of Mormonism and what it was like for me, born into a Mormon family in an island of Mormon culture. It is only by understanding the indoctrination of my youth that the reader will be in a position to grasp all the dimensions of the exit journey.

I was the fifth child of seven, and the fourth of six boys. My older brothers were evidently young scientists at heart, because they used me for experiments. They fed me crickets and on one occasion I consumed pieces of a garden snake they had captured. When I got old enough to be more selective in my dietary choices, the sibling experiments switched to the behavioral extreme, testing the limits of my emotional rage and despair under psychological duress. My brothers were expert teasers. Having endured the years of mockery, I became an expert in the art of psychological torture myself and freely experimented on my two younger brothers.

At age five I had a part in a church program. Even though I could not read, I insisted that my lines be written on a card, since the big kids had cue cards for their parts and I wanted to be like them. When it came time for me to perform, I recited my lines, word perfect, holding the card in front of me for reference. I was informed later that I had been holding the card upside down.

The neighbor around the corner had a couple of large chestnut trees. I discovered right away that chestnuts are just right for throwing, and it wasn't long before passing cars became targets of opportunity. A moving target is much more fun than a stationary object, because it involved leading the target and precise timing – it required analysis. [It is perhaps not surprising that later in life I found myself employed in missile and ordnance delivery systems.] One particular afternoon I managed to sail a chestnut through the open side window of a passing car and strike the driver. I was elated until he slammed on the brakes, jumped out of his car, and gave pursuit. He was not a happy camper. I ran into the house and ducked behind the couch in the living room. My older brother, who looked just like me, was sitting on the couch reading the paper. To this day, he swears that I framed him for the caper. I figure it was just payback for all those years of teasing, not to mention the crickets.

We didn't have much money, and my parents believed in keeping a huge garden and high-maintenance yard, which we cared for during the growing season. Winter was a blessing because it was a reprieve from the mowing, irrigating, planting, raking, weeding, trimming, and harvesting. As soon as I turned 16, I found a job outside the home to curtail the number of hours I was expected to toil in the yard and garden. I delighted in calculating my disposable income and projecting my buying power while making $2.10 per hour.

My dad grew up on a farm, has a BS in chemistry and a PHD in soil science. A distant cousin taught upper division mathematics at Utah State University, and my uncle Dave taught mathematics at Weber State. On a few occasions, I asked Dave about his job and we discussed some practical applications of probability theory. Practical applications of mathematics fascinated me. Three of my brothers have degrees in engineering like me; another has degrees in biology and dentistry, and one in business marketing.

My evolutionary computer chip evidently came equipped with strong math and analysis circuits, and a need to understand the workings of the power source under the hood rather than just how to drive the car. In many ways this has been an asset to me and surely arranged my eventual employment as a full-time aerospace engineer. My family will tell you, however, that in other ways it can make me a royal pain in the ass. On more than one occasion, I got in over my head due to my lack of fear of mechanical things and ruined implements and appliances. And then there is the computation of expenses and establishing cause and effect that drives the family bonkers. "For every degree cooler we maintain the thermostat this summer; it will cost an additional $50 per month." Many people think that engineers are cheapskates, but I think that is a bad rap. I maintain that engineers are just hard-wired for optimal resource management, which is perceived by others as pathological frugality. That is my story and I am sticking to it.

I would like to point out that there is no doubt in my mind that many of the women in the family are driving around more intellectual horsepower than me. The Mormon culture, which emphasizes that "the woman's place is in the home", has skewed academic accomplishments in a gender biased way.

In the late 1980s I was selected to be part of an aircraft accident investigation team, and received three weeks of intense subject training. The skilled accident scene examiner will never jump to a conclusion prematurely, and this ability has more to do with maturity, patience, and restraint than technical savvy. This training and practical on-the-job application of the concept reshaped my problem solving mentality. Once a problem is on the table, the gathering of evidence and data only stops when the preponderance of the data has been reviewed and a highly probable explanation is found that is consistent with all the evidence. This problem solving approach is in sharp contrast to what I have observed in deeply believing Mormons when they face tough issues. I will expand more on this later in the book, but I have seen a tendency to dismiss the issue(s) with little or no careful analysis, to jump to conclusions, and to focus on issues singly with no consideration of big picture patterns and cumulative probability effects.

In high school I ran the two mile event in track and field. Later in life, I resumed my distance running and have competed in marathons. I have always been a distance runner, not a sprinter. To some degree, this is an indicator of a character trait. The long hours of homework in engineering school came relatively easy to me. During my research into the LDS church, I felt compelled to develop my own summary of key findings and even write detailed book reports. In addition, mathematical analysis and the scientific method have always been integral parts of my worldview. In addition to my engineering profession, I have become a mathematics professor at the local community college, a very rewarding hobby.

One day I was talking to my father, who is now deceased, about our family characteristics. He was struck by the propensity of his children to take on large projects. It is telling that our family reunions are often accompanied by a family work project. Happiness for me is working on a project. In my case I salvaged a 1968 Dodge Charger from a Phoenix junkyard in 1990, did virtually all the restoration work; and now I drive it to work once or twice a week. I also successfully convinced my family it was wise to purchase a ~6000 square foot rundown home with no heating or air conditioning and make it livable. Looking forward to retirement, I already have projects planned that will easily consume twenty years. Even the writing of this book was not begun without careful analysis, data gathering, calculation of time available and time required, planned consumer trials, etc.

It has been said that many people spend more time planning a two-week vacation than they spend planning the rest of their lives. This is not the case with me. I go on vacation to STOP analyzing. Analysis of the housing market in the Los Angeles region in 1984 resulted in our move to Arizona in 1985; and purchase of a five-acre piece of prime Arizona real estate (with the large rundown home) in 1991. Analysis and research have driven all the major decisions of my life. I have found that the quality of my life decisions is proportional to the time invested doing analysis and research. "Connecting the dots" is not a universally acknowledged skill but it may be my strongest genetic aptitude. In retrospect, it now seems obvious that I would end up at odds with the LDS church; sooner or later I would realize that the causality and logic so plainly evident in nature and society was noticeably absent in my religious faith. Sooner or later, the crash investigating Rottweiler would get his teeth into the origins of the church and not let go until everything was thoroughly hashed out. The beauty of the doctrines, which inspire awe in many, amount to nothing to me if they are accompanied with illogical concepts and contradictory language. Excessive and undeserved flattery and depiction of good fortune is fundamentally illogical to me and was a huge red flag. I am going to blame my eventual showdown with the church as simply a genetic inevitability.

July 23 2007 Inca Trail, Peru

So there I was, looking at the faces in the tent, they were waiting for my answer to that dreaded question; was I a Mormon? "Yes", I said, "I am too." I hoped that this would be the last time I would ever have to answer the question that I was a Mormon in the affirmative. I had no idea of the wild ride the next few months would bring.

CHAPTER 2
THE RESTORED GOSPEL

He who knows only his own faith knows no faith. - Anon

Faith does not give you the answers, it just stops you asking the questions. - Frater Ravus

What follows is a description of Mormon beliefs, as I understood them while growing up. These descriptions should not be confused with my current beliefs. The basic doctrines of Mormonism are as simple as they are beautiful. A myth only need be appealing to become popular. I was taught that after Christ was crucified and the twelve apostles killed, the true church and authority of God was not on the earth and nobody had the authority to baptize, heal the sick, or perform the ordinances of salvation. The earth remained in this state through the dark ages, until 1820 when Joseph Smith Jr. was called by God to restore the true church upon the earth. I found out that Catholicism and Protestantism were simply inventions of men trying to duplicate the true church, and contained many truths, but lacked the true authority of God[3].

I was told that when Smith was fourteen years old, he went into a grove of trees in New York and asked God in prayer which church was true and which one to join. God the father and Jesus Christ appeared to Smith and told him that the true church was not found on the earth, but that if he remained faithful and worthy, he would become an instrument in Gods hand to restore the true church in its fullness, with a prophet and twelve apostles and the full authority to act in Gods name. I was taught that the restoration of all things good and holy took place between the spring of

---

[3] Joseph Smith, History; 1:19, *The Pearl of Great Price* (Mormon canon)

1820 and April 6, 1830 when the church was officially created. Along with the authority and organization of the ancient church, the restoration was accompanied by new volumes of scripture, The Book of Mormon, the Book of Abraham, the Book of Moses, the Doctrine and Covenants, all of which served as a witness of the divinity of the prophet Joseph Smith Jr. and also another witness of Jesus Christ. The Book of Mormon was accompanied with a special promise that those who read the book and pray would receive a spiritual witness from the Holy Ghost of its truthfulness[4].

Since Smith, there have been fifteen prophets, and members are taught that the true church will never be taken from the earth again. Currently, the prophet is Thomas S. Monson. LDS faithful believe he is literally a modern day prophet who receives revelation from God. Latter-Day Saints (LDS) believe they may become Gods and Goddesses in the highest degree of heaven, the celestial kingdom, through baptism, temple marriage, and keeping covenants and commandments.

The best way to describe Mormonism to the mainstream Christian is that it is basic Christianity on steroids. Mormonism takes everything one step beyond mainstream Christian normalcy. Virtually every concept and character is a little bit more personal, more tangible, more fantastic, or is amplified in some way, which is not necessarily a bad thing, it is just different.

A good example is the story of Noah and the ark. The flood episode, for Mormons, goes beyond just Noah gathering the animals two by two and God eradicating the wicked earth populace with water. We find out, through modern revelation, that the earth had need of baptism, just like us, because the earth has a spirit[5]. And furthermore, since Mormons believe that baptism is only valid if it is by immersion, then the entire earth was covered by water. The ramifications of planets having spirits are far-reaching, but not much is taught about that doctrine.

A similar narrative could be offered for Adam and Eve, Moses, Isaiah, and so on. Even The Book of Mormon itself is like the Bible with exclamation points. The characters are larger than life, the battles are grander, the intrigue more intriguing, the miracles more miraculous, and the visitation of Jesus more heart-warming and triumphant.

---

[4] Joseph Smith, *The Book of Mormon*, Moroni 10:3-5 (Mormon canon)
[5] The Church of Jesus Christ of Latter-Day Saints, *Ensign*, Jan 1998, p35

The cornerstone of Mormon doctrine is continuous revelation, the premise that God has always spoken to mankind through prophets, beginning with Adam. Revelation continued throughout Old Testament times, with each major prophet character heading up a 'dispensation' or mission from God. Adam, Noah, Enoch, Moses, Isaiah, etc. each had a dispensation, and given unique 'keys' which are special packets of authority. Christ's visit was a special dispensation, which was followed by the great apostasy, when the authority of God was taken from the earth for about 1700 years until Joseph Smith came onto the scene. Joseph Smith ushered in the last dispensation, which is also called the dispensation of the fullness of times, which required each of the previous head prophets (Adam, Noah, Enoch, etc) to visit Smith and give him all the keys. Today, Prophet Thomas Monson and the twelve apostles hold all the keys. So this dispensation is like the dispensations of old, except more important, this is the last and final dispensation before Christ returns to initiate his millennial reign.

Joseph Smith is like a prophet in the Old Testament, but he was a prophet the likes of which the world had never before seen. Instead of a burning bush, he received a visitation of the Father and the Son. Instead of the typical 50 or 100 pages of scripture, he gave us about 800 pages[6]. He did not limit his work to the living, but taught that we should be engaged in redeeming the dead as well. Smith revealed that the gospel is taught to the dead in the hereafter, but the ordinances of salvation can only take place here on earth. Therefore, the ordinances of salvation (baptism, marriage, etc.) must be performed here on earth, by proxy, for every human being who has ever lived on the earth in the event that the person accepts the gospel in the afterlife. These ordinances are conducted in dedicated shrines throughout the world called temples. The information about the dead is gleaned from genealogical research, and as a result, the LDS church has built the world's largest genealogical database[7]. In order to attend the temple and perform these ordinances for oneself and also for the dead by proxy, one has to be found worthy through what is called a temple recommend interview.

---

[6] *The Book of Mormon*; 531 pages, *Doctrine and Covenants*, Sections 1 thru 137; 286 pages, *Pearl of Great Price*; 61 pages. (All part of the Mormon canon)
[7] Currently found at www.familysearch.org

Not only is everything in Mormonism more grandiose, more personal, more recent, and more urgent, more effort is required of a Mormon than a mainstream Christian to obtain the highest reward in heaven. The member has to be extremely valiant and persevere in order to swim upstream through the labyrinth of life, accomplishing amazing feats of consistent meeting and temple attendance, missionary work, scripture study, church service, family and personal prayer, genealogical work, food storage, community service, etc.

The faith requirement in Mormonism is wholesale. Scholars speak of two different ways of thinking and learning; mythos and logos[8]. Myth was not concerned with practical matters, only the underlying meaning is important. Logos is the rational, pragmatic, and scientific thought processes that obtain practical results. Most religious traditions allow for myth in scriptural storytelling, such as the rich symbolism of the great cleansing flood and the parting of the Red Sea to allow passage of the Children of Israel. In Mormonism, there is no gap between mythos and logos. The great flood is taught as a real and literal event, as is the parting of the Red Sea, the Jonah and the whale odyssey, days of darkness at the death of Christ, etc. While literalism works for many religious believers, it eventually pushed me away when I was unable to reconcile the wholesale literalism with reality.

In stark contrast to mainstream Christianity, Mormons believe that the family is an eternal unit, that couples can only attain the highest reward together as a husband-wife team. Interestingly, the eternal family doctrine was not taught by any of the Biblical prophets or Jesus, and it not even mentioned in The Book of Mormon. According to biblical accounts Jesus taught the opposite.[9] Yet in the Mormon church today, young and old alike are taught that families are forever in both word and song. On the surface, this notion seems innocuous and even uplifting. After all, we all want to be with our loved ones, our families. The power of this doctrine as a control mechanism and a potential mortal enemy to family relations will be addressed in later chapters.

---

[8] Karen Armstrong, *The Battle for God*, pg xvi,xvii
[9] Matthew 22:23-30, Luke 20:27-35

CHAPTER 3
PURITY AND THE PERFECT TRIBE

Each ethnocentric group stresses its uniqueness and its differences in order to maintain its vitality and identity. Each builds walls against outsiders and foreigners. Ethnocentrism creates iron curtains, Zion curtains, and all kinds of barriers to keep out those who are different. Perhaps the most difficult challenge a person can ever have in this life is to transcend the limitations, narrowness, and ethnocentrism of his own cultural heritage in pursuit of truth. – Arza Evans

When one person suffers from a delusion, it is called insanity. When many people suffer from a delusion it is called religion. - Robert Pirsig

Church members are taught that their spirit, or intelligence, has always existed and has no beginning or end. This earth life is just one step in our progression. Mormons refer to the pre-earth life as the pre-existence, and are told that we dwelt with God there before coming to Earth. Jesus and Satan were there and there was a battle between them. Two thirds of the spirits agreed to follow the plan Jesus presented, and the remaining one third followed Satan and became angels of darkness.

Therefore, in Mormonism, it is not just God on the good side and Satan on the bad side vying for control of souls. Satan and all those spirits that followed Satan are now demons hiding behind every dark corner, in our closets and in our cellars. Their mission is to plot and plan ways to overpower humans and possess their bodies. It is a demon-haunted world, and Mormons have much to fear from Satan and his legions of dark angels. It is only through obedience, purity, and vigilance that church members are kept safe from the evil that surrounds them.

Affiliates are taught that science and book learning are fallible and should not be trusted implicitly. Revelation from modern day prophets, on the other hand, can always be trusted. The prophet of the Lord will never lead the LDS people astray. Rather than plunge the church into error, God would take the life of the prophet and a new one would step up to do exactly God's will, which is a fool-proof system[10]. Ultimately, the responsibility for discerning truth from error resides with the individual, because each member of the church is given the Holy Ghost when they are baptized which is age eight for members born into the church. The Holy Ghost serves as a moral compass, pointing the way to truth and purity. The compass, the members are told, only works when they are faithful and diligent.

Members find out when they are young that they are very special people, according to the teachings of the church. Their spirits were held in re-serve, because of extreme valiance in the pre-mortal life, to come to the earth at this special time, to accept the one and only true church. The primary reason for their existence is to be an instrument in God's hand to share the light and truth of the restored gospel to the inhabitants of the earth and build the kingdom of God. For parents, the glory of their life work is to teach their children the gospel, how to be obedient, and prepare the young men to be missionaries for the Lord. Parents teach their daughters that they should encourage the young men to serve mis-sions and then become mothers in Zion, destined to raise up another generation of valiant workers for the Lord and His kingdom. The scrip-tures admonish parents to diligently teach their children the gospel, how to pray, and ensure they are baptized[11].

Affiliates are taught from passages in <u>The Book of Mormon</u> that Ameri-ca is the Promised Land, the land of milk and honey and prosperity. So long as the people living on this continent do not, as a whole, become an

---

[10] Taught by prophet Wilford Woodruff, see Chapter 8 for complete quotation and reference

[11] *Doctrine and Covenants* 93:40,50; 68:25,28

[12] *The Book of Mormon*, 1 Nephi 2:20

evil people, they will flourish[12]. Being born on this continent is a very special gift and privilege that is accompanied with promises from God. Individual righteousness will always bring success and prosperity.

As members attend meetings and conferences, they learn that the technological advances that have been changing the world, are, in fact, part of God's plan to facilitate the gospel to be preached to the earth. Television, radio, air travel, immunization from disease, everything that science has given us, is really part of Gods plan to ensure that all of God's children have a chance to accept the only true church, the LDS church.

Like most religious institutions, the most intense indoctrination takes place during the teen years. In Mormonism, the three-hour weekly meetings on Sunday are augmented with a weeknight activity when the person reaches age twelve. Also at age twelve boys and girls may attend camp each summer. Things shift into high gear in the ninth grade when the young people begin daily seminary instruction during school hours, which continues through the twelfth grade. In addition, once every three years, the young people ages fourteen to eighteen are invited to a special reenactment of the pioneer handcart trek, where they are exposed to extreme physical and emotional hardship in combination with intense indoctrination.

Authority begins to play a vital role for the member at age eight when he/she is baptized and confirmed a member of the church, which includes the right to the Holy Ghost (Spirit) as a constant companion. The young men are given Priesthood authority in stages beginning at age 12, with added responsibilities at ages fourteen and sixteen. Age eighteen is a special milestone, young men can be given the 'higher' Priesthood and both young men and women are eligible to receive a special blessing called a Patriarchal blessing[13]. Young men can begin attending the temple at age eighteen when preparing for a mission at age nineteen, where they make special covenants and oaths of secrecy in the temple, usually while surrounded by expectant family members, respected church leaders, and friends who have already made the commitments to obey. A 'mission', is

---

[13] See chapter 15 for more discussion of Patriarchal blessings

a period of missionary service, usually geographically remote from the person's home, that can last from eighteen months to three years. The standard mission duration for young men is two years. Young men are asked to serve a mission from age 19-21, young women can also serve, if they choose, after age 21. The LDS church, with its emphasis on family, prohibition of pre-marital sex, etc. tends to motivate young people to marry early, most marry by age 23. The marriage vow is the final major ordinance involving authority, but authority continues to play a major role because the husband has Priesthood authority to perform ordinances for his family, such as baptizing, blessing the ill, and performing other ordinances for his family as required. It is interesting to note that all major commitments are made by about age 23; the importance of which will be discussed later.

Each member strives to obtain what is called a "testimony", which is a special witness or spiritual experiences that make up the core of the religious conviction. A person must have a strong testimony, and answer a question to that effect, to be found worthy of entering the Mormon temples. The most important portion of the indoctrination is how one obtains and retains a testimony. The method taught is the key to unlocking all truth in the universe, and we will refer to as the 'truth test'. The truth test is what turns doubting young people into life-long members, converts non-members to Mormonism, and opens a window to heaven for each member to receive revelation and truth from God. The truth test will be discussed in detail later.

So, what did it feel like to be raised in an LDS home in an LDS community? I will do my best to describe it. I felt very loved, very special, and very privileged. I had wonderful caring parents, wonderful teachers, great boy scout leaders, and great LDS friends. In fact, all my close friends were LDS, there were very few non-LDS in the community. Family life was very busy with seven children, and our parents taught us the value of hard work and education. Young Mormons are taught to live a strict moral code. No drinking, no smoking, no sex or masturbation, no cussing, no violence against others, no suggestive humor, and no immodest clothing. Even steady dating was discouraged. I believe I was among the most obedient of all my peers.

Probably the only real grave sin I committed in my teens was carving the initials of my high school on the front lawn and football field of the neighboring rival high school one late night after dark, using gasoline and rock salt. In fact, I think I was recruited for the crime because I was above suspicion, and it worked. After all, I was a leader in the student seminary organization, nobody ever dreamed that I could possibly be involved in such shenanigans.

Since my sister was about 10 years older than me, I was more or less raised in a fraternity and was clueless about the interests and thinking processes of young women. They nevertheless fascinated me as my hormones kicked in. I was as clumsy on the dating scene as my 6+ foot body was on the basketball floor. I tried making out with girls I was attracted to on the first date, only to have them decline going out with me a second time. Ouch. Then I became gun shy, backed off and waited for the girl to make the first move. I will never forget spending the day at a beach in Santa Cruz on a second date. I walked the girl to her door that evening to say goodnight, was about to turn and walk away, and she said; "I had a really nice time, and IF YOU DON'T KISS ME, I AM ABSOLUTELY GOING TO SCREAM." Since I didn't want the neighbors to call the SWAT team, I obliged.

The demand for purity was strong, and is portrayed as a Mormon legacy. I was taught that Joseph Smith was a pure and innocent boy and his life contribution to mankind was second only to Jesus Christ[14]. At age fourteen, Smith refused alcohol for a painful leg operation. I was also taught that later in life, when a mob tried to force whiskey upon him, I was taught that Smith suffered broken teeth rather than imbibe the vile beverage. (I would find out later that Smith did not drink on that occasion because he feared poison, and freely drank alcoholic beverages up to and including his dying day[15].) Joseph Smith had only one wife, Emma, to whom he gave his full love and devotion. I was taught (erroneously) that although the doctrine of polygamy was revealed to Smith, he resisted the commands of God to take more wives and went to his

---

[14] *Doctrine and Covenants* 135:3
[15] Richard Lyman Bushman, *Joseph Smith, Rough Stone Rolling*, page 549

grave like an unspotted lamb to the slaughterhouse having lived a pure and monogamous life. After his death, with the approval of subsequent prophets, additional women were married, by proxy, to Joseph Smith in the temple.

With all the attention and good will and service being provided to me, I felt glad to respect and honor my parents and teachers by attending church, to take seminary classes, and eventually serve a two-year church mission. It felt like the right thing to do, all of my friends were following the same course. By the time I was nineteen, I had invested a large portion of my life in the interest of the church, had paid ten percent of my income to the church (tithing), and I felt allegiance to 'Team Mormon', just like I felt allegiance to my high school and to the USA, only the church allegiance was stronger, more personal, required a deeper commitment, and was more exclusive. I trusted my parents, my teachers, my family members, and my friends who all seemed to believe with their whole hearts that we were in the one and only true church of God. During my adolescence, I never had any real deep-seated doubts for very long, there were just too many people that surrounded me that I trusted to call their integrity into question. Plus, I had experienced my version of answer to prayer, confirmation from the holy spirit that The Book of Mormon was true, and I was taught that this manifestation was something very special, not to be taken lightly. I was taught that The Book of Mormon was the most correct of any book[16], including the Bible, devoid of error, essentially pure truth.

I was expected to be pure and perfect, because purity and perfection surrounded me. Purity and perfection began with Old Testament prophets and Jesus, continued with Joseph Smith and subsequent prophets, was the legacy of the gospel, and the legacy of my forefathers. Strict obedience was the only way to honor my legacy and avoid overwhelming guilt and shame.

We have all seen the Natural Geographic programs about the Native American tribes and tribes in Africa where when the young men reach a

---

[16] Brigham H. Roberts, *History of the Church*, Vol. 4, page 461

certain age they have to go through some ritualistic event, usually pain-ful, such as scar tattooing all over the body. It is the final 'rite of passage' typical of societies throughout world history that marks the transition from childhood into manhood. Baptism and the first temple visits are classic initiation rites for all members. Missions represent the pinnacle rite of passage event in the Mormon male tribe. After enduring the two year mission, I had arrived. I had my battle scars. The tribal elders were satisfied. I was no longer an adolescent. I was treated as a man upon my return from missionary service. Now I was respected and my opinion carried weight. I was an adult member of the Mormon tribe. I had no idea how the tribe dealt with defectors, but I was going to find out.

CHAPTER 4
CERTAINTY AND THE TRUTH
TEST

The quest for certainty blocks the search for meaning. Uncertainty is the very condition to impel man to unfold his powers. Erich Fromm

When an individual knows he doesn't know, he is wise. Wisdom is the opposite of certainty. The knowledge of our ignorance is wisdom. Dr. Timothy Wilken

Psychologists refer to how humans come to think they 'know' something as epistemology. How can one know the truth? The LDS epistemic method is a process described as follows:

Read and study and contemplate the issue. Approach God in prayer with real intent, having faith, and then what you feel to be true by the influence of the Holy Ghost. If you do this, you will feel either a burning in the bosom or other unique feeling is unequivocal confirmation of the truth, or a 'stupor of thought' or feeling of confusion and you will know that the idea or concept is false[17]. Using this recipe is the method used to determine the truth of all things in Mormonism.

This is the ultimate truth test. According to the teachings of the church, scientists can make mistakes, but the Holy Ghost never makes mistakes. What the world thinks is true is suspect. Only the Holy Ghost and the Lords anointed, when speaking under the influence of the Holy Ghost, are reliable sources of truth.

---

[17] *The Book of Mormon 10:3-5, Doctrine and Covenants 9:7-9*

The truth test is a central doctrine in the theology of Mormonism. Any in-depth discussion with an LDS member will eventually come around to the truth test. It gives members the opportunity to find out the truth of the gospel themselves, and instills in each member a sense of ownership and personal relationship with God. It is akin to a mainstream Christian experiencing a change of heart and feeling of being saved by the grace of Jesus. For those who feel they have experienced the influence of the Holy Ghost, they feel that God has communicated His will directly to them. Some feel a burning in the bosom, a warm and peaceful feeling, a tingling in the spine, or other unique feeling on a regular basis, for some as often as daily.

Not only is the truth test the ultimate method to determine truth and allow personal revelation to flow from God to man, the penalty for denying the Holy Ghost is grave. There is only one sin that merits eternal damnation in outer darkness, and that is denial of the Holy Ghost. One can obtain a measure of forgiveness for murder, but having had that warm feeling and then saying that it was just a warm feeling and not the Holy Ghost is a more grievous sin than murder. For this sin, there is no forgiveness in this life or in the life to come[18].

With the truth test comes certainty. LDS members are more certain of the will of God, the divinity of the prophet Joseph Smith, the truthfulness of The Book of Mormon, etc., than they are that the sun will rise tomorrow.

Finally, only LDS members have the right to the Holy Ghost as a constant companion. This is by virtue of the ordinance of confirmation as a member, accomplished with the restored priesthood. No other religion has this right, or has full access to the truth test. Individuals of other faiths can, from time to time, be influenced by the Holy Ghost, but only under unusual circumstances. The truth test does not work for people of other faiths because they have not received the promise of the Holy Ghost as a constant companion by the authority of God, which was restored through Joseph Smith. The exception is The Book of Mormon promise. Every sincere investigator, if they read and study The Book of

---

[18] Mark 3:28-29, *Doctrine and Covenants* 132:27

Mormon and pray with real intent and faith will receive a spiritual witness that <u>The Book of Mormon</u> is true. This is the primary conversion tool used in missionary work.

Problems with Certainty and the Truth Test

First of all, certainty with regard to religious beliefs is preposterous. All religions and philosophers agree that there is no hard evidence that God exists; belief in a supreme being is an act of faith by definition. A sure knowledge is not possible in the religious arena, and defeats the first and inviolate ground rule of religious thought; which is faith.

The supposition that the truth test is unique to Mormonism is untrue. In reality, all religions throughout the entire world employ an identical recipe for cementing religious convictions. There is a man living in Mesa, Arizona, a personal friend of mine, who has traveled the world and made it something of a hobby of his to inquire as to how the rest of the religious world determines truth, how ministers feel they have been 'called' to the work, why people become devout and give their lives to their faith, and so forth. The formula is the same for other Christian religions and world religions alike: read, study, live according to the precepts, meditate, and pray and a unique feeling will eventually come over you and a curious feeling of certainty ensues. The conversion and life-changing event has occurred. Religious affiliates describe the event in many ways; the grace of Jesus has been felt, the soul has been cleansed, the prayer answered, forgiveness and comfort felt, the nagging psychosis healed, the evil spirit evicted, etc. It is absolutely and positively universal.

Epistemology is a fascinating subject. While there are many variables and extensive theories, the experts generally agree that the portion of the brain that registers the 'spiritual' response triggers an overpowering sense of certainty at the same time. This could be an evolutionary hard wiring in the human psyche[19]. If we, as humans, were not coached and nurtured as children to develop confidence, and were to cave in to all the self-doubts we innately carry with us, we would be completely dysfunc-

---

[19] Andrew Newberg, *Why God Won't Go Away: Brain Science and the Biology of Belief*

tional. As children, we become increasingly brave and begin to develop confidence. We become conditioned to project confidence and have to in order to function at all. As we grow older, the projection of confidence becomes habitual and our peers see us as mature, confident, and complete persons. Primitive man, with all his insecurities, relied on instinct to know when to fight, to flee, or attack when placed in a life or death situation. The causal operators employed at these moments are designed to promote survival and play the odds, not determine truth. When those life-changing moments arrived, only the humans that acted decisively and with complete certainty tended to survive and reproduce. The triggering of the overpowering sense of certainty in conjunction with a soul-moving 'spiritual' experience is therefore quite possibly a logical outgrowth of human evolution.

Those who have a mystical experience have the quality of a profound knowing and a curious sense of authority[20]. The person equates the mystical experience to a state of knowledge which brings about a feeling of having touched something far deeper and far more real than what is normally experienced by the five senses in our ordinary lives. This conviction itself becomes a source of validation of the objective reality of what they have seen: what they see in their minds, they assume, must exist outside their minds. Invariably, the experience is taken as confirmation that the beliefs of a particular system are correct, even though there is little evidence to support them. Even though the feelings are real and undeniable, the truth of any associated religious doctrine is not assured.

The amazing thing is that the process is fully automatic in humans. Uncertainty leads to anxiety, anxiety demands resolution, and the cognitive imperative drives the individual to an explanation[21]. What is offered first that is logical is generally accepted.

As a youth, I was coached for hours about how to set the stage for a spiritual experience and confirmation that The Book of Mormon was

---

[20] William James, *The Varieties of Religious Experience: A Study in Human Nature*
[21] Andrew Newberg, *Why God Won't Go Away: Brain Science and the Biology of Belief*, p 70

true. Absolute silence, reading, prayer, and prolonged meditation were the key ingredients. Then I was to ask myself this question, "Could an uneducated teenager have written this book?" If I was sincere, I was told that I would get a unique feeling or manifestation. I was also coached on how to recognize these feelings, and they were described to me. It might be a warm feeling in the chest or a tingling feeling in the neck or spine, or seeing light when I closed my eyes, or some other unique manifestation. Looking back, the coaching was in reality a recipe for self-hypnosis, which has been shown clinically to lead to seeing or feeling the pre-hypnotic suggestions. I eventually developed the capability to conjure these same feelings at will.

Steven Hassan describes a case study of "Jim" who had seen a golden light surrounding the leader of his cult and held onto that spiritual experience as an immovable anchor in his commitment to the cult. In only a few minutes of hypnosis, Steven was able to recreate a more spectacular hallucination of the same variety in Jim, which immediately allowed Jim to extricate himself from cult influence[22].

Another problem with certainty and the truth test is that the truth test is unreliable. Some examples that establish the test as unreliable are:

1.   Since the truth test is universally used by all religions, and most religions conclude that their way is the only true way to find God, they cannot all be correct. Therefore, there are hundreds of millions of false positives. The truth test formula is therefore proven unreliable.

2.   Many LDS have described the confirmation truth test feelings in relation to stories that were ultimately found to be fabricated. Examples include the faith-building stories told by Paul H. Dunn. These stories were absolute treasures to many, and accompanied by the warm feelings, tingly spine, and burning in the bosom for thousands. Dunn later confessed that the stories

---

[22] Steven Hassan, *Releasing the Bonds, Empowering People to Think for Themselves,* Freedom of Mind Press, 2000, pp 63-64

were contrived[23]. The truth test formula is therefore proven unreliable, even among LDS members.

3. Many LDS describe the burning in the bosom, the tingly spine, etc. as being indistinguishable from feelings when reading other inspiring stories (especially patriotic) or quotes that have nothing to do with religion or the plan of salvation. This is more evidence confirming the unreliability of the truth test.

4. Finally, unfulfilled and false prophecies made by prophets when 'under the influence of the Holy Ghost' are another indicator of the unreliable nature of the truth test. In 1835 Smith prophesied that the second coming would take place by the year 1891[24]. April 5, 1843, at the General Conference of the Church, while the Spirit rested upon him, the Prophet Joseph said: *"Were I going to prophecy, I would say the end would not come in 1844, 5, or 6, or in forty years. There are those of the rising generation who shall not taste death till Christ comes.*[25]*"* Since all those in the rising generation are now dead, the truth test failed Smith. The truth test is therefore also unreliable for LDS prophets.

The truth test could readily be laboratory tested and shown unreliable. The test would sequester 100 people who have no knowledge of an inspirational work of fiction who are also humble and teachable. Instruct them that to know truth, they should read and pray and watch for that "burning in the bosom", a 'tingly' feeling, or other sign from the Holy Ghost that what they are reading is true, which feeling may vary widely from individual to individual. Then give them a week to read and pray about the inspirational work of fiction. Keep score as to how many determine the book to be truth.

In the LDS culture of friendship and trust, affinity fraud schemes find fertile ground. Often, the victims describe using the truth test to determine how to make financial investments. Thousands of well intentioned

---

[23] *Salt Lake Tribune*, 16 Feb 1991; *Church News*, 26 October 1991
[24] Roberts, *History of the Church* Vol 2, page 182
[25] Joseph Fielding Smith, *Teachings of the Prophet Joseph Smith* page 286

LDS lose millions of dollars in these schemes, prompting top church officials to caution members against such investment scams. Often the perpetrator refers to his temple recommend and important church responsibilities as part of the setup to build trust. In 2006 Utah ranked number one in the nation for fraud[26]. In 2001, the FBI listed Utah number 1 for mortgage fraud[27]. While many of these crimes are not related to affinity fraud, affinity fraud is a pervasive problem among faithful church members. The truth test simply does not work, scam artists bank on it.

Another problem with the truth test in Mormonism is circular reasoning. Circular reasoning is established by asking questions to determine if one statement of fact relies upon itself. A simple example is The Book of Mormon.

Q. How do you know The Book of Mormon is historically true and accurate?

A. I have received a witness of its truthfulness from the Holy Ghost.

Q. How do you know that this witness from the Holy Ghost is certain and reliable?

A. It is promised in The Book of Mormon.[28]

Every tenet of Mormonism hinges on the validity of the truth test, which is built on circular reasoning. Noticeably lacking in Mormonism is any sort of check and balance system. The person(s) and institution that stand to profit from the truth test also devised the truth test. Those who say that this method of discerning truth is complete and has to be failsafe because it is described in modern scripture are caught in a no-exit track of circular reasoning or self-deceptive paradox. The truth test fails the independent check and balance characteristic that is requisite for an objective evaluation.

---

[26] Consumer Fraud and Identity Theft Complaint Data, 2006, Federal Trade Commission, 2/07, page 18

[27] *Deseret News*, 26 July 2005

[28] *The Book of Mormon*, Moroni 10:3-5

Finally, the truth test has to be classified as an emotional response to a stimulus. Trusting emotions over reason has a somewhat dubious track record in history. While the following comparison in no way implies that the objectives of these groups are similar, yet they do share a common folly. No offense is intended in this example, but the comparison is warranted because a strong misconception merits an equally strong counterexample.

Reason can treacherously deceive a man, but emotion is always sure and never leaves him. – Adolph Hitler

Do not seek Adolph Hitler with your brains, you will find him with your hearts. – Rudolf Hess

Compare these quotes to this one:

When confronted by evidence in the rocks below, rely on the witness of the heavens above. - Boyd K. Packer, currently sustained as a Prophet, Seer, and Revelator of the LDS Church.

The illusion of certainty created by the truth test doctrine permeates religious affiliates and leads to serious societal ills associated with unreasonable religious fervor. For example, church members are often willing to sacrifice familial relationships for religious fervor. Family members who leave the faith are often disowned, chased from the home, or forbidden to discuss religious issues with other family members. An unnecessary strain is placed upon the family; rifts and divorce are common in such situations.

Since LDS members are certain that Mormonism is the 'only path to salvation', they often look upon other belief systems with contempt and view the members of these other deficient belief systems as lacking in faith and commitment and in need of conversion. When their non-member friends do not convert to Mormonism, LDS members sometimes think that these people are somehow defective (how could they possibly reject the plain and precious truths of the gospel?) and no longer worthy to be their friends. Non-members, upon seeing the friendship disintegrate when they elect to not embrace Mormonism, are left puzzling over the motives behind the friendship and become wary of befriending other Mormons.

Religious affiliates typically are incapable of any sort of self-examination of their own belief system, and automatically label contradictory information as "anti" and contrived, no matter how compelling and well documented. All of this is due to the certainty that comes with the truth test. The illusion of certainty leads members into the 'us versus them' syndrome. Anyone who is not a member of the church does not have access to the Holy Ghost as a constant companion is automatically playing for the other team and cannot be trusted. When a 'them' person brings up a controversial issue (polygamy, skin color discrimination, etc), the affiliate automatically feels persecuted. Church members often become defensive or assume the role of combatant when the inquirer is generally just confused or seeking clarification.

The truth test is also at the foundation of the 'tying the myth to life experiences' syndrome. Church members believe that every unexplained or 'spiritual' experience confirms 'their' belief system – no other explanation is ever considered. The warm and tingly feelings are the telltale signs of the Holy Ghost at work, just as promised by the doctrine of the church, therefore the church HAS to be true. No other possibility is contemplated, largely due to the confirmation bias[29]. Members refuse to believe there could possibly be a valid intellectual reason for anyone to disavow their faith, and therefore condemn any who defect, and this is another symptom of the unreasonable fervor brought on by the illusion of certainty.

A tragic circumstance that accompanies certainty is all too often evident in the aged. After the death of a spouse, or in the face of a long illness, the LDS member often gives up on life and surrenders to death. After all, the LDS member is certain that the afterlife is full of joy, is pain free, and replete with friends and family that have already passed on, etc. Many let familial relationships wither and die as they curtail their activity and hope for the end to come. The joie de vivre is gone, and the last

---

[29] The confirmation bias will be discussed in detail in chapter 10.

years of their lives are devoid of any positive contribution to society. The treasures of wisdom and love that the aging have to offer are locked away into miserable Gollem-like creatures who have turned inward awaiting the grim reaper.

Certainty can handicap church members when faced with making critical life course decisions. Some examples: Many women are promised by church leaders that they will become mothers in Zion and their primary purpose is to raise children[30]. They become so certain of their role as homemakers and that marrying within the faith will be all that is needed – there is no need to become educated or develop a marketable trade or skill. Then when the husband dies early or the couple divorces, the woman is ill prepared to make a living for herself and her children. Another example occurs when one-half of a married couple leaves the church, the faithful member remains certain that attainment of the highest order of heaven is impossible (without a member spouse). This is according to the doctrine of the church. Therefore, the member feels justified in divorcing the apostate to try to find another mate who will take them to heaven. Certainty obscures from their view other very real possibilities.

Conclusion

Anyone who purports to have a sure knowledge of God, Christ, the divinity of a prophet or a book written by a prophet is trapped in self-deceit and is exhibiting unreasonable fervor by asserting such sure knowledge. Saying that they 'know' the unknowable basic tenets of faith is bearing false witness and is prideful. False certainty brings with it religious extremism and an array of societal ills associated with extremists.

So, is there a fail-safe, reliable method for discerning truth, or are we forever guessing? Well some things, such as in math and science, can be proven beyond any rational or reasonable doubt. Regarding historical events, we are left to judge for ourselves based on available information and our instincts and intuition regarding human nature. In most cases with church history, there are several possible explanations for any one

---

[30] This language if often found in Patriarchal blessings for women, see Chapter 15

event, document, journal entry, newspaper article, etc. Historians use multiple sources and other reasonableness tests to assign a most likely probability. Generally, 'Occam's Razor'[31] holds true: the most likely explanation is usually the correct one. When sitting on a jury and listening to opposing accounts of the same event, jurors generally can discern, after careful consideration, which account is true and which one is contrived. The contrived accounts have inconsistencies, require people to do unreasonable things, and break down under examination of physical evidences and are not corroborated by third-party accounts. These same tools are useful in assigning probabilities to events and claims of religion to establish the truth beyond a reasonable doubt. When presented with a plausible argument, it is important to analyze the thread of logic involved. Ask yourself objective questions, such as: is this argument/ scenario intuitive, or does it require mental contortionism? Does the explanation "make the path straighter," or does the explanation "make the path crooked?" Is the scenario compatible with the facts, environment, and other events? The final test is one of cumulative probability. When the story relies on a string of low probability events, its probability of holding truth becomes so small that it can generally be safely discarded.

The objective researcher will also consider the possibility of plagiarism when examining stories or questionable 'true history'. Shared inaccuracies are strong evidence of plagiarism. A large number of shared ideas, events, and especially a sequence of events also constitute strong evidence for plagiarism.

To some degree, our understanding of the past is limited by the finite experience base of our lifetime. Luckily, historians have been able to recreate the moods, current events, gossip, and superstitious mindsets of the era being examined. In many cases, understanding event sequences and motivating factors require an in-depth examination of all surrounding circumstances, including the current events and prevalent superstitions.

The human need for certainty is a popular social pathology. Uncertainty brings fear and discomfort whereas certainty brings a sense of peace and

---

[31] Attributed to Franciscan friar William of Ockham, see http://en.wikipedia.org/wiki/Occam's_razor

security. It helps a person make sense out of this world and avoid the painfulness of ambivalence. A strong leader is one who knows what he is talking about. A person who only states opinions and speculation does not inspire deep loyalty or spark great enthusiasm. Human nature craves certainty. This tendency has created serious problems for the world. Jesus was crucified by certainty. The airliners that flew into the World Trade Center were piloted by certainty. The Nazi concentration camps were built and operated by certainty. Certainty carried out the Mountain Meadow Massacre. Beware the man who is certain of the will of God.

A 'certain knowledge' philosophy creates a cycle of arrogance, ignorance, error, and guilt or denial when the errors are exposed. In order to break the chain, humility and uncertainty must replace the foundational epistemology of certainty. Gardiner[32] explains:

> To be free, man must be free from not only the control of walls, bars, strong arms, and weapons, but must be free also, from the control that comes from the allure of security [or the threat of eternal pain].... Faith must be the only mover, a faith that is forever tenuous and defies certainty. As soon as certainty enters, security is founded and the need to continue that security can be used to control, coerce, and confine...

Unfortunately, accepting uncertainty runs counter to the human tendency to seek comfort and security. As can be seen, that security comes with a high price. Adherence to irrational religious ideas that offer security, despite overwhelming contradictory evidence, is a manifestation of social pathology.

Religionists would have us believe that all the great injustices in human history are attributable to Satan and his legions of demons, and that the solution is to turn to God. However, the common thread throughout the history of human strife is the unreasonable fervor brought on by the very same illusions of certainty fostered by religious institutions. It is

---

[32] Shame and the Destruction of Agency, Ed Gardiner, see http://www.postmormon. org/main.swf

time that humanity swallows a humility pill and discover the wonder of uncertainty and the beauties of the mysterious. Certainty, as it pertains to religious thought, is clearly not working for humankind.

The spirit of liberty is the spirit which is not too sure it is right. – Learned Hand

Doubt is uncomfortable, certainty is ridiculous. - Voltaire

The most beautiful thing we can experience is the mysterious. It is the source of all true art and all science. He to whom this emotion is a stranger, who can no longer pause to wonder and stand rapt in awe, is as good as dead: his eyes are closed. - Albert Einstein

As our island of knowledge grows, so does the shore of our ignorance. - John Archibald Wheeler_

The trouble with the world is that the stupid are cocksure and the intelligent are full of doubt. - Bertrand Russell

CHAPTER 5
SEEDS

The longing for certainty and repose is in every human mind. But certainty is generally an illusion and repose is not the destiny of man. – Oliver Wendell Holmes

Illusion is the first of all pleasures. – Oscar Wilde

Feb 1986   Mesa AZ

I set down my pencil and turned around to face my coworker. "What happened?" I asked. My coworker replied: "They arrested a guy named Mark Hofmann for those bombings in Salt Lake City. It turns out that he was selling forged documents to LDS authorities, and he was about to be exposed as a fraud, and was trying to cover his tracks. But it gets more interesting than that. The documents bought by high-ranking church authorities were being purchased primarily to keep them hidden[33]. Why would they need to do that?"

Why indeed, I thought to myself. This makes no sense. Something is definitely amiss here; I could feel it in my gut. I made a mental note to study this when I had some time to get all the facts. For the near term, it would just have to wait. Plus, I didn't know where to go to find the real facts. I was just too busy to worry about the rat I smelled that spring day. Eighteen years would pass before I would eventually act on that gut feeling. It was a seed.

Another seed was planted when I was in my teens. A lesson was taught discussing the depth and breadth of the atonement of Christ. In Mor-

---

[33] Robert Lindsey, *A Gathering of Saints: A True Story of Money Murder and Deceit* (Simon and Schuster, 1988)

monism, Christ didn't just die on the cross for our sins and overcome death by being resurrected. No, the big event was the atonement in Gethsemane that preceded the crucifixion. This was where he took upon himself the sins of every person and suffered for us so we wouldn't have to, if we only accept him as our savior. But wait, there is more. Christ didn't just suffer for the sins of the inhabitants of the earth, he suffered for everyone everywhere, in every world throughout the galaxy – the atonement was both infinite and eternal[34]. So, people in other worlds like our earth, would have different scriptures describing an extra-terrestrial named Jesus, who would suffer for the sins of the people, but would never live on their own world. I learned that Jesus was sent to our earth because we had, here on our earth, the most cruel people in the galaxy, the only ones that were wicked enough to crucify the perfect person.

This doctrine, the infinite and eternal atonement, was a huge problem for me for several reasons. First, there was the probability aspect. I was already reeling with the improbability of my selection to be born in a special time, a special promised land, to special parents, in the only true religion. I was chosen in the pre-mortal life due to my extreme valiance against incredible odds. The flattery was transparent and did not set well with me, it seemed too contrived. Now, I had to factor in an astronomical probability about how this earth was special above all other worlds. It just didn't work for me. There comes a time for every individual when the story becomes too tall. I had reached my limit.

Secondly, the people in other worlds would not be able to relate to the story of Jesus, the Jewish culture and Roman rule, or have a chance to visit the Holy Land and see the landscape of history. This was not fair; it just seemed that God's plan would not put people in other worlds in such a dreary condition. People in other worlds would have their most honored hero an extra-terrestrial and not even part of their civilization. This was nonsensical and offended my intellect. Surely somebody was mistaken. I anxiously awaited clarification – I felt that in my heart of hearts that there would come a day when this doctrine would

---

[34] Russell M. Nelson, *Ensign*, "The Atonement" Nov 1996

be expounded upon and brought back in the realm of reasonableness. I waited for 30 years for somebody to help me understand this or correct it to no avail. This became another seed.

Thus, the seeds were sown. As with most members, the seeds of my doubt and misgivings remained hidden and repressed for decades. Members of the church are conditioned to look for the good in the church and tend to forget about those things that gave us pause at one time.

Other seeds that caused mental discord include:

- I always thought polygamy was wrong, but to be a good Mormon, I had to find a way to justify it. Mental contortionism ensued.
- I always thought the church discriminated against blacks, but to be a good Mormon, I had to justify the priesthood being withheld from blacks[35] until 1977, figuring it was God's plan, not mine.
- I did not really want to go on a mission, but to follow God's prophet, I had to change my thinking and get in line. I figured as long as I had to go, I might as well try to enjoy it.
- The temple ceremony was replete with secrets and oaths, which directly conflicts with the teachings of The Book of Mormon. But I tried somehow to make it work in my mind.
- I thought the earth and our human ancestors were more than 6000 years old, but the church told me I was wrong and I better get comfortable with it.

Over time, intellectual issues can stack up and intrude on the conscious mind. Eventually, the dissonance pushes faithful religious types to a place where they have to step back and examine their belief system objectively. It pushes people to edge of their belief plateau, the precipice.

The continued suppression of intellectual discord presents a risk to the long-term mental health of the individual. The health of our mind is the

---

[35] *Pearl of Great Price*, Abraham 1:26-27

key to survival in this life. When we don't come to grips with the dissonance, we are essentially sending a signal to our mind that it cannot be trusted. At the very minimum, confidence in one's intellect suffers, because the mind is uncertain when it can be trusted to properly evaluate issues and when it cannot. In the long term, if the disharmony is strong, and the self-talk remains consistently negative, symptoms of mental illness can result. Some of the phrases I have heard used by LDS members when they are consciously repressing their intellect and supplanting irrational faith for reason are:

1. "We will just have to have faith on this issue"
2. "It is unhealthful to delve into the mysteries"
3. "This is something we will learn about in the next life"
4. "More intelligent men than us have already resolved this, we don't need to rehash it"
5. "This is one of those tests to determine who is really faithful"

It is appropriate to point out how these groupthink phrases fall into two categories: they are either (a) thinly-veiled guilt pills or (b) excuses to be lazy and ignorant. If you can't just have faith, then you must be overly prideful and not a true disciple. The more you get wrapped up in mysteries, the more damage you will do yourself (of course the opposite result is in fact much more likely). Why can't you just believe? Humble yourself, study, and pray, use the truth test, and you will find your answer. Are you so impatient that you cannot wait for the millennium or the hereafter to find your answers? The underlying tenet is that if you cannot find the proper answer, it is your own fault. You are too proud, too impatient, not 'in-tune' with the spirit, or lack enough intelligence to understand.

Many live their entire lives in the church and never consider the irrationality that plagues the Mormon groupthink. The church for them is not much more that a social fabric, thinking deep thoughts is not really required to live, love, be happy, and be saved. I was not one of these people. I saw things in a more pragmatic light. I saw the teachings as a requirement for celestial redemption from our sin-filled lives. I fought my inner self to get into compliance with the church's teachings.

To me "the church" was supposed to be the restoration of God's truth on earth and it all had to make sense. The cognitive dissonance was now spilling over the edge of my cup. I was finally ready to take an objective look at the religion of my youth. The real truth was now more important to me than the warm fuzzy blanket and need to belong to the tribe. At age 45, my intellect had pushed me to the edge.

CHAPTER 6
MIND CONTROL, PART 1

Man is an animal suspended in webs of significance that he himself has spun. – Clifford Geertz

None are so hopelessly enslaved as those who falsely believe they are free. - Goethe

From the day we are born into this world, circumstances and human influences vie for power over our thought processes. The great irony in our human existence is that it is virtually impossible for us to discover how we have been influenced, or break out of mind-controlling habits by ourselves. We have built our own walls, which constrain our beings, and these walls in no small measure define who we are as individuals and lend us comfort and security. The prison inmate with a life sentence hates the walls for the first 10 years, learns to tolerate them for the next 10 years, then becomes comfortable inside the walls over the next 10 years. After 30 or 40 years, the thought of trying to live outside the walls becomes terrifying. The inmate at this point is institutionalized and begins to view the walls, the guard towers, and the routine as sanctuary from the menacing world outside. The same holds true for those subjected to mind controlling indoctrination, whether it is religious, political, or societal. As humans age their capacity to break away from a mind-controlling group or significantly alter the ingrained thought processes becomes diminished. The groupthink, the doctrines, the images of Jesus on the cross, the thought that God is above watching over them becomes as much a comfort to them as the walls, the barbed wire, and the guard towers are a comfort to the incarcerated.

Destructive mind control[36], in a nutshell, is a social process that encourages obedience, dependence, and conformity, while suppressing autonomy and independence. It is a system of influence that seeks to disrupt a person's authentic identity and displace it with an alternate cult identity[37]. It usually preys upon the emotions of guilt and fear, and generally promises great rewards for 'correct' behavior. Conforming to the group think and obtaining the reward(s) become everything; all else is irrelevant.

Through a series of small, seemingly innocuous choices, endorsed by the group, the individual slowly surrenders their free will and capacity for critical thinking to the group. Once immersed in the group, very few will be able to free themselves. Steven Hassan explains it as follows[38]:

> The key to mind control's success lies in its subtlety, the way it promotes the "illusion of control." The individual believes he is making his own choices, when in fact he has been socially influenced to disconnect his own critical mind and decision-making capacity. In other words, he believes that he has freely chosen to surrender his free will to God or to a leader or ideology. When one steps back and objectively evaluates the vast amount of social influence used to get him to "surrender", the degree of manipulation becomes very obvious.

Mind control techniques can be beneficial when they are used to empower the individual to act autonomously and take responsibility for himself and his actions. The end result of positive mind control techniques is that the subject, after being indoctrinated, no longer has any need for any organization or additional indoctrination. In other words, the end result is complete freedom and autonomy of the individual.

Mind control is destructive when it coaxes the person to lose his identity and divest himself of independent thoughts and decisions. The end result of destructive mind control is that the individual becomes more and more dependent on the group and life is not worth living without the group and the promised rewards of staying within the group.

---

[36] Hassan, *Releasing the Bonds*
[37] *Releasing the Bonds*, pg 5
[38] *Releasing the Bonds*, pg 40

First, let us list some of the telltale characteristics[39] of destructive mind control:

- Fostering a new identity
- Threatening prophecies
- Secret meetings, Exclusivity, Shrines Reserved for Elite
- Deception
- Manipulation and Psychological Blackmail
- Dependency
- Incentives to spend more and more time with the group
- Confession, privacy infringement
- Extraction of as much money as possible
- Hyper-vigilance – thought stopping
- The demand for purity

Now, let us consider each characteristic individually, and determine if Mormonism, as currently implemented and practiced, does or does not exhibit, teach, or indirectly instill these attributes and attitudes within the membership. Some of these characteristics overlap, of course. It is acknowledged that many of these characteristics are shared by other religions, but only Mormonism is being tested in this narrative. Affiliates of other religious groups are invited to test their own belief system as they follow along in this discussion.

Fostering a New Identity

Mormonism encourages the members to become as little children and yield to the enticement of the holy spirit and be born again, taking upon them the name of Christ at baptism. Becoming as a child, innocent and devoid of critical thinking skills, is the perfect regression technique to displace adult logical thinking skills. Another common technique employed in developing a new identity is a new name[40]. In the Mormon temples, each inductee is given a new name, which will become the person's name in the eternities. [Interestingly, the husband learns his wife's new name when they are married, but the woman only discovers the new

---

[39] *Releasing the Bonds*, Chapter 2
[40] *Releasing the Bonds*, p 56

name of her husband in the afterlife.] Having been reborn into a new community, and given a new role in life, the person in effect becomes an actor, at times even feeling as if he is on a stage, and is careful to play the role programmed by the group. As time passes, the role, the alternate identity, displaces the authentic self and is falsely thought to be real and genuine.

People generally underestimate how profoundly social pressures influence a person's identity. In 1971 Dr. Philip Zimbardo, in a now famous experiment[41], took 21 mature middle-class adults and structured a mock prison, dividing them up to be either inmates or guards. In only six days time, the experiment had to be cut short, due to threats, rebellion, violence, intimidation, and sadistic behavior. And all this mayhem was spawned from subjects that were specifically selected based on their emotional stability. Social psychology has demonstrated time and again that humans are deeply affected by their environment and tend to evolve into entities who conform to what is perceived to be 'correct' behavior. Dr. Zimbardo went on to teach a course at Stanford University called "The Psychology of Mind Control".

Threatening Prophecies

Joseph Smith taught that the second coming was imminent in his day, and each successive prophet has warned of the second coming, signs of the times, and impending calamities. The church recommends that each family accumulate a two-year supply of food and consumables in the event of a disaster. Preparedness seminars are held regularly throughout the church to prepare the membership for impending calamitous events. While being prepared is laudable, it is the motivation for being prepared that is being examined, and the motivation is impending catastrophe to fulfill prophecy.

With each hurricane, tsunami, volcanic eruption, war or conflict, economic crisis, etc., LDS cry "these are signs of the times", "Christ is knock-

---

[41] M. Hunt, *The Story of Psychology*, 1993, pp 411-412

ing at the door", "repent and get your house in order", and so forth. Threatening prophecies give to the member a feeling of urgency, immediacy, and tends to limit the opportunity to critically examine the foundational claims as they pertain to current events.

The second coming, Mormons are taught, ushers in a new age, and a partial judgment takes place. Many of the inhabitants of the earth are supposed to be 'burned at His coming'[42]. There is no question that Mormonism contains threatening prophecies, as do all Christian religions.

Secret Meetings and Exclusivity, Shrines Reserved for the Elite

The church holds several meetings that are both secret and exclusive. In Mormonism, the local congregation is called a ward, which is presided over by a bishop and his counselors and clerks. This group of local leaders is called a Bishopbric. The weekly Bishopbric meetings are secret, in that the discussions of members and policy implementation are confidential. The lay member cannot attend a Bishopbric meeting, therefore also making it exclusive. Many other meetings fall into the secret and exclusive category: Priesthood Executive Committee, auxiliary presidency meetings, stake high council meetings, stake presidency meetings, and many others, are all exclusive and confidential. The lay member knows the meetings are being held but has no way of knowing what or who is being discussed and what judgments are being made. Temple worthiness interviews are also kept secret; to the extent that other members are not told which other members may or may not have had a recent temple worthiness interview. So these meetings are secret in two different ways: (1) that the meeting took place and (2) what was said and the outcome of the interview.

The church social hierarchy is built on exclusivity. In order to obtain 'temple worthy' status, the member has to pay his tithes (10%) and answer worthiness questions correctly. Only the temple worthy members can attend the temple and hold certain elite and important offices in the church. The next rung of exclusivity is the leadership rung. Leadership

---

[42] Malachi 4:1

meetings, both on the ward and stake levels, are reserved for those men and women in leadership positions; the lay members are not invited. The final rungs are the top offices at the ward and stake level, such as Bishop, Relief Society President, Stake President, etc. A bishop presides over a congregation of about 500 members called a ward, the Stake President (Stake President) presides over six to twelve bishops, making a 'stake', or collection 'wards'. While it is said that these positions are not sought after, most people in the church look upon the most elite leaders as being head and shoulders above the lay membership in terms of righteousness and ability to know the will of God.

The LDS culture includes both secret meetings and exclusivity attributes. On top of that, the temple rites themselves include strict oaths of secrecy. Members who are not temple-worthy are looked down upon as having a flaw in need of correction. Temple worship is a special activity in a shrine reserved for the 'few', only the most deserving and devout, and is a very effective type of societal elitism. Certain rooms in the temples, such as the Holy of Holies, and rites (such as 'Washing of Feet') are reserved for the super-elite.

Deception

The lay member would swear that there is no deception in the church. And, among the lay members, there is no overt and conscious intent to deceive. But unintentional deception is still deception. The most rampant form of deception in the church is manifest in the form of 'testimony bearing', where the member makes outrageous claims that he/she knows without any doubt the church is the only true church on earth, that Joseph Smith was a prophet of God, that The Book of Mormon is a true historical account, that the president of the church (currently Thomas S. Monson) is a living prophet who speaks for God, that Jesus Christ is the son of God, etc. Of course, these tenets are, by definition, religious beliefs that cannot be known beyond reasonable doubt. Therefore, the illusion of certainty is, at its core, a deception. And it is a powerful deception, which is as dangerous and far reaching as it is outrageous.

It is interesting that this mammoth deception is self-perpetuating. The adults teach the children that it is praiseworthy to pretend to know, as they are coached to stand and 'bear testimony' at a very young age. The testimony bearing occurs every Sunday. Each teacher in every lesson is obligated, if they follow the lesson manual, to bear testimony of the subject matter. Certainty about feelings and basic gospel precepts like the golden rule, good begets good, etc. is fine. However, all too often, the subject matter deals with the aforementioned unknowable basic faith tenets. Thus the deception is perpetuated and reinforced every Sunday. It is an environment where everyone is guilty, so there is no one to blame.

There are other top-down deceptions that are basic church policy. The so-called 'faithful history' policy white washes the history of the church, allowing the lay member to believe that the whole story has been told. The obfuscation of church financial holdings and Hinckley asserting that the church has divested itself of money making investments[43] can only be described as deception.

Manipulation and Psychological Blackmail

A mind control environment sets next to impossible standards for performance, thereby creating an environment based on guilt and shame. No matter how hard a person works, he will always fall short of the standard, or at least feel that more could be done, feel guilty, and then resolve to work even harder in order to avoid shame pain.

The aforementioned threatening prophesies are manipulative in nature in that they instill a sense of urgency. Psychological blackmail is a positive or negative psychological consequence for an action or inaction. Guilt is the consequence for the sins defined by Mormonism. Happiness is promised for the righteousness, also defined by Mormonism. These blackmail tools are obvious.

The less obvious blackmail is the guilt for inaction or sloth. If one forgets to say a prayer, there is guilt. If a family fails to hold family home evening, it is expected that discord will invade the home. Every month that one fails to attend the temple, the Lords blessings are withheld. The

---

[43] See full quote and reference in chapter 17

foreshadowing of Gods malevolence becomes reality as the subconscious in the individual works to fulfill the embedded psychological expectation.

The church member is told how to pray, and how often, how often to read scriptures, how to teach lessons, how to teach their families every Monday evening, virtually everything is scripted. [Many members become disappointed when leaders restrict lesson materials to what is presented in the lesson manuals. This type of restriction is becoming more prevalent in the church.]

How does the church manage to motivate its members to do all these things? How does the church manipulate its members? One method is through guilt and the need to avoid shame pain. At church, you often hear statements such as: "Have you done your home teaching this month? I feel so good when I get my home teaching done the first week of the month. My husband and I had such a wonderful spiritual experience at the temple this week." The lay member is left to wonder why they do not have the wonderful spiritual experiences, why they cannot be enthusiastic about doing their visiting teaching or home teaching early in the month. Guilt engulfs the lay member when he or she falls short of the advertised standard. Guilt is an ugly motivator, but an effective one for most people.

Why do so many LDS accept foreign exchange students? One motivator is guilt reduction. Every member is reminded, approximately monthly, that they have a responsibility to do missionary work. Most are uncomfortable discussing religion with their friends and coworkers, and guilt sets in. A foreign exchange student solves this guilt problem. The student is obligated to be part of family activities, which exposes him/her to the gospel every day at home and once a week attending church meetings and youth activities. By default, the member family is doing their missionary work every week, so they are guilt free, at least in regard to missionary work.

Another manipulation tool is flattery, also referred to as "love bombing", making people feel special by showering them with praise[44]. Members are told that they were especially courageous and obedient (valiant) in the pre-existence (life before this life) and that is why they are members of the church in this life. Members are taught they are special and unique in many ways, and that God favors them as they are vigilant. They are a chosen people, a royal nation, and the elect of God. The flattery extends to the prospect of becoming Gods and Goddesses in the after-life. The flattery and enticements are also strong in the day-to-day operations of the church. Members regularly compliment each other, and seeking approval becomes a constant and overarching contest among members. Contests for approval become the lifeblood and motivator for the social-ites. Some succumb to the contest completely and become sociopathic, flirting with depression between the approval highs.

The single most important blackmail tool is the family unit and the eter-nal family doctrine. When coupled with the father's priesthood respon-sibilities and the sacred shrine of the temple, this doctrine becomes a sledge hammer to manipulate members to toe the line. A courageous young man who is willing to risk his life going into combat has no armor to protect him from his mother's pleas to keep the commandments so the whole family can be together forever in the eternities. The tears of mothers and wives and children are fearful weapons, and the church has enlisted them into its service. The church teaches that the faithful will be separated from the unfaithful in the afterlife, so leaving the church is commensurate to leaving the family. Due to their unwavering loyalty to the church, many faithful members ostracize family members who leave the church, not wanting to jeopardize their eternal salvation. They feel justified in cutting the ties in mortality since the defector(s) will not be part of the eternal family anyway. Thus members must carefully con-sider the gravity of their decision if they are to leave the church, because it often also means being cut off from family.

Weddings are among the most joyful family events, and a Mormon temple wedding is cause for great celebration and family togetherness. However, if some family members are not faithful members, they can-not, by rule, attend the temple wedding ceremony. This results in one of the most distasteful realities in Mormonism; families are segregated for

---

[44] *Releasing the Bonds*, pg 53

the marriage ceremony and other important rites and ceremonies which can only be accomplished in the temple. Those who are not temple worthy wait in the parking lot while the temple worthy elite witness the ceremony or event. Bob McCue points out that[45]:

> This is how I explain the Church's temple building program. The temple recommend interview process is the primary control tool the Church has with respect to adult members. If there is no temple within a reasonable distance of a population of Church members, this control tool does not work. ... Based on the foregoing information, it does not require much cynicism to posit that the main purpose for temple work for the dead may be to ingrain conditioning in the living.

Similarly, fathers must be faithful in order to baptize and ordain children when these important age milestones are reached. A father who cannot perform these ordinances is a disgrace to his family and a discredit to his gender, stifling any chance for family celebrations. Thus many disaffected members simply play along, praying, paying, and obeying in order to enjoy these family events.

All too often, missionaries who become disillusioned with missionary work cannot bear the thought of returning home – it would be too humiliating to the other family members. So they plod along, depressed and uncomfortable and resentful, hating every minute of every day until they can return home and resume a normal life. I personally witnessed this as a missionary.

Dependency

In Mormonism, members depend on the church network for virtually everything. The outside world really becomes superfluous for the totally immersed member. Need friends? The church provides them. Need a social life? Ready made for you. Need programs for your kids? The church has you covered: primary for ages three to eleven, scouting for

---

[45] Bob McCue, "Out of My Faith", p 86 http://www.mccue.cc/bob/spirituality.htm

the boys and young women's groups for ages twelve to eighteen, plus seminary indoctrination beginning at age fourteen or fifteen, after that, institute instruction thought the college age years.

Out of work? The church has employment placement and welfare if things get bad. Need some work done on your house, or a new home built? Ask people at church. No need to hire anybody outside the church. The church member is taught to depend on the other members, to serve one another.

The encouragement to have large families tends to result in more dependency on the church, since the parents often feel overwhelmed with raising the children and are relieved to have ready-made programs and friends with sanctioned moral values for the kids.

Incentives to Spend More and More Time With the Group

The incentives to spend more and more time with the group are varied and seductive. The more time the member spends with the group, the higher on the social rung the member tends to climb. Praise from one's peers becomes almost a narcotic, because it is not only praise from a human, but also it implies approval from God and heaven, which carries with it the potential for eternal consequences. This flavor of praise is the heroin of all incentives.

The only way to be found among the elite in Mormonism is to spend an inordinate amount of time with the group. Going beyond the norm, devoting oneself, doing more than others, these traits lead to rewards of increasing responsibility as the person climbs into exclusive circles. Thus, the incentives to spend more time with the group, be in service of the group, and distance oneself from the corrupt world are very enticing.

Evidence suggests[46] that people are the least likely to be open-minded when they are under time pressures. Thus the busy person is less likely to jettison a bad or illogical belief. Successful mind control always involves making the subjects intensely busy, even to the point of sleep deprivation in extreme circumstances[47].

---

[46] Ben Dean, PhD, CoachingTowardHappiness.com

Confession, Privacy Infringement

The role of confession in mind control groups is well established[48]. Confession is an integral doctrine and process in Mormonism, as it is in many religions. Affiliates are taught that serious transgressions must be confessed before God will forgive and forget. The confession process increases dependency on the group and erodes privacy. Counselors who have LDS patients are often surprised at how readily they divulge profoundly personal information, which is indicative of LDS conditioning and a distorted sense of personal boundaries.

In addition to confessions, members are subject to probing personal interviews by untrained lay clergy, without a parent present, beginning at age eight. Mandatory annual interviews begin at age twelve. Some youth are asked about masturbation before they even know what it is in these interviews. Monthly home visits from other members (referred to as 'home teaching' or 'visiting teaching') generally involve personal conduct questions such as how often the family prays together, reads scriptures together, and whether the family is having weekly gospel discussions and activities. Although the visits and questioning is done in a spirit of love, it is essentially prying and spying and a form of self-policing.

Extraction of as Much Money as Possible

It is estimated that the LDS church, with a membership of thirteen million[49] collects about six billion dollars a year, and in the period of 1984-1997 donated $30.7 million to non-Mormon charity, or an average of $2.2 million per year[50], which is only a few dollars per member per year. While humanitarian aid efforts from the church have increased in recent years, and is laudable, the percentage of net revenue and net assets being given back to humanity is still less than most US businesses. Says Richard Ostling: "I don't know of any religion that is so invested in stocks,

---

[47] Conversation with Steven Hassan, former member of the 'Moonie' cult and sleep-deprivation victim.

[48] R.J. Lifton, *Thought Reform and the Psychology of Totalism*, 1961

[49] http://www.mormonhaven.com/stats07.htm

[50] Richard N. Ostling, *Mormon America: The Power and the Promise*

bonds, cattle ranching, etc.,"[51] Elaborating on the preoccupation of the LDS with wealth, Heinerman and Shupe add[52]:

> The much publicized "televangelists" of the "electronic church", such as the Reverends Jerry Falwell, Oral Roberts, and Jim Baaker, are small time by comparison [to the LDS church]. Likewise the millions of dollars of self-appointed messiahs like Sun Myung Moon, much ballyhooed by the sensationalist press, are not even in the same league.

We have legalized robbery, and called it belief. – Dire Straits

In comparison to other religions, being a Mormon is expensive. The ten percent tithing commandment taken at face value is nothing short of staggering. The way that tithing is explained to the member is somewhat nebulous and left open to interpretation, which is a sort of psychological blackmail by itself. Tithing is an "all or nothing" proposition, which adds to the nervousness on the part of the member, because if only 9.9 percent of the member's increase is donated, the ten percent threshold was not met, and the member receives zero blessings. And the theological rewards for coughing up the ten percent are huge. The Lords promise is that "he who is tithed at the coming of the Lord shall not be burned"[53]. So here we see a remarkable combination of a threatening prophecy, psychological blackmail, and monetary extortion all rolled together.

The nervous and insecure member will tend to pay more, not wanting to miss the ten percent threshold and be a candidate for being 'burned at the coming of the Lord'. Many agonize over this and find that paying ten percent of gross income is worth it for peace of mind. It is akin to the person that purposely errs on the conservative side when doing their tax return, just in case they are audited. Others, including bishops and stake

---

[51] Book Probes LDS Wealth, Power, *The Salt Lake Tribune*, November 13, 1999

[52] John Heinerman and Anson Shupe, *The Mormon Corporate Empire, The Eye-Opening Report on the Church and Its Political and Financial Agenda*, Beacon Press, 1985

[53] *Doctrine and Covenants* 64:23

presidents, realize that ten percent of increase can readily be interpreted as net income after all expenses. This often computes to be around one or two percent of gross income, and they have complete peace of mind. Thus the law favors the liberal chance-taker and makes the worrywart a beast of burden.

Interestingly, many church members break about every commandment in the book, but rely on the 'get out of purgatory free' tithing card to save them. It is a thinly-veiled absolution for money scheme.

But the church does not stop at just tithing. There are monthly 'fast offerings', missionary fund contributions, and a whole litany of donation categories. When a calamity strikes, the church rallies the members and encourages special additional contributions.

As is common in virtually all religions, there are additional expenses required to serve and participate. Members are encouraged to donate the use of their automobiles and other personal property. Members are regularly called upon to donate food for social events.

Hyper Vigilance – Thought Stopping

Members are psychologically conditioned by the group to believe that they must be hyper-vigilant about their thoughts, emotions, and behavior. This is a central aspect of Mormon doctrine. Scriptures such as "As a man thinketh in his heart, so it he"[54], and "he that looketh upon a woman with lust hath already committed adultery in his heart"[55] are discussed frequently.

Members are taught that the hymns sung as a congregation serve a dual purpose. No only are they a form of worship in a group setting, they may be used to displace evil thoughts by singing softly to yourself when the need arises. The memorization of scriptures and other church-provided materials such as the Articles of Faith, the Mission of the Aaronic

---

[54] Proverbs 23:7
[55] Matthew 5:27, *The Book of Mormon*, 3Nephi 12:28, *Doctrine and Covenants* 63:16

Priesthood, the Young Women's Promise, the Standard of Truth, etc. are also mentioned as vehicles that members can use to push bad thoughts out of one's mind. Members are taught that evil thoughts or thoughts that contradict the groupthink must be forced out of the mind, and are poison to eternal salvation. These are thought stopping techniques, typical of mind control groups[56].

The Demand for Purity

The demand for purity permeates Mormonism. Purity of thought, purity of action, purity of motives, pure love, pure charity, and especially moral purity are demanded of the member. The body is to be kept pure and clean, which includes complete abstinence from alcohol, tobacco, coffee, tea, drugs. After all, the members all know the scripture "no unclean thing can enter into the kingdom of God" and understand that purity is vital to salvation.

The degree of purity and the standards go beyond mainstream Christianity in many categories. For example, the youth of the church are taught that sexual relations outside the bonds of marriage are sins "like unto murder"[57], and that masturbation is a deplorable sin[58]. Young men with a masturbation habit are not allowed to serve missions[59]; young couples that have had difficulty abstaining from premarital sex are not allowed to wed in the temple and are looked upon as unclean.

Church members are taught that modest dress is close to Godliness. Worthy LDS church members are required to wear special underwear, next to the skin, both night and day. The underwear, referred to as the 'garment of the holy Priesthood', covers the entire torso, extending to the knee of the legs, and a few inches down each arm. The temple garment is to be worn at all times, except when not practical for sports, swimming, and bathing. If the garment pieces are completely removed for marital

---

[56] *Releasing the Bonds*, p 184
[57] *The Book of Mormon*, Alma 39:5
[58] Mark E. Peterson, "Steps to Overcoming Masturbation", (Pamphlet)
[59] Spencer W. Kimball, *The Miracle of Forgiveness*, page 77

relations, they are to be put back on immediately, to leave them off for an extended period is transgression.

[Note: Repression breeds obsession, and when the value of human sexuality is repressed, it returns as pornography[60]. When sex is removed from love, we only succeed in removing love from sex. Many believe this is the reason that pornography is particularly pervasive in Utah[61].]

Other Mind Control Tactics

Other mind control tactics used very successfully in Mormonism include:

- Conformity/uniformity in appearance: The first step to conformity in behavior and thinking is conformity in appearance. Women who have attended the temple automatically have a dress code dictated by the temple undergarment; the white shirt and tie combined with the dark suit for men is standard attire.
- Constant reminders: special clothes, symbols, marks (including the marks in temple undergarments), jewelry (CTR rings, standing for 'choose the right' are popular among young and old alike)
- The social hierarchy is the cult hierarchy. Those who think and look like the group are popular, accepted, and rise to lofty positions in the church.
- Tying life experiences to the myth. In Mormonism, every faith healing, every inspiration, every tear shed, every epiphany of thought, every good experience confirms the truth of the myth. Every man is a Priesthood holder and can bless, heal, and baptize. The 'Priesthood' makes every man a medicine man, which combines flattery with a sense of ownership.

---

[60] John Shelby Spong, *Why Christianity Must Change or Die*, page 160
[61] "Porn Pervasive in Utah", *Deseret News*, 20 Jan 2007, "Utah is No. 1-for Online Pomography Consumption", 3 Mar 2009, *Salt Lake Tribune*

Conclusion

In order for humans to retain control of their own thought processes, precautions can be taken. Some of these precautions, which will serve to weaken mind control groups and fight faith abuse are:

- Avoid institutions that ask one become as a child, discourage critical thinking, or promotes taking a new name or employs other identity suppression strategies.
- Always challenge threatening prophecies or doomsday predictions. Demand to see the data.
- Mandate open meetings, never exclude anyone.
- Never be 'guilted' into anything. Live your life on a want-to, choose-to basis.
- Distance yourself from any situation that involves deception, manipulation, flattery, or dependency.
- Never surrender time to a group unless some tangible benefit to humanity is derived thereby.
- Contribute for humanitarian aid reasons, never give money for guilt or 'salvation for money' reasons, only donate to organizations that give a full accounting of every dollar and try to spread contributions around.

Many people carry the misconception that each mind control organization has an evil designer and mastermind that founded it, to serve the sinister purposes of the mastermind. This is not the case. Strong mind control organizations are a product of evolution, survival of the fittest, and trial and error.

And speaking of trial and error, the LDS church spends millions doing surveys and statistical cause and effect social research to determine how to perfect its methods, specifically, how to help young people remain faithful. Scouting, boys and girls camps, team sports, co-ed activities, theater productions, and goal setting programs have been shown effective in helping young people remain faithful members into adulthood, and therefore, the church emphasizes these elements of its programs for the youth. In a similar manner, gangs, drug cartels, and military units also spend considerable time perfecting their programs and policies to obtain maximum performance, efficiency, and loyalty. Those institutions that continuously improve rise to the top and thrive. Those that do not will wither and die. There is no sinister plot to rule the earth, it is simply good business.

It is not surprising that the US citizenry is hesitant to consider an LDS member a sound choice for President. While most would expect that unreasonable religious fervor would be bridled in the Oval Office, there is the nagging doubt that in a crisis, the reaction of an LDS chief executive might revert to the base cultism. For example, retaining a core belief in an impending Armageddon conflict and expecting the imminent second coming of Christ might lead to the wrong choices of conflict escalation when the opposite reaction is needed. It is unfortunate for Mitt Romney that he did not take time to do some in-depth research into Mormonism about 5 or 10 years ago and renounce his membership. He seems like a reasonable man, capable of squelching his human biases, and would probably have reached the same conclusions the author has reached. If he had, he may have become President of the USA.

CHAPTER 7
RUDELY AWAKENED

If a faith will not bear to be investigated: if its preachers and professors are afraid to have it examined, their foundation must be very weak. - George Albert Smith

Each of us has to face the matter – either the Church is true, or it is a fraud. There is no middle ground. It is the Church and kingdom of God, or it is nothing. – Gordon B. Hinckley[62]

July 2005

My awakening from the hypnotic 'ignorance is bliss' state begins with two major events only a few weeks apart. The first was during an early morning fitness run. My non-member running partner had just read the book Under the Banner of Heaven by Jon Krakauer, and had questions about the origins of polygamy. The book described polygamy, beginning with the wives of Joseph Smith. I accepted the book on loan, with a promise to read it and verify the facts.

I had not started reading Under the Banner of Heaven before attending the Lamborn family reunion. The reunion was held near Brigham City Utah. After the main festivities and traditional work project were over, several of my sibling brothers and I sat down and we discussed the church, its doctrine, and how much of the information that was coming out about the church and its history did not square with what we had been taught. Although our upbringing was the same, our experiences

---

[62] LDS General Conference Address, Spring 2003

and doubts regarding the church varied greatly, from atheism to true-blue faithful. Although I had been pushed to the edge of my intellectual comfort zone, I considered myself completely faithful and a "true-blue Mormon", having done zero research and attempting to squelch my doubts and intellectual dissonance.

The impact of this discussion with my brothers cannot be overstated. We discussed many topics, including problems with the <u>Book of Abraham</u>, troubles with the historicity of and witnesses to <u>The Book of Mormon</u>, and the questionable conduct of Joseph Smith in many situations. We also discussed the refreshing honesty of our father, Reuel Lamborn, regarding the church and 'testimony'. It had only been three years since our father had died, and this was really the first time we talked about him at length since the funeral. Reuel was not prone to repeating hollow assertions or relying on borrowed knowledge which is so prevalent and even encouraged in the church. He was his own man and made his own judgments and decisions based on the available information. He was also a man who respected and had tolerance for other opinions.

During this discussion with my brothers, for the first time in my life, I felt like I could be honest about my innermost thoughts and feelings about Mormonism, knowing that with brothers, blood was thicker than religious holy water. Not only was this group understanding and sympathetic, there was no closed-mindedness or tendency to be judgmental. There was only brotherly love and concern that we were making the best choices for ourselves and our families. It was immediately obvious that these men were entirely capable of thinking for themselves. What a breath of fresh air. People regularly pay hundreds of dollars for such a valuable therapy session. The best things in life are free, and this experience fits that description. We resolved to help each other, share our thoughts, feelings, and discoveries, and knew that while our individual paths would all be different, we were and would always be a band of brothers.

We also agreed that we would do our level best to spare our dear mother any unnecessary pain and anguish, should any of us decide to leave the church. We knew that mom would likely never understand a defection from the church and she would consider her life a partial failure should one of her chicks fall out of the Mormon nest. We all knew that we had the best mother that any member of the human race could ever wish to have, and none of us wished to hurt her in any way. On that warm summer night, I never would have imagined that I would be the one to cross the line and inflict that pain we agreed to avoid. I will expand on this issue later.

I returned home to Arizona and figured that Krakauer's book was as good a place to start as any. I read it and was surprised at how much history of the church and background information regarding the church was woven into the murder story. While it did not seem likely that Krakauer would be dishonest with the portrayal of Joseph Smith as an accomplished womanizer and dyed-in-the-wool polygamist, I nevertheless checked the names and dates on familysearch.org, the church's own genealogical website, and then purchased Mormon Enigma[63], for my wife as a Christmas present (so I could borrow it and read it too).

I had been taught in my youth that Joseph Smith had received revelations regarding polygamy, but that during Joseph's mortal life he had only Emma as wife. Not only that, I was taught that Smith was extremely reluctant to consider taking other women as wives due to his unwavering love and devotion to Emma. Thus, he resisted the commands of God to take other women, promising that he would later in life, but was murdered before he could make good on his promise to God, and that his promise was made good in the afterlife as he had several women sealed to him in the temple. In short, he was painted as a saint of the highest order, with impeccable honesty and monogamous devotion to Emma.

While some members have scoffed at this misinformation, others have honestly admitted to me that they were taught the same thing. There appears to be much non-uniformity in what facts are taught to the members. The lesson plans in my day, apparently conveniently omitted the polygamy issue in total, when it came to the life of Smith. It should also be pointed out that an entire religion, "The Reorganized Church of Jesus Christ of Latter-Day Saints" (RLDS) officially believed implicitly and

[63] Linda King Newell and Valeen Tippetts Avery, *Mormon Enigma, Emma Hale Smith*, 2nd Ed, 1994

completely that Smith only had Emma for his wife until the evidence of other marriages became incontrovertible. The RLDS organization officially changed their name to "Community of Christ" in 2000[64].

My son Joe recounted to me what was taught to him regarding Smith and polygamy, in 2007, in seminary at Red Mountain High School (Mesa AZ). The current lesson plan allegedly includes discussion that Smith took other women as wives, and emphasizes Smith's reluctance to follow God's commands. Of course, the teacher allegedly mentioned that there was no welfare program and there had to be a way to take care of the widows and excess women, at best a half-truth, since the men actually outnumbered the women on the frontier. (The whole 'reluctance' angle makes me ill, since it does not square with the facts and obvious motives, but nicely coats the bitter pill with sugar for easy swallowing by church members). The current seminary lesson plan, according to my understanding based on this discussion with my son, still conveniently omits the following facts[65]:

1. Smith married women who were already married (polyandry).
2. Smith was caught in an adulterous affair with Fanny Alger before any 'revelations'.
3. Emma was not initially told about the marriages.
4. All women married to Smith were sworn to complete secrecy, and the women received no sustenance from Smith.
5. Smith's favorite method of persuasion involved an angelic visitation and threat of death to the prophet by the sword if the women did not consent.
6. That, to a large degree, the gunfight at Carthage jail that resulted in Smith's demise was a direct result of Smith's womanizing (proposing marriage to Jane Law) and subsequent lawlessness in destroying the free press that had so eloquently exposed Smiths foibles. Nothing is more of a threat to tyranny than the truth, and the truth was the one thing that Smith could not stand to have printed.

---

[64] *Salt Lake Tribune*, 9 April 2000
[65] These facts are well established in *Mormon Enigma, Emma Hale Smith*, Newell and Tippetts

Of course, I realized that I had been hoodwinked and I had been sold a piece of swampland. How is it possible that a four-year seminary graduate, a returned missionary, a life-long member, and perennial Priesthood leader (me) knows less about the personal life of the founder of Mormonism than a non-member coworker?

After reading <u>Mormon Enigma</u>, I was struck by two aspects of the polygamous relationships Smith formed. The first aspect was the secrecy. Secrecy has no place if the subject is revealed truth from God. The second was Smith's unscrupulous method in securing the affection of these women. Several women related the same experience when Smith approached them with a proposal. Smith described an angel of the Lord appeared with a sword and commanded that he propose marriage to the woman or the angel would slay him. To me, this amounts to manipulation, preying on the woman's belief in angels and his 'prophetic calling', along with fear and compassion. No woman would want to be responsible for the death of a prophet of God. Thus Smith was able to add liberally to his harem. I was physically ill reading about this. I could not believe in a God that would participate in such folly; therefore Smith had to be, in my estimation, either a fallen prophet or a complete phony from start to end. The only thing left for me to discover is when the deceit began.

Up to this point, polygamy was never a huge issue for me – most of the male members of the church simply accept it. After all, it favors the male. I was no different. I simply went along with it. If it is God's will, then I was willing to just count my blessings even though it seemed wrong. So, make no mistake, it was not polygamy in general, or Smith's polygamy in particular, that gave me heartburn at this time (since this time I have reconsidered, see Appendix B). It was the secrecy, the story of the angel and the sword, and the manipulation perpetrated by Smith that set me on a path of discovery. I was, however; far from reaching any conclusion about the veracity of the church at this point. I simply became fully engaged in my research, and with a completely open mind, for the first time in my life.

At this point I made a conscious decision to put my research and findings completely out in the open. My thinking was this: (1) I dearly wished others would have shared these facts and events with me earlier, and I should adhere to the Golden Rule, and (2) the truth has nothing to fear from examination. Surely the true church of God can withstand any fact or series of facts and the facts can be discussed openly, honestly, and objectively in any church forum. The truth would never shrink when faced with facts; rather, our understanding of truth is always enhanced by facts and evidence.

I told my wife about the books I was reading, invited her to join me, and left the books out for her to read. Even though <u>Mormon Enigma</u> was a Christmas present, and she was genuinely excited to read it on Christmas morning, her enthusiasm waned after I quickly read it, recommended it as an informative book, and put it back on the shelf. She realized that it was probably not overly complimentary of Joseph Smith and was therefore patently evil. For the member, the facts should only be examined when they do not detract from the spirit.

Now, I return to my investigation. Obviously, the church had hidden Smith's polygamous and polyandrous relationships and deceptions from me for some reason. It was also plain to see from Smith's public denials of his polygamous relationships that he was capable of deception on a grand scale. I also realized that while serving a mission in Belgium and France and since my mission to my non-member friends, I was guilty of spreading false information. I repeated the lies that Smith only had other women married to him after his death, that the women in the church outnumbered the men, that the days of polygamy were over and would never return, etc. This upset me on several levels. First, I did not fancy being affiliated with any organization that adopts a hide and deny approach to information control. Second, now that I know I am guilty of perpetuating the deception, how do I right the wrong? And lastly, I would have dearly wished to know about these issues before giving up two years of my life on a mission.

The obvious question then became: What other skeletons are lurking in the closets of church history and origins that have been obscured from my view? I soon discovered that Smith's womanizing was the tip of the iceberg. I was transformed into a ravenous wolf, devouring book after book, researching on the internet, trying to get answers to my deepest questions.

I proceeded to read BH Roberts <u>Studies of The Book of Mormon</u>, which was an eye-opener to a horde of problems with the historicity of <u>The Book of Mormon</u>. Now my radar was on full strength scan, there was no turning back now.

CHAPTER 8
MIND CONTROL, PART 2

We don't receive wisdom; we must discover it for ourselves after a journey that no one can take for us or spare us. - Marcel Proust

Faith means not wanting to know what is true. - Friedrich Nietzsche

There are three primary reasons why intelligent and stable people fall into destructive mind control[66]:

1. Lack of awareness or denial that destructive mind control institutions exist
2. Environments and situational vulnerabilities
3. Psychological profile / personality

Among the prime personality characteristics which make people susceptible to mind control are difficulties with critical thinking, a belief in destiny and the supernatural, vivid imaginations, insecurity, low self-esteem, and pre-existing phobias. People-pleasers, those who seek approval of their peer group, are particularly vulnerable.

Other potentially destructive mind control tactics[67] are:

*   Doctrine over person
*   Loading the language
*   Group pressures
*   Obedience to authority
*   Information censorship

---

[66] *Releasing the Bonds*, p 86
[67] *Releasing the Bonds*, Chapter 2

- Controlling a person's spiritual life
- Gaining control over a person's thinking time
- Creating fear in members, defectors are shunned
- Providing models that demonstrate "correct" behavior
- Closed system of logic, sacred science, dissenters shamed
- Major time commitment required for indoctrination sessions and group rituals
- Intense indoctrination during the teen years
- 'Heavenly soldiers for God' theme

Doctrine over Person

There is no official allowance for an individual to tailor or modify doctrine to suit individual needs in Mormonism. Members who cannot comprehend or hesitate to accept a certain aspect of doctrine are invited to humble themselves and pray fervently, and are promised that with the proper combination of humility and prayer, they will eventually understand and agree with the group. The underlying message is that if an individual cannot agree with the group, the individual lacks the proper humility and sincerity in prayer. The member can only trust his intellect when it conforms with church doctrine. The doctrine itself is intrinsically perfect and supposedly unchanging, although new prophets tend to foster doctrine drift over time. An example is the recent wording change in the introduction to The Book of Mormon[68], which de-emphasizes the long-held tenet that Native Americans were direct descendants of the Lamanite people described in the book.

Loading the Language

Such phases as "magnifying one's calling", "lengthen your stride", "having one's calling and election made sure", "returned missionary", "family home evening", "word of wisdom", "the brethren", "the endowment" are examples of loading the language. There are many other Mormons terms and acronyms that mean nothing to others, such as wards, stakes, home teachers, visiting teachers[69], MIA (Mutual Improvement Association), PPI (Personal Priesthood Interview), Relief Society, Elders Quorum, Seven-

---

[68] "Single Word Change in Book of Mormon Speaks Volumes", *Salt Lake Tribune*, 8 Nov 2007

[69] All active adult male members are home teachers and active adult female members are visiting teachers. Home teachers and visiting teachers make home visits to other members each month, sharing a lesson and asking about family needs.

ties, PEC (Priesthood Executive Committee), and so on. Mormonism loads the language as well as any institution.

Linguistic terms unique to the group tend to reinforce the groupthink and serves to insulate the group from outsiders. Newcomers are anxious to learn the lingo, and with the mastery of each expression, acronym, and term feel more and more accepted. Outsiders automatically feel left out of the conversation when insiders begin discussing church events and activities. Steven Hassan explains:

> Words are the tools we use for thinking. If you can control the words people use, you can control their thoughts.[70]

Group Pressures

There is tremendous group pressure in Mormonism. The daily pressures are related to scripture study and prayer. Weekly pressures include attending meetings, preparation for meetings, and family home evening. Monthly pressures are applied to complete home teaching or visiting teaching, attend the temple at least once, and for many, monthly reports are required. There are quarterly leadership meetings, semi-annual stake and semi-annual general conferences to attend and assimilate, and annual tithing settlement. And there are dire consequences if everything is not completed. The member who does not perform is pushed to a lower and lower social status, is not given prestigious responsibilities, and probably the worst consequence is family and spousal disappointment, blame, and shame.

Obedience to Authority

The church has a trump card regarding obedience to authority. Mormon Prophet Wilford Woodruff stated, when he was president of the church:

> The Lord will never permit me or any other man who stands as President of this Church to lead you astray. It is not in the program.

---

[70] *Releasing the Bonds*, pg 50

It is not in the mind of God. If I were to attempt that, the Lord would remove me out of my place, and so He will any other man who attempts to lead the children of men astray from the oracles of God and from their duty. [71]

This trump card, simply stated is this: God will never punish a member for taking direction from church leaders. This takes away any objection to obedience, because the leader and the directive does not have to be correct, the leader's direction does not have to make any sense, the instruction could actually be immoral and it wouldn't make any difference. The member is obligated to obey, and questioning is often met with impatient dismissals. Ezra T. Benson describes the depth and breadth of the blind obedience expectation[72]:

> First: The prophet is the only man who speaks for the Lord in every-thing. Second: The living prophet is more vital to us than the standard works [Bible, Book of Mormon, etc]. Third: The living prophet is more important to us than a dead prophet. Fourth: The prophet will never lead the Church astray. Fifth: The prophet is not required to have any particular earthly training or credentials to speak or act on any matter at any time. Sixth: The prophet does not have to say "Thus Saith the Lord," to give us scripture. Seventh: The prophet tells us what we need to know, not always what we want to know. Eighth: The prophet is not limited by men's reasoning. Ninth: The prophet can receive revelation on any matter, temporal or spiritual. Tenth: The prophet may be involved in civic matters. Eleventh: The two groups who have the greatest difficulty in following the prophet are the proud who are learned and the proud who are rich. Twelfth: The prophet will not necessarily be popular with the world or the worldly. Thirteenth: The prophet and his counselors make up the First Presidency – the highest quorum in the Church. Fourteenth: The prophet and the presidency – the living prophet and the First Presidency – follow them and be blessed – reject them and suffer.

An example of this is when I asked a leader to explain the reasoning why young men who came to church without white shirts and ties should

---

[71] LDS General Conference Address, October 6, 1890
[72] *Mormon Corporate Empire*, pg 200

be denied the opportunity to administer the sacrament. What was so special about a white shirt and tie, and why is it appropriate to risk hurt feelings over an arbitrary dress code? The answer was a curt: it is at the discretion of the stake president and bishop; the membership is expected to obey and enforce. No discussion, no rationale, no chance to gain a deeper understanding, no chance for compromise, just a command to obey.

The young children are taught that peace is found through obedience. Among the many songs taught to young children is *Follow the Prophet!*, with nine verses, the refrain, repeated after each verse, is:

Follow the prophet,
Follow the prophet,
Follow the prophet,
Don't go astray!
Follow the prophet,
Follow the prophet,
Follow the prophet,
He knows the way.

The hymn '*Keep the Commandments*', sung by young and old alike says:

Keep the commandments;
Keep the commandments!
In this there is safety;
In this there is peace.
He will send blessings;
He will send blessings.
Words of a prophet:
Keep the commandments.
In this there is safety and peace.

Information Censorship

When the information that a person has access to is controlled, his ability to develop and exercise critical thinking skills is greatly diminished. The church accomplishes censorship of information in several ways.

The most overt method is the closing of church archives and hiding historical documents that call into question the divinity of church origins or contain teachings contradicting current doctrine. Censorship began with Joseph Smith with the destruction of the Nauvoo newspaper "The Expositor"[73] and continues today with the closure of church archives and the purchase of historical documents from Mark Hofmann[74].

The church makes no apologies regarding the tactic of selective storytelling. The premise is that the church is engaged in a war between good and evil and has assumed the role of advocate for good only, and is therefore justified in abandoning balance in reporting facts. Apostle Dallin Oaks stated:

> Balance is telling both sides. This is not the mission of the official Church literature or avowedly anti-Mormon literature. Neither has any responsibility to present both sides.[75]

Another apostle, Boyd K. Packer goes on to say:

> In the Church we are not neutral. We are one-sided. There is a war going on and we are engaged in it. It is the war between good and evil, and we are belligerents defending the good. We are therefore obliged to give preference to and protect all that is represented in the gospel of Jesus Christ, and we have made covenants to do it.[76]
>
> *"That the lie is permitted as a means to pious ends is part of the theory of every priesthood.[77]"*

---

[73] Richard Lyman Bushman, *Joseph Smith, Rough Stone Rolling*, p 539

[74] Robert Lindsey, *A Gathering of Saints: A True Story of Money Murder and Deceit*, see also Chapter 17

[75] Conference for Church educators, August 1985

[76] Boyd K. Packer, "The Mantle is Far, Far Greater than the Intellect", given at the 5th Annual Church Educational System Religious Educators' Symposium, 22 August 1981

[77] Friedrich Nietzsche, *The Will to Power*, p. 89

More subtle methods of information censorship are dilution and misdirection. This is achieved using two methods. The first is dissemination of new teaching materials. If the gospel is 'the same yesterday, today, and forever', why the need for new lesson manuals every few years? The second dilution method is through 'continuous' revelation. Articles in the monthly magazines[78], including semi-annual general conference addresses, and new publications from church leaders form a continuous stream of information to occupy the membership.

How does dilution work? If a person's time is consumed assimilating the new materials, there is little time to research the old materials to detect changes and inconsistencies. Dilution also allows the church to downplay certain controversial issues or doctrines over time. Some examples: Brigham Young taught that Adam was God[79], Christ was a polygamist[80], and blacks would never be able to hold the priesthood[81]. Spencer W. Kimball taught[82] that the time had arrived that the skin color of the righteous Native American (Lamanite) people was changing and becoming lighter, a great confirmation of the prophecies of The Book of Mormon. If the church members only had the old magazines, conference talks, and original teachings of Kimball and Young, these embarrassing doctrines would be brought up every year or two and would be devastating to the membership. The current lesson manuals that describe the teachings of Young and Kimball make no mention of these troublesome doctrines; they have been scrubbed clean.

The final method is a smokescreen which is deployed by amplifying the doctrine of persecution. The members are taught that persecution confirms the divinity of the true church of God. Satan won't waste his time throwing his barbs at other religious institutions; only the true church of God merits his full attention. The members learn that one of Satan's best tools is anti-Mormon literature. Anything that is not condoned by

---

[78] Monthly LDS publications include *The Ensign* for adults, *The New Era* (formally *The Improvement Era*) for teens, and *The Friend* for children.
[79] *Journal of Discourses*, 1:51, 4:1, 2 Diary of Hosea Stout pg 435 (April 9, 1852)
[80] Brigham Young, quoted in Eliza Young's, *Wife No. 19*, Chpt. XXXV
[81] Brigham Young, *Journal of Discourses*, Vol. 7, pp. 290-291, 1859
[82] *The Improvement Era*, December 1960 pp.922-923

church headquarters or confirms the groupthink is automatically labeled as sinister 'anti-Mormon' literature, the work of Satan. Undoubtedly, this book will achieve this label immediately, even though it is not intended to be anti-anything. It is about giving people the opportunity to make informed and unencumbered choices and breaking out of manipulative circumstances.

Thus, the doctrine of persecution and cautioning the members to be wary of anti-Mormon literature and websites is the final, and perhaps the most effective method of information censorship.

Controlling a Person's Spiritual Life

Self-control is not an automatic response or natural behavior for believers. Giving yourself to Christ, putting your life in the hands of God, or similar experiences are regularly expressed by members when describing their life experience. However, a member of the church would deny with their dying breath that the church controlled his or her spiritual life. Only those who step outside the group are in a position to recognize this control, and the subtlety of the willing transfer of command from the individual to the organization. Ironically, both Christ and Buddha taught that power should be transferred from institutions to individuals, but Mormonism and most organized religions capitalize on the names and (alleged) teaching of these philosopher kings to accomplish the polar opposite.

The church gains control over the spiritual dimension of humanity by thought channeling and vaunted philosopher gurus, tied together by the Holy Ghost doctrine. This sounds complicated, but it is terribly simple and terribly effective. The member is taught that everyday uplifting thoughts and ideas that come to them are given to them through the Holy Ghost, there is no other source of pure truth. The member then attributes everything to their church membership (which gives each member rights of continuous guidance via the Holy Ghost), reinforcing their conviction on a daily basis. Other beautiful possibilities regarding spiritual gifts are not ever contemplated. Thus the spiritual machinations of the individual are channeled to the church and the boundaries are iron clad. The member is blinded to other possibilities before even leaving the gate.

Members are taught that if a prophet (vaunted philosopher guru) said something, then reason and critical thinking must be set aside and blind faith, humility, and obedience are required. This is disingenuous and limits the possibility for the person to discard a misconception from a prior generation or replace an antiquated or bad idea with a better one. With the current set of fifteen prophet, seers, and revelators pontificating profusely on all sorts of subjects, there is little need for the member to do any independent thinking. The thought engine with all critical thinking processes gradually shuts down. The end state of the member completely assimilated by the group think is one devoid of original thinking and blind to what has happened to them. They are completely dependent on the group on how to live their lives day-to-day, which is another example of dependency.

Gaining Control Over A Person's Thinking Time

The control of a person's thinking time is accomplished by task over-loading and excessive direction. The standard of personal conduct includes such a consuming and varied array of activities that there is usually little time left over to do any thinking outside the box built by the church. The member has been given so many volumes of comprehensive advice on how to live, learn, act, think, raise children, etc. that there is hardly time to remember all the particulars and remain organized enough to execute it properly. The thinking regresses to focus only on the 'how' to get everything done, not 'why'.

Members are encouraged to have a large family, which, by itself, drastically limits available thinking time. If, per chance, the member winds up with time to do something else, the temptation is to vegetate or look for a mental escape like television or a fictional book. Very few ever reach the point of feeling motivated to research the true history of religion.

Creating Fear in Members, Defectors are Shunned

Fears and phobias (fear of the irrational) in the members come in many forms. The fear of God's judgments is an example of doctrinal fear. Members typically think that this is healthy fear, since it motivates the member to repent and prepare for death or the second coming. The threatening prophecies and talk of 'signs of the times' make this fear more real and more urgent. Fear of the demons of Satan, numbering in the billions, who are ever-present here on earth, haunts every member. Safety may only be found by being hyper-vigilant and staying close to the herd. There is the ever-present fear of the anti-Mormon network, working diligently to destroy the Kingdom of God. Phobia indoctrination is the single most powerful mind control tool to foster obedience and make affiliates dependent[83].

The other fears and phobias that play into the Mormon psyche relate to the society more than the doctrine. Since everyone in the Mormon community has a responsibility, there is a nagging fear that one is not performing up to standard. There is always fear of offending others. Then there is fear of what others might think if family members fall into sin or renounce the faith.

The final fear is the awful infernal state of those who leave the fold. They are viewed as the most miserable creatures in existence; it would be better if they had never been born. The gossip and rumor mill regarding those who leave the church reinforces this fear. The most common reason discussed is that the dissenter was "offended" or "decided he was smarter than the prophets", which are thinly-veiled accusations of false pride. It is usually accompanied by a vocalization of sadness, implying that the defector has lost his soul and merits the pity of the faithful. Other typical phrases the author has heard include "gone off the deep end", "got addicted to drugs or pornography or something", which assassinates the character of the defector and paints a picture of misery and pain. Erich Fromm explains:

---

[83] *Releasing the Bonds*, chapter 10

Man as man is afraid of insanity, just as man as animal is afraid of death. Man has to be related, he has to find union with others, in order to be sane. This need to be one with others is the strongest passion, stronger than sex and often even stronger that his wish to live... For this reason the individual must blind himself from seeing that which his group claims does not exist, or accept as truth that which the majority says is true, even if his own eyes could convince him that it is false. The herd is so vitally important for the individual that their views, beliefs, feelings, constitute reality for him, more so than what his senses and his reason tell him.... There is almost nothing a man will not believe or repress when he is threatened with ostracism.

Providing Models that Demonstrate "Correct" Behavior

Living models who illustrate correct and acceptable behavior abound. The local ward and stake leaders are the most apparent. The local membership, when discussing gospel principles and conduct, often use local leaders as examples. The living prophets, seers, and revelators are showcased on a regular basis. Book sales are an indicator of how much these men are revered.

Deceased models are regularly discussed. For example, the current study curriculum showcases a latter-day prophet each year. The lessons always focus on the positives and events in the lives of these men that illustrate proper conduct and Godliness. Pioneer experiences and stories from valiant ancestors are regularly called for in lesson plans. Church affiliates are presented with models of correct behavior at every turn.

Closed System of Logic, Sacred Science, Dissenters Shamed

Mormonism creates a tightly controlled logical system. All revealed doctrines are absolute truth and true science will always align with revealed truth in the end. The Holy Spirit is thus the source of all truth, and those who are in tune with the spirit will hear and understand the truth, which always agrees with the teachings of the church. All members have access to the truth test, which is a foolproof method to know what is true and what is false. This logical system is airtight and completely circular.

It is the core of the force field that surrounds each member and is virtually impenetrable.

Those who dissent are made to feel as though their questioning indicates that there is something inherently wrong with them, and this is backed up by the core logic system. If the dissenter is not in harmony with the group, he or she is obviously not in tune with the spirit due to sin or worldliness or pride. There is no other explanation contemplated by the membership. When a controversial or illogical topic is discussed, members who feel uncomfortable with what is being said just remain silent. The silence is assumed to be agreement, which is how lies and falsehoods flourish in mind control organizations.

Major Time Commitment Required for Indoctrination Sessions and Group Rituals

If the three-hour meeting block each Sunday is not time commitment enough, most members have callings that require meetings each week or each month and many also have responsibilities to work weekly with the youth for 90 minutes on a weeknight. Virtually everyone has quarterly training meetings to teach them how to properly dispense their responsibility.

The ultimate group ritual in Mormonism occurs in the temple. Most faithful members attend about once a month. Each visit soaks up a minimum of three hours, when preparation and travel time are included. Temple attendance is replete with group affirmations including group movement, group prayer, and language and signs and handshakes familiar only to the group. Many will spend hundreds of hours in the temple each year. At least once a month, there is a stake or ward 'temple night' to encourage participation. Twice each year, the members are challenged to attend the temple for an entire day in the week before stake conference. Some take vacation time off work to attend the temple for these challenge days and will spend 12 hours or more in the temple in a single day. Temple rites are begun early in life (usually age 19-22) and combines verbal public commitment with repetition, an effective behavioral control technique, well proven in selling cars, Tupperware, books, insurance, political ideals, and other products and services.

Intense Indoctrination During the Teen Years

Mormonism certainly qualifies in this category with weekly young men/ young women activities, four-year seminary during the high school years, boys and girls camps, and the pioneer reenactment which combines extreme hardship with intense indoctrination.

It is during the teen years that the identity of the individual takes shape, and the desire to become independent from parents is strong. Therefore, the church provides programs where third party teachers (not parents) are there to indoctrinate the youth. When the tools of mind control are wrought upon the youth during this volatile transition time, the chances are very good that the objectives of mind control can be attained. Key teen attributes which facilitate mind control tactics include heightened sensitivities to guilt and shame, an intense need to be identified with a group, fears and phobias of many kinds, and a proclivity to search for and select a life course.

There is another organization that perfected the teen indoctrination method. [Once again, this example is not intended to offend or compare the purposes of these organizations, only point out common methods.] The demand for moral purity, complete abstinence from sex, tobacco, and alcohol, and hyper-vigilance were taught and practiced. Role models showing correct behavior were provided. The children were convinced of how special they were, how they had been divinely chosen. The parents described the transformation of their children and watched helplessly as their children were literally kidnapped right under their noses. The party had complete control; the parents were powerless to deter their fanaticism. The organization: Nazi Germany in the 1930s.

'Heavenly Soldiers for God' Theme

The portrayal of the affiliate as being a warrior hero on the side of good against the world of evil is a recurring theme in mind control groups[84]. The soldier mentality facilitates the top-down authority structure of the

---

[84] *Releasing the Bonds*, pg 181

organization, reinforces the black/white images of the world, and leads the member to believe that his sacrifices for the army of God are holy and will be rewarded with glory.

Heavenly soldiering in Mormonism extends to every member, not just the missionary force. Church hymns such as "Onward Christian Soldiers", "Behold a Royal Army", and a popular Mormon play called "Saturdays Warrior" all teach the members their divine role as combatants in the war against evil.

Conclusion

Some things to remember in retaining control of thought processes and fighting faith abuse with its associated unreasonable fervor:

- Avoid groups that load the language (have excessive tribal vocabulary terms)
- Avoid groups that require strict obedience to leaders
- Never take action due to fear of the group or fear of the supernatural inventions of the group
- Avoid groups that have "correct" behavior models, major time commitments, or shun dissenters

In addition to religious cults, gangs, drug cartels, pyramid sales schemes, and military units are other examples of organizations that could potentially qualify as mind control entities.

Are destructive mind control subjects happy? They will, almost without exception, declare that they are the happiest people on the planet, and they believe it. Steven Hassan explains[85]:

> When the cult member says he is "happy", it is usually the cult identity that is talking. The cult self is doing what it has been instructed to do…. "When I was in the cult, I told everyone that I was happier that I had ever been in my life. But when you are a Moonie, being

---

[85] *Releasing the Bonds*, pg 117

close to God makes you happy, and God is defined as a suffering parent. Therefore, the more you can feel God's suffering heart and sacrifice, the happier you will be.

Mormonism, as currently implemented, qualifies as a mind control society, and a very efficient one. So, is Mormonism a destructive cult or not? This question is under constant debate among members (especially disaffected members) and non-members. There is no clear answer, because it all depends on the definition of a destructive cult.

World leading experts in cultism[86] have suggested that a destructive cult, in addition to the elements of destructive mind control and preoccupation with wealth, exhibits the following characteristics:

- Includes a pyramid-shaped authoritarian regime with a person or group of people who have dictatorial control, with no meaningful accountability. Leaders claim to be prophets, apostles, or the Messiah, and profess to know the true meaning of scripture[87], always knowing what is right. There is no tolerance for critical inquiry. The LDS church meets this criterion with its organizational structure with both a prophet and apostles and top-down obedience requirements. *When our leaders speak, the thinking has been done. When they propose a plan – it is God's plan*[88].

- It uses deception in recruiting new members (e.g. people are NOT told up front what the group is, what the group actually believes and what will be expected of them if they become members). The LDS church does a relatively good job of being upfront with basic doctrines and expectations for new recruits. The exceptions are dodging controversial issues and giving half-truths as explanations. Recruits are told of the great blessings, the honor, and privilege of attending the temple, which they can do after a one-year waiting period. The recruits are not told

---

[86] Example: Steven A. Hassan, website is currently freedomofmind.com
[87] *Releasing the Bonds*, pg 5
[88] *Mormon Corporate Empire*, pg 197 citing a June 1945 Ward Teachers Message published by the Church

that in the temple they will be asked to consecrate everything they possess and will ever possess to the church. They are also not told that they will learn secret signs, words, and phrases that cannot be divulged under penalty of death. Does this qualify as deception or just reverence for the sacred? The reader is left to decide.

The reader is also left to decide if Mormonism qualifies as a destructive cult based on the evidence presented. I have not listed and discussed every single characteristic mentioned in the reference materials regarding mind control tactics, I have culled the list to what I felt are the most interesting for Mormonism. Steven Hassan clarifies the cult judgment criteria[89]:

It is not necessary for every single item on the list to be present. Mind-controlled cult members can live in their own apartments, have nine-to-five jobs, be married with children, and still be unable to think for themselves and act independently.

Perhaps the more important question is whether Mormonism uses destructive mind control and represents a toxic environment for the human intellect. Again, the reader is left to decide. Is the mind control destructive, fostering an ever-increasing dependence on the group and discouraging autonomy of mental processes, or does it promote autonomy and diminished dependence on the Church?

---

[89] *Releasing the Bonds*, pg 46

CHAPTER 9
THE RAGGED EDGE

He who will not reason, is a bigot: he who cannot is a fool; and he who dares not, is a slave. -William Drummond

It demeans both life and art to call Mormon falsehood 'paradox'. – Bob McCue

I continued teaching the High Priests Group once a month. My research crept into my lessons. I was far too interested in what I was discovering to keep tidbits of interesting information from my friends at church. Thus began my fall from grace.

My first foray into presentation of non-scripted lesson material occurred when a lesson came up on the life of Joseph Smith, Jr. I went to the church's own genealogical website, familysearch.org, and printed the list of the wives of Joseph Smith, Jr. I then printed the information for some of the wives of Smith, showing that they were already married, and that their husbands were very much alive at the time of their marriage to Smith. I asked, by show of hand, how many were aware that Smith had wives other than Emma in his mortal life. Three raised their hand (out of about 25 present). I then asked, by show of hand, how many were aware that Smith had married women who were already married to living men. There were no hands. I asked how many knew that Smith had married a fourteen year old, Helen Mar Kimball. There were no hands. I presented the proof and passed it around the room. The men eagerly examined the printed sheets. The lesson went well, there were no negative comments or repercussions, only compliments.

The following month a lesson included some scriptural references in the Book of Abraham. For some reason, the younger men (Elders Quorum) were combined with the older men (High Priests) and I was teaching a larger than normal group of men that day. At this point, I had not read any books on the origins of the <u>Book of Abraham</u>, but had just done some limited Internet research, and was vaguely aware of the central issues. I opened by asking, "By show of hands, how many are aware that the original papyri from which the <u>Book of Abraham</u> was translated were discovered in 1967 in a New York museum?" Three people, of about 40 present, raised their hand. I followed with "I am in a situation and need your help. I have a friend who claims to be able to prove that Joseph Smith was a fraud based on the <u>Book of Abraham</u> and the papyri. Is there anyone here with information that could help my friend understand the origin of the book?" A brief discussion and some testimony bearing ensued, and the assertion that 'all you need is the truth test' argument to help my friend. I said that testimonies would not help this situation, that testimony bearing is simply declaration-ism, the last bastion of the unreasonable fanatic, and would have no positive effect on my questioning friend. A single attendee, a neighbor of mine, who remains a good and open-minded friend, spoke to me after the class, offering to lend me a book[90] on the subject. I readily accepted his invitation and read it in the following weeks. I made notes as I read, and essentially wrote a book report. I then read <u>By His Own Hand Upon Papyrus</u>, by Larson. The facts in the two books were the same. To me, the facts spoke for themselves. The papyri were basic funerary documents, having nothing to do with Abraham, and post-dated the time of Abraham by many centuries. Smith was obviously incapable of translating Egyptian and had no gift from God for translating. He conjured the <u>Book of Abraham</u> and passed it off as a translation of the papyri, the deception was obvious to me, and I think it is obvious to anyone who objectively reviews the facts and evidence.

Even though the pile of evidence contradicting a divine origin of the church was mounting, I refrained from making a final decision regarding the truthfulness of the church. I was in data collecting mode, playing the role of the accident investigator. I was full of questions, and held hope that I would be able to find the answers I was seeking. Only after all the

---

[90] James R Harris, <u>An historical & doctrinal commentary on the Pearl of Great Price ; "The facsimiles of the Book of Abraham ; A study of the Joseph Smith Egyptian papyri"</u>

evidence was reviewed would I decide if I could continue believing in an orthodox manner.

I taught my final lesson to the High Priests in September 2005. The lesson was on building testimony, and it was a subject that I had been contemplating daily for about a month anyway. I began the lesson with a simple geometrical proof of the Pythagorean theorem, illustrating how the logical arguments are made, how the sum of the squares of the two sides have to equal the square of the hypotenuse, how the results are irrefutable. In addition to be ironclad truth from the logical development and geometrical proof, it is readily tested and useful in everyday life, especially in construction or laying tile.

I then contrasted the truth of the theorem with a five-year old member of the church who says, "I know the church is true". Is this real truth? Is the youth really sure? The class agreed that the youth was just repeating what he/she had heard and a child could not know the truth of the at age five. What about those of us who bear testimony of The Book of Mormon, calling it truth, as grown men? Can the truth of the book be established beyond a reasonable doubt, and can anyone actually KNOW of its truthfulness, and be absolutely sure? The class thought this was possible because the truth test. Of course, this response was anticipated, and I was ready with a counter-example.

I related to the class the story of BH Roberts, and his struggle to understand and resolve some fundamental historicity problems with The Book of Mormon circa 1922[91]. Here we have perhaps the most knowledgeable and informed historian on the earth at the time regarding the origins of the church, and a general authority of the church, in an honest intellectual struggle. After trying long and hard to answer his own questions, he sought advice, enlightenment, and counsel from the First Presidency and the Quorum of the Twelve Apostles. Roberts scheduled several hours with these men and described to them the issues with which he had been struggling:

---

[91] Brigham H Roberts, Brigham D. Madsen, ed., Studies of The Book of Mormon, University of Illinois Press

- The numerous domesticated and other animals (horses, cattle, sheep, elephants) cited in The Book of Mormon were not present upon arrival of the Europeans and are not found in the fossil record. I added that none of the glyphs that I have personally encountered on this continent show domesticated animals — only deer and birds and such. Also, silk and wheat cited in The Book of Mormon were not present upon arrival of the Europeans, and references to the crops and animals prevalent on this continent (llamas, bison, corn, potatoes are examples) are noticeably absent.

- Linguists agree that the variety of languages found among the native Americans suggest thousands or tens of thousands of years in development/isolation and a non-Hebrew, non Aramaic origin (the only languages possibly spoken by emigrants from Jerusalem in 620 BC). It is just not logically plausible that at least some Indian tribes were speaking Hebrew or an Aramaic dialect at 421 AD as asserted by The Book of Mormon.

- The evidence that the American Indians are not of Hebrew origin is overwhelming (language, skeletal structure, skin color, customs, stone-age technology). Every serious, unemotional, and unbiased anthropologist concludes that the origin of the American Indian is eastern Asia.

- Parallels between Ethan Smith's A View of the Hebrews and The Book of Mormon appear too numerous to be a coincidence. A View of the Hebrews was published some 7 years prior to The Book of Mormon, and Joseph Smith almost certainly had access to a copy of the book (it was published only 30 miles away from his home). The assertion that The Book of Mormon is an original work is questionable for any who take time to study and read A View of the Hebrews. I mentioned several of the parallels, here is a partial list:

1. Both books begin with the destruction of Jerusalem and banishment of Israel.
2. Use of the words "remnant" and "Gathering of the dispersed of Judah" in the introductions.
3. Use of the literal gathering of Israel as a theme.

4. Native Americans are of Hebrew origin, also a shared inaccuracy.
5. Stick of Judah, stick of Joseph, Ezekial 37 prophecy fulfilled (View of Hebrews, pg 34)
6. The people were of one color skin originally (p 114, 157)
7. Savage hunting tribes annihilated the more civilized tribes (pp 130-131, 143)
8. Ancient works, forts, mounds, vast enclosures, skill in fortifications (p 130-131)
9. Advanced metal working of all kinds (p 144)
10. Breastplate description (p 149)
11. Burying records in boxes (p 168-169)
12. Use of the phrase "Bring them to a knowledge of the gospel" (p 177)
13. Allegory of the olive tree and the House of Israel
14. Sacred records being handed down from generation to generation and then buried in a hill
15. Even though the migrating peoples were Hebrew, somehow Egyptian languages are involved
16. Both books use the terms "Zion" and "Mt. Zion" to designate restoration/gathering places.
17. Both books call upon the American people to preach the gospel to the Native Americans
18. Both books predict the eventual conversion of the "remnants" and that they will become white before the burning of the world.

Well, as I related to the men these historicity issues with The Book of Mormon, I could see that some of the men were visibly shaken. I mentioned that even though Roberts was addressing the highest authorities of the church, some of them were actually crying upon hearing him recount all the difficulties that are really insurmountable to a reasonable person. The world was crashing down around the Twelve Apostles, the sky was falling; everything they had worked for and dedicated their lives to was reduced to ash by their most trusted church historian in a few hours. If the highest authorities of the church can have their beliefs decimated by a single man with a few facts in a few hours, then how can we sit here in Mesa, Arizona and pompously state that we know the book to be true beyond any doubt? It is the pinnacle of false pride. Such religious beliefs cannot and should not ever be associated with a statement of sure knowledge, because such an assertion is preposterous. Religious tenets are not possible to know, only believe. There was some significant squirming going on amongst those present.

I should mention at this point that the Stake President was in attendance and seated in the front row for this lesson. As expected, he took issue with my argument, asserting that it was indeed possible to know these things for a certainty using the truth test, that the spirit of the Holy Ghost and God were the ultimate sources of truth, etc. The usual unsubstantiated rhetoric, made without any reasonable basis, and fundamentally fanatical in nature, was reiterated for the LDS members present. We agreed to disagree.

Looking back, these were great discussions and I am sure they were very stimulating to those present. I was perfectly content to continue being a member and sounding the voice of reason amongst the rank and file believer, and fully expected to do it in this manner for a very long time. Apparently, members cannot be disciplined for verbal discussions. I was growing bolder each month, and I liked where it was taking me. I continued to get very positive feedback from my peers in the quorum, but the congratulations seemed to be offered in more private situations, as if the person offering the compliment did not want to be seen or heard being complicit with a borderline heretic such as me. In a church full of gospel music, I was the rock and roll band. In my heart of hearts, I knew that introducing some balance to the discussions each Sunday was doing a great service to these men I cared about. I can understand why many choose to remain in the fold, believing that more good can be done from the inside out than from the outside in. I experienced this first hand. However, I was woefully unprepared for what would happen to the Lamborn family in the next three weeks.

CHAPTER 10
COGNITIVE HUMAN BIASES

One of the saddest lessons of history is this: If we've been bamboozled long enough, we tend to reject any evidence of the bamboozle. We're no longer interested in finding out the truth. The bamboozle has captured us. It's simply too painful to acknowledge, even to ourselves, that we've been taken. Once you give a charlatan power over you, you almost never get it back. - Carl Sagan

People are very open-minded about new things... as long as they're exactly like the old ones! -Charles Kettering

Humans are inclined to evaluate the world around them with some bias. Some of these biases are instinctual, some are instilled in us by conditioning, some we learn by trial and error. What follows is a discussion of some important human biases, and how organized religion, particularly Mormonism, tends to reinforce and exploit them. An understanding of human biases was tremendously helpful to me in my recovery period from the Mormon groupthink.

Groupthink Bias

The groupthink bias is defined as a tendency and bias for humans to lend credence to the predominant opinion held by the group. This bias could be instinctual, a product of the evolution of the human species, the theory being that those who went along with the group had the benefits of living in harmony with a group. Living in harmony with a group meant protection, opportunity for trading, specialization and division of labor, and the like, all of which tended to give longer life expectancy and more opportunity to reproduce.

Irving Janis[92] devised eight symptoms that are indicative of groupthink.

1. **Illusions of invulnerability** creating excessive optimism and encouraging risk taking.
2. **Rationalizing warnings** that might challenge the group's assumptions.
3. **Unquestioned belief** in the morality of the group, causing members to ignore the consequences of their actions.
4. **Stereotyping** those who are opposed to the group as weak, evil, disfigured, impotent, or stupid.
5. **Direct pressure** to conform placed on any member who questions the group, couched in terms of "disloyalty".
6. **Self censorship** of ideas that deviate from the apparent group consensus.
7. **Illusions of unanimity** among group members, silence is viewed as agreement.
8. **Mindguards** — self-appointed members who shield the group from dissenting information.

It has been noted that almost all of these are seen in totalitarian dictatorships, such as the Third Reich and North Korea.

We see manifestation of the groupthink bias all around us. Children born into Christian homes tend to be Christian. Children born in a home where both parents ascribe to a particular political party tend to align themselves with that political party. As the person matures and becomes an independent critical thinker, these alignments that have defined their field of view may change, which usually take place after adolescence.

Humans tend to be relatively uncritical of their own group, even to the point of turning a blind eye to its shortcomings. In contrast, humans tend to be highly critical of other groups and are quick to amplify their foibles. These characteristics are part and parcel to the groupthink bias.

---

[92] Janis, Irving L. *Victims of Groupthink*. Boston. Houghton Mifflin Company, 1972

All successful religions, including Mormonism, reinforce and use the groupthink bias to their advantage whenever possible.

First and foremost, the church encourages large families. The advantages of large families for mind control have already been discussed. In addition, large families favor the growth of the religion, given the predisposition (bias) of the children to accept the religion of their parents. Once again, this is simply good business.

Group prayer is particularly effective in achieving consensus of thought in a group. Members are encouraged to pray together as husband/wife couples and families at least daily, and group prayers are offered at every church meeting. There is even a special group prayer in the temple, referred to as "the true order of prayer" reserved for the elite, and can only take place in the shrine of the temple.

Mormons are encouraged to hold family home evening every week, to discuss family and household needs, make schedules, and a gospel lesson is always to be included. Thus the children are indoctrinated in a manner that places the groupthink of the religion right alongside the planning of family vacations and who takes out the trash next week. In other words, the groupthink is woven into the fabric of the family group as well as the ward family group, and the worldwide church group.

Even the doctrine reinforces the consensus opinion. Mormons are told that they are a peculiar people, and it is a badge that is to be worn with pride. Thus the group expects to be different and expects to think as one from a doctrinal viewpoint.

Every church meeting and activity reinforces the groupthink bias. With a three-hour meeting block on Sunday and responsibilities that bring members into contact with each other in a working relationship, friendships are a natural result. For the young people in the church, an additional 1.5 hour meeting with peers is held during the week, in addition to daily seminary classes, imparting to the youth a strong predisposition to select friends who are also Mormon. Thus another group is formed to insulate and protect the member from intrusion of other influences that might contradict the consensus view. This is often the strongest and most influential group to which people ascribe, because they have a hand in selecting the closest of their friends, giving them a sense of ownership and agency, however meager.

Anxiety in a group setting can be a powerful force. In Mormonism, where it is a taboo to question authority or the groupthink, the individual is often left feeling that he is the only person in the room to 'not get it', whether it be understanding a doctrine, feeling the spirit, agreeing with the person in authority, etc. This is akin to the "Emperors New Clothes" effect. The individual immediately is put into a desperate situation and seeks relief wherever he can find it, and he generally does manage to construct some logical pathway and find relief. Bob McCue[93] observes:

> "Hence, group dynamics themselves can create a self-perpetuating cycle of anxiety and relief upon which religious testimonies can come to be based. This is the religious equivalent of the economist's money machine – something is created out of nothing."

Authority Bias

The authority bias is the tendency for humans to place credence in experts and those placed in a position of authority. This is mostly a conditioned bias, and is usually reinforced by trial and error. It is also intertwined with the groupthink, since the group also tends to follow the guidance and direction of experts and those in authority. This is generally a good bias; after all, to consult a doctor and then go against his expert advice is usually a bad course of action. However, when over-amplified or misapplied, the authority bias can also be destructive.

In addition to experts who have earned a credential through education, the authority bias extends to elected officials, law enforcement officials, company executives, and religious leaders. [Notice here that I did not include immediate work supervisors in this list. In the early 1900's, they would have been on the list of those whose opinion is generally held in high regard. In the workplace today, at least in the USA, the boss is as

---

[93] Bob McCue, "Out of My Faith", p 81 http://www.mccue.cc/bob/spirituality.htm

much a target of criticism and faultfinding as anything else. Thus, the authority bias is eroding with time among humans, which is probably a good thing, as it leads to more creativity, autonomy, and ownership for the individual.]

Authority has been a central tenet of Mormon doctrine since its inception. During the first vision, where Smith purported seeing the Father and the Son, he was told that the religions found on the earth denied the "power of God"[94]. The key events of the 'restoration' revolve around the reestablishment of the authority to act in the name of God. Visitations of John the Baptist, Peter, James, and John, and a host of others to restore all the authority and 'keys to the kingdom of God' are central to the belief system. The authority and rights to revelation are clearly defined for each office and individual. The father is the final authority in the home, the elders quorum president for members of his quorum, the ward Relief Society president for the adult women in the ward, the bishop has the authority over all the ward leaders, the stake president has authority over all the bishops and wards in the stake, the prophet and apostles have the authority to guide the whole church.

The members are instructed that they will never do wrong in the eyes of God if they obey those placed in positions of authority over them. Every person who is called to such a position is called by revelation and their installation in the office is the will of God himself. Not only that, when the person is called, he or she is 'set apart' by laying on of hands and given the necessary authority keys to officiate in that office bestowed upon them. This is an effective method of impressing upon the minds of the members that they should obey those in authority and heed their counsel since God has sanctioned their authority.

There are constant reminders given to the members regarding respect and deference to those in authority. Each week, at the main group meeting (sacrament meeting), the bishop and his councilors sit up on the 'stand', an elevated platform above the members and facing the members. When the sacrament (emblems of the body and blood of Christ) are of-

---

[94] *Pearl of Great Price*, Joseph Smith History 1:19

fered to the membership, the bishop is always served first. If the bishop is absent, his first councilor is the first to partake, and so forth. The pecking order is clearly established and the reminder to have respect for those in authority is thus physically acted out each week. Each subgroup has a called leader, who has authority over the others in the group or subgroup. Those in authority often sit in front of the others and decide who should be the voice for group prayers, take charge in meetings, take notes, give lessons, set policies and rules, etc. Authority figures abound in the church hierarchy and since they are called of God, the others are compelled to obey. When anyone in the congregation is called to a position, he/she is presented before the congregation and each member is invited to indicate that they sustain the person in their new responsibility by raising the right arm to the square. This happens at least once each month and as often as weekly, depending on the demographics and dynamics of the congregation. Reinforcement of the authority bias is strong in Mormonism.

Regarding the long-term ill effects of an authoritarian environment, Ed Gardiner[95] notes:

> Authoritarian systems, by their very nature, enforce a mistrust of the self. This, in order that they, the authoritarian system, may stay in power. The result of this self-mistrust is a divided psyche with an inner wall that is fought with weapons forged by shame and steeped in self-loathing.

'Saying is Believing' Bias

As humans pronounce their beliefs or opinions, they become less likely to find fault with or change their position. With each repeating, the bias becomes stronger.

In Mormonism, 'saying is believing' equates to 'testimony bearing'. Virtually every lesson plan in every lesson manual has at least one portion of the lesson dedicated to testimony bearing by the instructor. Home

---

[95] Ed Gardiner, "Shame and the Destruction of Agency", see http://www.postmormon. org/main.swf

teachers and visiting teachers are asked to bear testimony as part of their monthly visits. All told, virtually every member is asked to bear testimony at least once a month.

Once a month the membership meets for what is called 'fast and testimony' meeting at the ward level, a public opportunity to reinforce this bias. Pressure is exerted upon the young people to stand and pronounce their sure knowledge of the unknowable. Even little children who are vying for attention and parental approval stand and say how they "know the church is true", that "Joseph Smith was a true prophet", that "The Book of Mormon is true", and other assertions of sure knowledge. This is not an intimate forum with a few people. Several hundred people typically attend fast and testimony meeting. Thus the person has made the pronouncement to virtually his whole social universe, including some strangers. It is a powerful reinforcement of the 'saying is believing' bias.

The membership is not only instructed when to bear testimony, but also that for general testimony bearing, there are three key elements: (1) Joseph Smith was a prophet of God, (2) The Book of Mormon is the word of God, and (3) that the Church of Jesus Christ is the only true church on the face of the earth. Traditionally, the members also add that the current prophet (now Thomas S. Monson) is God's living oracle. Note that these scripted points, in addition to being unknowable, are among key factors that differentiate Mormonism from mainstream Christianity, thus reinforcing the groupthink and fortifying cultural barriers at the same time.

Testimony bearing is simply declarationism, and declarationism is the last bastion of the unreasonable fanatic. – Vernon Lamborn

The Confirmation Bias

The confirmation bias is the human predisposition to retain the initial idea or method presented and reject subsequent ideas or methods. The first idea to take hold generally remains. It takes much more evidence and energy to displace the first idea than what it took initially to embed it. The more ambiguous the issue, the more likely embedded belief will survive scrutiny. On the importance of this bias, psychologist Raymond Nickerson concludes[96]:

> If one were to attempt to identify a single problematic aspect of human reasoning that deserves attention above all others, the confirmation bias would have to be among the candidates for consideration. It appears to be sufficiently strong and pervasive that one is led to wonder whether the bias, by itself, might account for a significant fraction of the disputes, altercations and misunderstandings that occur among individuals, groups, and nations.

What typically happens when an individual is reviewing evidence that might disagree or contradict the initial idea or belief is the 'makes sense – STOP' perfunctory analysis syndrome. The person begins reviewing the information, focuses on a single topic or tenet, finds a way to discount it or explain it away and then immediately concludes that all the information can be explained away or dismissed in a similar manner, and going through each and every fact is a waste of time. The impatience felt by the investigator is a manifestation of the confirmation bias. Many cannot overcome it and fall victim to the 'makes sense – stop' perfunctory analysis syndrome.

Highly intelligent people are readily sucked into the process of finding complex methods to explain the embedded belief, and thereby become heroes. In fact, the smarter a person is, the less likely they are to change their mind once it has been made up. For those familiar with Mormon church history, a prime example of such a highly intelligent person was Hugh Nibley. He could string together arguments and introduce far-out hypotheses and explanations like no other. He was truly an apologist hero. Some of his arguments are so elegant, one becomes awestruck. Most of his arguments have been found, in the final analysis, to be either bunk, fluff, or of extremely low probability. He would often use linguistics, about which most people know very little, to support his arguments and wow the audience. It is amazing how impressed we humans are by things with which we are unfamiliar.

---

[96] Michael Shermer, *Why People Believe Weird Things*, p. 299

Every time we recall an event, we must recreate the memory, and with each recollection the remembrance may be changed – affected by succeeding events and personality evolution. Thus those in a strong faith lifestyle will tend to color their memories of the past more and more toward a faithful and doctrinally consistent life collage. Our past, even that which we would swear was real, has been biased by our life experience and our opinions. The older the memory, the more likely it is that it has been colored by succeeding events. Memories do not fade, they expand[97].

Escalation of Commitment Bias

This bias has also been referred to as 'the Sacrifice Trap'. Humans tend to hold dear that in which they have made heavy investments.

When I divulged my doubts regarding the 'restoration' to the bishop, as I recall it, the first words out of the bishop's mouth were "but look at everything we have worked for!" A person tends to value that for which he or she has paid a very dear price. Mormonism has always demanded great sacrifices: money, time, even all the members possess if necessary.

Most members are born into the sacrifice trap. From childhood they hear stories about the great price their parents and ancestors and pioneers have paid to preserve and build Zion. Children are saddled with a 'legacy of faith' responsibility at an early age. To shirk this responsibility is equated to being disrespectful of parents, grandparents, dead ancestors, and brave pioneers. They begin paying tithing at age eight (or earlier) and sacrificing time and effort for the church in a myriad of ways. One example: even though the church could easily pay for building maintenance, member families are asked to volunteer their time to maintain the buildings, thus the sacrifice trap grips the members ever tighter. Once a person has sacrificed much for a long time period, his or her ability to objectively examine information that may contradict the 'cause' is compromised.

---

[97] *Why People Believe Weird Things*, p. 182

For the young men and some young women, giving up two years of their life at age nineteen (21 for the young women) is a huge sacrifice. Most cannot bear the thought that those two years were wasted. To many, the mission sacrifice launches them into an orbit above the logical world and the information age. They exist in a stratosphere that cannot be touched by facts or reason, no matter how compelling. Too much has been invested.

For faithful members the financial sacrifice is enormous. Tithing alone is a tremendous sacrifice that for many makes leaving the religion all but impossible. How many of us would simply walk away from a cause to which we have donated $100,000? In addition to the ten percent tithing, many families simultaneously support a missionary which is a significant cost (LDS policy is that missionaries are to pay their own way). Many LDS forego retirement planning to pay tithing; others go into debt at the end of the year to pay tithing, incurring more debt on top of an already large debt burden. The Book of Mormon teaches that prosperity is tied to righteousness. Therefore, members are often caught up in keeping up appearances and take financial risks to appear prosperous in order to project righteousness. Thus many members buy large homes, expensive cars, and nice clothes for their large families. Utah has recently had the worst personal bankruptcy rate in the nation[98].

The great cementer of the sacrifice trap is persecution, either real or imagined, because enduring persecution is a sacrifice. Nothing brings a culture together and steels their resolve more quickly than persecution. Brigham Young gloried in persecution because he knew of its power:

> Well, do you think that persecution has done us good? Yes. I sit and laugh, and rejoice exceedingly when I see persecution.[99]

This is not an isolated quotation. Dozens of similar quotes may be found in the Journal of Discourses, it was a finely honed tool of the trade for Young. There is no doubt that persecution shaped the church in its

---

[98] *Deseret News*, 10 Jan 2005
[99] *Journal of Discourses*, Vol 2, page 538-539, 23 Oct 1853

infancy. Without polygamy and the Mormon theocracy doctrines and the persecution these doctrines brought, there would have been no west-ward migration (no need for isolationism), no pioneer sacrifices, and no catalyst to steel the resolve of the people to establish Zion.

'Dominant Thought' Bias

Humans tend to evolve into that which they think about the most. Humans tend to believe that the images or behavior they are determined to emulate will somehow bring automatic happiness, bring huge rewards, and/or make their dreams come true. Advertizing agencies try to capitalize on this bias by associating happiness and beauty with their product, and placing those images in front of us often enough to have them become part of our desired self-image. The Marlboro man is the classic example of this type of image association. The Marlboro man is the epitome of self-reliance, toughness and manliness. Smoking then becomes linked, in our mind, to these desirable qualities, and therefore smoking becomes desirable by association.

This bias is not necessarily bad; it can be used to help people in many ways. The important thing is that we understand how this bias works so that we recognize when it might be preventing us from being completely objective.

The LDS church reinforces the dominant thought bias in numerous ways. The visual cues are everywhere in LDS homes. Quotations from Mormon prophets are typically found on the refrigerator or framed and on the wall. Many have pictures of the prophet(s) or temples on the walls. Each home is encouraged to subscribe to the monthly church magazine(s) which are usually conspicuously placed in the living room for ready access.

The temple undergarment is a continuous reminder to the faithful member of the covenants made in the temple and their status as a member, how they are unique from the rest of the world. The youth often wear CTR (choose the right) rings as a reminder. Young men memorize the 'Mission of the Aaronic Priesthood' and the 'Standard of Truth', the young women memorize 'The Young Women's Promise' (all quotes of

Mormon prophets). Young men and women are also encouraged to memorize scriptures and scriptural references and competitions are held as motivation.

Daily prayer, scripture study, church responsibilities, memorization, all lead to defining the dominant thought of the member, which is the aim of the church. The church reminds the members regularly that Mormonism is Gods plan of happiness, creating an association between happiness and church membership. This association tends to blind the members to the social problems associated with Mormonism, and overcoming the blindness is difficult when it runs counter to the dominant thought.

Reciprocity Bias

The reciprocity bias is the human predisposition to feel indebted when given a gift. Businesses have thrived by giving away a trinket or simple service, causing the person to feel indebted, who in turn often voluntarily returns the value of the trinket or service to the business many times over.

In Mormonism and most religions there are overwhelming illusory gifts given to the members, especially in the hereafter. Examples include the gift of salvation, eternal life and bliss, the gift of knowledge, the gift of saving ordinances such as baptism, the holy spirit, grace, God's love, the holy scriptures, etc. Gifts that are somewhat unique to Mormonism include personal priesthood authority, patriarchal blessings, the ordinances of the temple, eternal marriage and families, and advice from latter-day prophets, seers, and revelators.

There are also tangible offerings associated with church membership. Some of these gifts are: teaching services from members, the nice buildings and comfortable accommodations, the tokens of the blood and body of Christ, free use of church resources, planned social events, youth programs, a ready-made circle of friends, counseling services, employment specialist services, marriage and funeral services, a welfare program, etc.

All of these gifts, tangible and intangible, create a feeling of indebtedness among the membership and reinforce the reciprocity bias.

Survival Instinct Bias

Each of us is preoccupied with survival, and even though religious beliefs are not normally viewed as important for survival, humans are generally not able to differentiate between survival beliefs and religious beliefs. Indeed, many people, when shown incontrovertible evidence that a core belief is nonsense simply scratch their head, turn away, and continue to believe. How is this possible? While this seems illogical and strange on the surface, it is actually completely consistent with elements of human nature. To understand this, we must understand the nature of belief and how humans have evolved to interact with the world around them.

The human mind is our primary tool of survival, and our senses alone are inadequate to ensure survival success. We must constantly evaluate the possibility of dangers that are unseen. For example, it is instinctual for us to suspect dangers when faced with alien surroundings, which is why we innately feel nervous in unfamiliar situations. This ability to extend our perception of our environs beyond our tangible sensory perceptions substantially improves our ability to survive. The (caveman) jungle dweller has a much greater ability to stay alive if he imagines a tiger or other dangers even when his senses tell him otherwise. Thus our beliefs are necessarily independent from our sensory data systems. Gregory W. Lester, PhD, observes: [100]

> This means that beliefs are designed to operate independent of sensory data. In fact, *the whole survival value of beliefs is based on their ability to persist in the face of contradictory evidence.* Beliefs are not supposed to change easily or simply in response to disconfirming evidence. If they did, they would be virtually useless as tools for survival... As far as our brain is concerned, there is absolutely no need for data and belief to agree. They have each evolved to augment

---

[100] Gregory W. Lester, PhD, "Why Bad Beliefs Don't Die", *Skeptical Inquirer,* November/December 2000

and supplement one another by contacting different sections of the world. They are designed to be able to disagree.

Even beliefs that do not seem clearly or directly connected to survival (such as our caveman's ability to believe in potential dangers) are still closely connected to survival. This is because beliefs do not occur individually or in a vacuum. They are related to one another in a tightly interlocking system that creates the brain's fundamental view of the nature of the world. It is this system that the brain relies on in order to experience consistency, control, cohesion, and safety in the world. It must maintain this system intact in order to feel that survival is being successfully accomplished.... This means that seemingly small, inconsequential beliefs can be as integral to the brain's experience of survival as are beliefs that are "obviously" connected to survival. Thus, trying to change *any* belief, no matter how small or silly it may seem, can produce ripple effects through the entire system and ultimately threaten the brain's experience of survival. This is why people are so often driven to defend even seemingly small or tangential beliefs.

Skeptical thinkers must realize that because of the *survival* value of beliefs, disconfirming evidence will rarely, if ever, be sufficient to change beliefs, even in "otherwise intelligent" people. In order to effectively change beliefs skeptics must attend to their survival value, not just their data-accuracy value.... Data is always necessary, but rarely sufficient.

Thus humans are biased toward retaining beliefs, no matter how irrational, in the face of contradictory evidence, because they are intrinsically linked to the survival instinct. The capacity of humans to jettison bad beliefs is not linked to intelligence but only to open-mindedness.

The LDS church, and indeed most popular religions, very effectively reinforce the survival aspects of their belief systems. The demon-haunted world and the perceived peril to the soul outside the belief system, in this life and the next, are among the doctrines aimed at making the belief system appear necessary for survival.

Conclusion

Persons who are normally viewed by their peers as being closed-minded are generally significantly affected by human biases. It is therefore not surprising that there appears to be a correlation between closed-mindedness and strong religious belief. Michael Shirmer[101] observes:

> In the study on religiosity and belief in God that Frank Sulloway and I conducted, we found openness to experience to be the most significant predictor, with higher levels of openness related to lower levels of religiosity and belief in God. In studies of individual scientists' personalities and their receptivity to fringe ideas like the paranormal, I found that a healthy balance between high conscientiousness and high openness to experience led to a moderate amount of scientism. This was most clearly expressed in the careers of paleontologist Jay Gould and astronomer Carl Sagan. They were nearly off the scale in both conscientiousness and openness to experience, giving them that balance between being open-minded enough to accept the occasional extraordinary claim that turns out to be right, but not so open that one blindly accepts every crazy claim that anyone makes.

Organized religions in general, and Mormonism in particular reinforce, amplify, and exploit our innate cognitive human biases to keep the members faithful and insulated from contradictory information. The fully orchestrated program envelops each member with a force field that is virtually impenetrable.

In order to overcome our human biases, education and recognition are the first steps. Education must always go beyond an examination of the data. The implications of the data and the change wrought upon a belief system must consider survival of humanity, wholeness, consistency, and order. Information fidelity alone is insufficient.

Here are some ideas for judgment criteria when examining new information or during self-examination which can aid in suppressing human biases:

---

[101] *Why People Believe Weird Things*, p 293

1. Is this simply the groupthink, or are there sound reasons to believe or think this way? Where is the data to back it up? Groups have been wrong before. Most of the world thought the world was flat at one time. Is this perhaps another one of those instances?

2. When consulting an expert or authority, ask: What are his credentials? How likely is it that he is in a better position than I am to make this judgment? Experts are often wrong. Is there public domain data that might confirm his assertions? Should I get a second opinion?

3. How sure am I when I assert a belief or opinion? Is my belief or opinion based on facts and hard evidence, or have I become stubbornly attached to this belief simply because I have been vocalizing it for so long? There is no shame in admitting an error and accepting truth anew.

4. Am I simply reinforcing my imbedded belief here, or am I truly open-minded to new information that might dislodge my imbedded belief? How much of my imbedded idea is based on hard facts and irrefutable evidence, and how much is simply due to the idea being the first to take hold? Am I feeling impatient when reviewing new information? Impatience has no place with the objective investigator. A jury always considers ALL the evidence carefully before making a decision, and I owe it to myself to be just as cautious.

5. How much have I invested in a particular belief or idea? Am I holding onto this belief because of my investment or because of its merits? If I had nothing invested in this idea, would it still be worth championing?

6. What are my dominant thoughts, and where are they leading me? If I step back and objectively examine my dominant thoughts, are they helping me evolve into the best version of myself? Are my daily visual and audio cues helping me visualize the best possible me or should they be changed?

7. Am I acting out of obligation because of illusory or tangible gifts? If the organization gave me nothing and promised me no reward whatsoever in this life or in the hereafter, would my attitude and support be changed?

8. Am I acting on a belief that I have always considered part of basic survival, yet in reality has nothing to do with survival? Are the survival aspects of the belief system intangible and fabricated by the group?

Recognizing and overcoming our human biases is a lifetime challenge and should become a driving and thriving aspiration. The task is not so much seeking knowledge, rather it is to seek and find all the barriers within ourselves we have built against accepting knowledge. Only through suppression of our biases will we be able to exercise objective judgments and become the best versions of ourselves while protecting our minds from emotional disturbance. Wise and knowledgeable people are portrayed as those who have studied and know a subject better than anyone else. While this learning method is positive, the more transcending and sublime advancements in understanding come from escaping that which has deceived us and held us captive. It is always a painful process, but ultimately the most rewarding.

CHAPTER 11
HERETICS AND HARPOONS

The fact seems to be that we are least open to precise knowledge concerning the things we are most vehement about. Vehemence is the expression of a blind effort to support and uphold something that can never stand on its own. – Eric Hoffer

Men never do evil so completely and cheerfully as when they do it from religious conviction. — Blaise Pascal

September 20th, 2005   **Mesa, AZ**

It was not long before my annual temple worthiness interview was due. We met at the church building early in the evening, in the privacy of his office. I happened to be reading BH Roberts <u>Studies of The Book of Mormon</u> at the time. After the usual preliminary cordial chit-chat, he launched into the standard scripted questions that make up the temple recommend interview. When asked the question regarding firm testimony, I told him that I was having some deep-rooted doubts concerning the restoration and the divinity of the prophet Joseph Smith. The bishop looked like he had been kicked in the stomach. Rather than try to answer the questions I brought up about Joseph Smith and <u>The Book of Mormon</u>, he told me that "men more intelligent than you" had already looked into these matters and reconciled them all. There was no need for the lay member to research such issues. When he saw that I was not buying that line, he shifted into guilt mode. "What sins are you concealing that have led you to this disbelief?" "How often do you pray and read <u>The Book of Mormon</u>?" When this led nowhere, he shifted gears again and went into damage control. "To whom have you been talking?" I mentioned that I was discussing some issues with non-members, I often discussed things with my brothers, and that we had formed an on-line discussion group. I emphasized that the discussion group was not a one-sided bunch of apostates, rather, we discussed both sides of each issue, recommended to each other objective books to read, and our discussion group was mostly made up of active members, including a bishop's councilor. I gave his a list of questions and issues I had for him to consider and perhaps direct me where to find some real answers.

I walked out of the church building on that warm September evening and felt genuinely relieved that I had shared my doubts (with specific facts and examples) to my local church leader. The true church of God should have no problem with the doubting member trying to reconcile facts and information. In fact, no organization would be better equipped to help the doubting member than the true church of God. I hated the idea of harboring these doubts in a closet. Hiding it just didn't feel right. Now at least he might start to do some studying and help me get answers to these questions. After all, weren't we on the same team? I was completely oblivious to my naiveté. The possibility that the bishop considered me an enemy of the church at this point never crossed my mind.

Five days later (September 25th, 2005) I was summoned to meet with my Stake President, and basically went over the same ground. I made a point of telling both my bishop and stake president that I was far from making up my mind, and fully expected to be researching for 5 years or so. I picked 5 years because I knew that both the Stake President and bishop would be replaced in the next 5 years, since in Mormonism, these leaders usually have about a 4-6 year tenure, and both had been installed in their positions for a few years. I wanted them to have the expectation of a long haul with me as a questioning member with lots of interesting data to share with the membership. At this point, I didn't really care that my open and sharing attitude would make them nervous, and would potentially put them in an awkward position. It just didn't occur to me. I was determined to share the facts and discuss all the skeletons with whoever would listen. If such discussions shook people up and caused them to question their faith, so be it. Later on, I began to feel somewhat reticent about the discomfiting situation I was thrusting upon the local leaders of the church, because it would probably cause them extra work and worry.

Less than a week later, I got a call from my oldest brother Vern, who was living in Henderson, Nevada. Out of the blue, he had received a visit from his bishop, who had never been to Vern's house before. Vern managed to extract from his bishop the reason for his visit: he had received a call from a concerned bishop in Arizona, suggesting that the convictions and motives of each of the Lamborn brothers was in question, and recommended a visit and heart-to-heart talk. At first Vern felt like his privacy was being compromised and was angry. As the discussion evolved, however, it became therapeutic for Vern to vent his concerns to his bishop. In the end, he actually enjoyed the visit. It became crystal clear as the discussion progressed that his bishop had no desire to know about the warts of church history. It was a game of 'one-hit tennis', where the disaffected member brings up one troublesome issue after another, and the faithful member has no intelligent responses. The one-hit tennis matches are typical when uninformed members are confronted with real issues contradicting core beliefs.

I hung up the phone after listening to Vern describe his visit with the local church leaders. Now it was my turn to feel like I had been kicked in the stomach. I had been betrayed. My deepest thoughts and concerns, expressed in what I thought was a confidential interview, had now thrust my brothers into a very embarrassing and potentially volatile situation. Casting doubt upon one's allegiance and religious conviction in Mormonism is commensurate to accusing one of being a traitor to his country. No good could possibly come of this inquisition, and I wrote the bishop an epistle to let off some steam and hopefully give him a dose of reality. My letter to him is shown in Appendix C.

The bishop told me that the church handbook of instructions gave him license for notifying the bishops of my brothers in order "to protect the good name of the church". Apparently, the "good name of the church" takes priority over family relations, confidentiality, and trust. This was a complete surprise to me – a real head-scratcher. What possible threat could a band of brothers pose to the true church of God? At this point I came to appreciate, first-hand, this quote:

With or without religion, you would have good people doing good things and evil people doing evil things. But for good people to do evil things, that takes religion. - Steven Weinberg

At this point I was placed on restriction, which is a disciplinary action executed at the discretion of the bishop. I was not allowed to attend the temple, use my Priesthood power outside the confines of my home, teach any lessons, or pray in public. I was released from my teaching capacity sometime in October, and only spoke up and made comments from the audience after my last lesson on testimony. I ignored the 'no praying in public' restriction, and prayed in church when called upon. I felt I had as much right to pray as anybody who walked through the church doors, regardless of what doubts I was harboring about Joseph Smith. Plus, I knew there was no way the bishop could practically enforce this rule. I was the voice for group prayer about eight or ten times while supposedly on restriction.

The line between investigating the actions of a member and persecuting the member is a very fine one. This church has stepped over this line repeatedly, and certainly did in my case. The church regularly confuses dissent and refusal to conform with disloyalty - my case is an example, as I was at this point a loyal, active, and faithful member.

As I continued my study, I was careful to avoid books that would be viewed as anti-Mormon works. So to this day, I have never read any book that I consider to be anti-Mormon. The first book I read was Krakauer's <u>Under the Banner of Heaven</u>, which is 100% neutral. Many would say that Fawn Brodie's <u>No Man Knows My History</u> is anti-Mormon, but I had heard members discuss points brought up in the book in Sunday school and felt that it would be easy to separate the facts from the opinions, and it was. Brodie's book is a masterpiece of investigative journalism, and set a very high standard for subsequent exposés on church origins. I have also heard glowing reports on books written by the Tanners, but did not read any, since most members view them as anti-Mormon, even though I suspect they are mostly just factual with astute commentary.

I then read the following works:

- <u>Studies of The Book of Mormon</u>, BH Roberts
- <u>An Insider's View of Mormon Origins,</u> Grant Palmer
- <u>The Keystone of Mormonism,</u> Arza Evans,
- <u>Mormon Enigma</u> by Tippets and Newell
- <u>Farewell to Eden</u> by Anderson,
- <u>A View of the Hebrews</u> by Ethan Smith,
- <u>Rough Stone Rolling</u> by Richard Bushman
- Sections of the <u>Journal of Discourses</u>
- Sections of <u>The Comprehensive History of the Church</u> by BH Roberts
- <u>An historical & doctrinal commentary on the Pearl of Great Price ; The facsimiles of the Book of Abraham ; A study of the Joseph Smith Egyptian papyri</u> by James R Harris
- <u>By His Own Hand Upon Papyrus</u> by Larson

I consider my research materials extremely well balanced and I defy anyone to prove otherwise. The facts are essentially the same in all the works, and it is easy to separate the opinion from the facts and events, regardless if it is being told from the faithful or naturalist viewpoint. To me the facts speak for themselves and really do not need amplification, although many of the authors are adept at pointing out the most likely explanations for the events, as well as exposing patterns of behavior that leads to understanding of motives.

The Kinderhook episode was also a very telling event that fit the pattern of deceptions perpetrated by Smith, and was an important discovery for me. I had never heard of the Kinderhook plates until I was deep into my research. Smith's commentary regarding the Kinderhook plates is as follows:

> I insert fac-similes of the six brass plates found near Kinderhook... I have translated a portion of them, and find they contain the history of the person with whom they were found. He was a descendant of Ham, through the loins of Pharaoh, King of Egypt, and that he received his Kingdom from the ruler of heaven and earth.[102]

---

[102] Quotation of Prophet Joseph Smith, Jr., *History of the Church*, v. 5, p. 372

The six brass plates were actually fabricated out of a copper alloy, with engravings and an acid etch to make them look old, then placed where they were sure to be found. Smith fell headlong into this trap and was caught in a lie. The Kinderhook plates remain in the possession of the Community of Christ church.

With all these facts and events swirling around in my head, I felt I needed a timeline to sort it all out. A timeline is sometimes helpful in identifying trends and patterns of behavior and opinion, and the evolution of a culture. I searched the Internet to no avail. Eventually, I decided to build my own timeline, showing what I felt were significant events. My formulation of the timeline was technologically primitive, but it was of great value to me in bringing out key events in church history. The timeline is shown in Appendix D. [This is the same document I would later share with the members of the high council at my disciplinary council.]

The facts, events, forensic evidence, and disinterested expert opinions were overwhelming and conclusive to me. I began to freely share my research and discuss issues and disconfirming evidence of the divinity of Mormonism with church members, thinking that they would be open-minded and we would have profitable discussions. Of course, this was not the case. Initially, it boggled my mind that anyone who is true to his intellect could review all the facts presented in the books I mention above and still consider the church to be the only true church of God. In fact, I have only found a handful of individuals on the planet earth who are familiar with the facts recounted in these books and remain orthodox believers. Yet they are out there. Some will read this book and remain completely convinced the LDS church is true, which is not surprising given the power of cognitive human biases.

It has been my experience that the large majority of members, when confronted with a disconcerting fact or two, simply ignore the facts thinking that there is no point in dwelling on mysteries for someone who already has the truth. In addition to being a defense mechanism, this behavior is a manifestation of false pride in that it is a presumption of superior knowledge. It is amazingly ironic that an organization that is dedicated to elimination of false pride exhibits it so blatantly when faced with simple real facts, real events, science, and expert opinions. Yet it is understandable, given the nature of humans to mentally segregate belief and data processing.

I liken this defensive mechanism that each member has to the individual force fields portrayed in science fiction movies. Mormons are all equipped with the force field, and it is on full automatic mode at all times. It is strengthened and reinforced with each prayer, at every church service, and is especially strong after quarterly conferences (Stake and General Conferences).

I continued to read and study and attend church, although I increasingly found reasons to miss church, since I felt my time spent there was bringing decreasing return on my time investment. Sometimes I would sit through the entire three hours and never really have an opportunity to speak up, since the subject matter at times was not conducive to adding some reality-based balance.

I had always been proud of my roots, my heritage. The fact that I had polygamists on both sides of the family tree added spice and color. The fact that my fourth-great grandfather Abraham Hunsaker had served in the Mormon Battalion added valor and determination to the mix. It was all good. Or so I had thought for 45 years. As my sphere of research expanded, I found reasons that killed, to a great degree, the pride, color, and spice I associated with my heritage.

I found that the Mormon Battalion episode was tainted with a deception by Brigham Young. Young had sent Jesse Little to negotiate with President Polk for a 1000 man battalion, Polk reluctantly agreed to 500 men. Then Young made the Mormons believe they were being persecuted when Captain Allen came to take command of the battalion. This is an example of a situation Young turned into a perceived persecution to toughen team Mormon.

Polygamy seemed kooky to me when I was younger, but then I read about how Young used polygamy as a manipulation tool. He regularly rewarded his top henchmen with additional wives. Those were strictly obedient and loyal to Young improved their chances of scoring an additional wife. The rules were that once approved by Young, the man could find any wife of his choosing and seal the deal without the consent of the other wife or wives, as if he had just purchased a horse and wagon of some other material possession. I came to find the entire institution shameful. With my new understanding of how polygamy was practiced, my enthusiasm and pride of my heritage waned.

I did not realize it at the time, but I had embarked into a new stage of faith. I no longer trusted the church or its leaders. I no longer trusted the members to be reliable sources of information. They were just as full of disinformation as I had been. While my thought processes were mostly logical and causal, this discovery and deconstruction stage was not a time devoid of emotion. In fact, the emotions were all over the map: disillusionment, betrayal, loss, anger, disappointment, and wonderment. The most astounding revelation was that millions had been deceived on such thin arguments. Later I would realize that if thirteen million could be so easily deceived by the flimsy claims of Mormonism, 39 million by the Nazi party, it is a very small step to postulate the deception of hundreds of millions by the claims of Islam, Christianity, Judaism, Hinduism, Buddhism, etc.

May 1-3, 2007

A key event for me was when PBS aired the outstanding program "The Mormons". I watched with keen interest, and came away with the impression that PBS had treated each subject fairly and objectively. Many of the more damaging and controversial items had been omitted. The faithful believer viewpoint was offered at appropriate intervals. I was more excited to go to church the following Sunday than probably ever before in my life. I felt that the program had placed many issues into the spotlight, and that now the gloves were off for open discussions. The program came up about six times in conversations, during the course of testimony bearing, and lesson delivery that Sunday, 5/6/2007. I was so glad to be there to hear all the discussion and opinion. My High Priests group leader said he watched about 30 minutes and then had to turn it off, saying that the anti-Mormon bias was too much for him. In contrast, others thought that the program would open up doors for missionary discussions among our friends, and was very fair in its presentation of the events and doctrines. Every portion of the spectrum was evident among the members. It was tremendously interesting to witness such diversity in reaction to a single program. Overall, it was a breath of fresh air, and emboldened me to discuss tough issues more often and with less restraint. I no longer felt obligated to smother my inclinations to speak up.

One of the women in the congregation asked me right after the three-hour meeting block what my opinion was of the PBS' "The Mormons". I mentioned the fair and equitable treatment of the subject, which allowed for the faithful believer viewpoint. I told her that PBS had been kind to the church. After considering our conversation, I stopped by her home after work one day and left her a copy of my timeline (Appendix D), which I thought was a good summary of the PBS program, with some additional events and facts that might spur some follow-up discussions with her. She was not home when I stopped by, so I left the timeline with her husband. I began taking a copy of my 'Search for Truth' summary (Appendix E) and timeline to church each Sunday, with the intent of giving them to a member of the congregation. Typically, somebody would ask me how things were going and what was new. I would respond that I had been doing some research into church history and then ask if they like to see a summary of my findings. They would always respond in the affirmative and I would simply give them the materials on the spot. It made me feel good to be sounding the voice of reason and giving my friends some balance in information.

Looking back, I realize that this practice is probably what landed me in front of the disciplinary council and resulted in an escalation of conflict between the Stake President and me. Sometime in June I received a call from the executive secretary to schedule a meeting with the Stake President. Our schedules were pretty packed for that summer, thus we did not have a chance to meet prior to my leaving for a trip to Peru in mid July. I went to Peru with all these facts in my head, coupled with anticipation of meeting with the Stake President upon my return. The stage was set for me to experience that moment of clarity in Peru when I realized that I could no longer remain a member of the church.

The stake president's executive secretary contacted me upon my return home from Peru and scheduled a meeting between me and the Stake

President. We met on or about August 5th 2007. The Stake President eventually got around to the main reason for the meeting: "Lyndon, why are you still a member of the church?" I can still hear him ask that question. It was a totally fair question. I said that is was probably a good idea that I have my church records removed. I wanted to do it quietly in the hope that my mother would not find out. We agreed that it would best that my records be removed. I needed a one-way ticket out of 'Duck and Dodge' City. I inquired as to how it was done. Would he send me some papers? How can we make this easy? As I remember it, he said I would be getting some papers that would be self-explanatory. I thought that leaving the church quietly was the polite thing to do. The members of the church had done nothing to offend me. Many of my friends were faithful church members. Raising a raucous was not warranted. My mind flashed back to that lunch break in a tent in Peru. I was going to get my wish, and sooner than I thought. I left the meeting in calm optimism.

During that meeting I made a tactical error without realizing it. When discussing the process of leaving the church, I asked "Who is told that I am no longer a member? Who finds out?" The Stake President answered that he would tell no one. The reason I asked this was mostly due to my desire to spare my mother any distress. I believe that the Stake President made a mental note regarding my concern over publicity. Later, I believe he tried to exploit this perceived weakness as he chose to escalate the battle.

About ten days later, I did receive a letter, but it was a summons to a disciplinary council, with no provision for simply signing something and returning it. This was irritating. I had made the decision to resign quietly and leave with no fanfare. Now I really didn't know what to do. If I didn't attend the disciplinary council hearing, this would be tantamount to sending the message that I didn't care about my membership and speculation regarding my attitudes and reasons for leaving would have no boundaries. If I did attend, what would I say? "You have all been bamboozled and should think about doing some objective research?" It would serve no positive purpose, and making the men sitting on the council uncomfortable for a few minutes really would not bring me any comfort for having thrown away 40 years of my life chasing a myth.

The summons letter could have easily been accompanied with instructions on how to request record removal with pre-prepared papers. The fact that no such option was offered meant one of two things: (1) Either the church does not train its leaders to help the member take the easy way out, or (2) the Stake President wanted to hold a disciplinary council and escalate the conflict for some reason. Not including a simple form made me angry. Do I not merit the simple courtesy of a quiet and easy exit? I knew I could elect to not attend the disciplinary council, but I was afraid that the council might just 'dis-fellowship' me, which does not remove my records completely and I would technically remain a member, subject to harassment. I would eventually have to go through the whole thing again, which I wanted to avoid at any cost. I wanted to make certain that they would excommunicate.

The days came and went and I pondered my disciplinary council dilemma. Slowly, an idea began to emerge. If I could help the men on the council understand the quandary of the disaffected and intellectually honest person, the next person that travels my road might have an easier time. I might also be able to help the men be less fanatical and more humane toward their own friends and family members who might leave the church in the future. I would also be assertive enough in the delivery of my speech to assure an excommunication. The potential positive aspects of addressing the disciplinary council began to take shape in my mind, and I made some notes. I was now ready to address the council, it was going to be an exit interview they would not soon forget.

CHAPTER 12
THE FAITH CORRAL

You can't convince a believer of anything; for their belief is not based on evidence, it's based on a deep seated need to believe. - Carl Sagan

Enlightenment is man's release from his self-incurred tutelage. Tutelage is the incapacity to use one's own understanding without the guidance of another. Such tutelage is self-imposed and its cause is not lack of intelligence, but rather a lack of determination and courage to use one's intelligence without being guided by another. -Immanuel Kant

To a very great degree, the success of any religion is directly proportional to the extent it has tailored its doctrine and programs to exploit cognitive human biases and mind control techniques. This does not make these organizations inherently evil, just adept at keeping their members committed and faithful. Once again, it is simply good business.

The religions of the world are as varied as the cultures of the world. The religious alliance demographics are largely determined by one's birthplace. The probability that a person being born in Logan, Utah will become a Hindu is just about as great as the probability of a person being born in India will embrace Mormonism.

In this chapter, the idiosyncrasies of Mormonism will not be mentioned, since the faith corral applies to all popular religions and the elements of belief and mechanisms of retention are universal.

With the dawn of the information age in the 1980s, the opportunity for people to explore the available information has jumped several orders of magnitude. Although people are becoming better informed with the passage of time, mankind does not seem to be increasing in intelligence.

Take, for example, organized religion. There is no hard evidence of a Supreme Being or creator. More and more phenomena that were thought to be supernatural and impossible to explain are finding natural scientific explanations. More and more people are concluding that the existence of the earth and intelligent life is completely natural, not supernatural. If there is an organized higher power which governs the universe, mainstream religions with which I am familiar have utterly failed to paint a box around it.

Yet most of the worlds population of five billion remain convinced that they have found the truth about religion and remain faithful to an organized religion. Many are convinced not only that a Supreme Being exists, but that they know the will of the Supreme Being and have taken up the cause. Many are so fervent in their religiosity that they will strap bombs to themselves and perform suicide missions for the cause. How does this happen? Is it healthy? Do humans have a desperate need for religion? Why do so many choose faith and devotion on such thin evidence? That so many religious organizations have been successful in retaining and boosting their membership in spite of contrary evidence is a testament, primarily, to the reluctance of human beings to address their existential uncertainty.

Many theories exist as to why human civilizations naturally become religious. What is it in human nature that compels the overwhelming majority of the populace to embrace a religion? Many articles and books deal with this question, and there are a plethora of plausible theories. Some suggest that it could be partially explained by pedomorphosis. Pedomorphosis is the retention of childhood character traits into adulthood[103]. Many people describe their thought process, especially as children or adolescents, as sort of a dualist dialogue between themselves

---

[103] Dawkins, *The God Delusion*, p 391

and an imaginary protagonist inside their head. This is often portrayed in Hollywood as a child's imaginary friend. The imaginary friend of childhood thus transitions to God or the constant companion of the Holy Spirit into adulthood, a devoted consoler and counselor. Another theory suggests that religious tendencies may be simply a manifestation of traits that benefit the group in a natural selection process[104]. The important thing to realize that the fact that so many choose religiosity is, by itself, not an indicator that God exists, nor even that religious belief is more healthful than an atheistic view.

The development of faith for most humans is an integral part of the emotional maturation process and part of their cultural upbringing. Just as our emotional spectrum partially defines who we are, so does our faith spectrum. It is not something that just comes up in conversation one day then, boom, we decide that we have faith and religion is going to be an integral part of our life; it is an evolution, that happens in stages:

1. Childhood faith stage
2. Adolescent faith stage
3. Faith corral stage
4. Faith deconstruction stage
5. Reclamation stage

Between ages of about three to seven, the childhood stage, our psyche has unprotected exposure to the subconscious mind. Our imaginations run wild in this stage, we are uninhibited by logic and there are no boundaries. For the first time, we become self-aware, and identify ourselves as a unique entity at the same time becoming familiar with the concept of a group membership. For the first time, we are made to learn about boundaries, and we are exposed to cultural and group taboos. We are exposed to the concept of good and bad, and rewards and punishments. A rough concept of cause and effect takes root. We develop some capacity to differentiate between make-believe and reality for the first time. The locus of authority lies with the parents, teachers, and other adults.

---

[104] Dawkins, *The God Delusion*, Chapter 5

The adolescent stage, about ages seven to eighteen, is best characterized with a black or white theme. The individual has a strong sense of justice and reciprocity. [How many times do we hear adolescents complain about something not being fair?] In this stage of emotional development, thinking processes are linear, and all filing is digital: something is a one or a zero, there are no other choices. Things are good or bad, right or wrong, fair or unfair, perfect or flawed, real or fake, correct or incorrect, profitable or unprofitable, a reward or a punishment, and so forth. There are no gray areas in adolescence. The vibrant imagination of childhood is bridled and becomes subject to boundaries. Religious symbols and ideas are taken to be literal there is little or no consideration of mysticism, accepting uncertainty as an end state, or metaphoric symbolism. An objective and critical evaluation of religion or myth is difficult during this stage, although some simply rebel and others question religious tenets with emerging intellectual development. The locus of authority remains with those in authority and mature adults, although the adolescent begins to challenge and push back to test authority limits. It is interesting to note that most religions ask for commitments from adolescents during this handicapped stage.

While the overpowering sense of universal reciprocity is like a boat carrying adolescents through troubled water, it also traps them. Since the person has an overwhelming sense of justice, perfectionism, and causal relationships, he can easily become convinced that he is irredeemable after doing something he was taught was wrong. Even realizing that sooner or later he will step over the line can be just as devastating. Despair can ensue with dire consequences.

While some remain in the black and white adolescent stage for life, most leave this stage behind. With maturing emotions and a greater array of life experiences, most begin to see wider possibilities. The person begins to allow that perfection can be in the eyes of the beholder and may not be attainable, that one person's punishment might be another person's reward; that some portions of religion might be symbolic and not literal, and gray areas exist in moral questions. The strong sense of justice and reciprocity softens and the person enters a new stage that is characterized by conformity and trust, which we will refer to as the faith corral.

The majority of the population finds its permanent home in the faith corral. Faith becomes a primary factor in the ordering of one's world. The person trusts the group, the clergy, the books and materials circulated by the group, and wants to conform to be identified with the group. People in this faith stage are usually acutely concerned about what other members think of them and invest a disproportionate amount of their energy to conform to group expectations. Faith and beliefs shape one's identity and plays a strong role in life decisions. The person has completely internalized the symbols of right and wrong and is quick to judge right and wrong and react accordingly. Those who differ in opinion or are not in the group are seen as different kinds of people.

Interestingly, mind control groups tout their doctrine as absolute truth and the only answer to the people's problems[105]. "We are the way! We have the truth! We know, and you do not know. We are not lost, but everyone else is, and are in need of our divine guidance." Thought control groups use black and white thinking, dividing the world into simplistic dichotomies: good versus evil, us versus them, which caters perfectly to the Stage 2 and Stage 3 faith corral mentality.

Faith corral adherents surrender authority to the group and especially the leaders of the group. It is important to note that the locus of authority lies outside of the individual for these first three stages of faith.

Hundreds of millions of people today find themselves in this stage of faith. Despite the onslaught of the information age, advances of science, clergy corruption, and life experiences that contradict core beliefs, surprisingly few question their faith. Why is this? What is it about humans that keep them from a critical examination of religion?

1. Trust and betrayal. There is little or no opportunity to reflect on belief system critically, because critical examination would constitute a betrayal of trust and be seen as wrong. Nobody wants to be seen as a traitor, especially when the belief system is tied to family relations.

---

[105] *Releasing the Bonds*, pg 50

2. Identity loss. For many, the glimpse of another possibility cannot be contemplated, it is simply too daunting. It attacks a core belief and would invalidate, in some cases, the person's reason for living and erase themselves – they would become a non-entity, a nothing, and life would appear instantly meaningless and not worthwhile. Of course, this glimpse of apparent despair is only an illusion and is a symptom of a mind that has surrendered itself to a mind control entity and cannot remember its authentic self. Unfortunately, a mental illusion is totally real to the person totally vested in the mind trap. For those that step outside the groupthink for an objective look at their beliefs, many become frightened and stop prematurely. Arresting the investigation is simply an act of identity self-preservation, nothing else.

3. Pride. For many, the admission of having been deceived is too traumatic. Losing face among one's peers is not an easy thing to do. Once a person has championed a cause, particularly among family and friends, turning away from the cause is almost impossible due to pride and saving face. It is amazingly ironic that the humility touted by organized religion somehow evaporates when it comes to pointing out that the emperor has no clothes.

4. Human Biases. The cognitive human biases reinforce the walls of the corral to keep the herd together. Those in authority and the experts always recommend the sheep to stay in the flock, reinforcing the authority bias. The individual is always going to innately want to stay in the comfort zone of the group; therefore the groupthink bias plays a key role. When information or life experiences encroach on the belief system and push the member to the edge of the corral, the confirmation bias kicks in. Typically, the questioning member falls into the 'quick-look, stop' syndrome, which immediately bounces him back into the center of the corral with the rest of the herd. The escalation of commitment bias also tends to raise the corral rails. It takes much more effort to leave something in which one has invested so much time, money, and emotion.

5. Social Implications. For many, especially the women, it has been the author's observation that the social network of the herd is of huge significance and value. Leaving the herd and not knowing

if there is any possibility of replacing the society with which one has identified for years is frightening. The need to belong and fit in is strong. The rails on the corral grow higher and higher.

6. <u>Societal/Cultural/Geographical/Economic/Governmental Pressures and Biases</u>. Many people are born into circumstances that virtually demand adherence to the groupthink for survival. In the early days of Mormonism after the exodus to the Great Basin, this was the case. These scenarios still exist in various locations throughout the world. The residue of these pressures and biases in the USA are still evident. Some examples: the phrases 'e pluribus Unum' and 'In God we Trust' found on currency, the pledge of allegiance including the 'under God' phrase, traditional repetition of the pledge and customary prayer or moment of silence observance in schools and civic meetings.

7. <u>Fear</u>. There is comfort and security feeling that God has sanctioned your life choices, and God's anointed representatives are instructing you how to live your life. The warmth and security of the group is reassuring. Just as the institutionalized prison inmate is petrified of the world outside the prison walls, so the idea of leaving the group and the security of the faith corral is terrifying to the religious affiliate.

8. <u>Survival</u>. The belief system, over time, is viewed as the primary tool of survival in an evil world, and the only way to ensure survival into the afterlife.

For the overwhelming majority, the faith corral becomes a permanent home. It has been the observation of the author that leaving the corral, if it is going to happen, typically occurs during the first half of the human lifespan, although there are exceptions.

The two great motivators that bind people together and spur action are fear and aspiration. Faith corral reinforcements use both. The fear of encroachment from outsiders binds the people together, and the construction of this protective wall also creates a sense of aspiration as the wall goes higher and higher and the members sense the building of a kingdom of vital importance and security. The members are taught that the temple undergarment is a shield and a protection against the evils of the world, so each faithful member has a constant reminder of the wall of faith separating them from the rest of the world. Interestingly, the Great Wall of China is not much of a military deterrent to invasion, it serves rather as a psychological placebo for the people. It was built mostly during times of Chinese military weakness, as the insecurities of the people motivated extensive wall construction. During times of military strength and good relations with neighbors, work on the wall stopped.

There is an array of dangers associated with those who stay in this faith stage. One's life situations may drive one into despair. Such situations may include contradictions between authorities, the revelation of authoritarian hypocrisy, emerging intellectual knowledge, and life experiences that contradict core beliefs. It is a classic example of helping the butterfly out of the cocoon and thereby crippling the butterfly. The group that the individual relied upon to be nurtured has left the individual woefully unprepared for the real world.

The faith corral can lead to various degrees of unreasonable fervor as the human psyche reaches out for deeper and deeper meaning in life. The ills associated with unreasonable fervor include depression, discrimination, family strife, and the arrogance that accompanies the certainty illusion. It also diminishes one's capacity to empathize and understand those of other belief systems.

Albert Ellis[106] describes the correlation between religiosity and emotional disturbance:

> Devout, orthodox, or dogmatic religion (or what might be called religiosity) is significantly correlated with emotional disturbance. People largely disturb themselves by believing strongly in absolutistic shoulds, oughts, and musts, and most people who dogmatically believe in some religion believe in these health-sabotaging absolutes. The emotionally healthy individual is flexible, open, tolerant and changing, and the devoutly religious person tends to be inflexible, closed, intolerant, and unchanging. Religiosity, therefore, is in many

---

[106] "Psychotherapy and Atheistic Values", *Journal of Consulting and Clinical Psychology*, 48, Nov 1980, 637

respects equivalent to irrational thinking and emotional disturbance.

The struggle to overcome guilt and retain a positive self-image can lead to extreme discouragement. Gardiner[107] explains:

> In the face of shame there is no way to believe in a loving God. Destruction is imminent, always. Unconditional love does not exist. The pain is intense and escaping/avoiding that pain is the dominant force in life. This is why, with shame-based people, I see the formation of a reactive identity that protects and destroys ability to live and grow in a way that honors choice and freedom. There is only one choice; doing whatever keeps me safe from shame-pain. This may include ceasing to be an autonomous human being or succumbing to the forces aligned to convince one that their very person has been found so wanting that further effort is a waste....

For those who break out of the faith corral, there are other stages of faith. These stages involve deep introspection and reshaping of ones reality. Leaving the corral is a roller coaster ride of emotion, and will be discussed in a later chapter.

Conclusion

Human emotional maturation is often accompanied by faith stages. Beginning with adolescence, there are real dangers associated with the development of faith. For those growing up in a religious environment, faith becomes part of how the world is perceived and dealt with. Organized religion, by design, emphasizes natural human biases to retain its membership and immunize them against encroaching reason and logic. Very few are able to break out of the faith corral to the next stage.

With children, parents should strive to instruct them **how** to think, rather than **what** to think. Critical thinking is a skill that will help them throughout their lives, religiosity tends to hamper critical thinking abilities.

---

[107] Ed Gardiner, "Shame and the Destruction of Agency", see http://www. postmormon.org/main.swf

There is in every village a torch – the teacher: and an extinguisher – the clergyman. – Victor Hugo

In the Foreword, I pointed out how facts and information have little effect on human emotional battleships. The blueprints for construction of these battleships have now been revealed, and we can now begin to understand the complete organism. Love begins with understanding.

With a hull forged from certainty and immune to logic and the engine fueled with an intense need of guilt avoidance and fear, the human emotional battleship slices through life waters. The helmsman has a radio tuned to a single station, which announces the same orders over and over: "Full steam ahead, Christ is coming! Pray, pay, and obey and safety is ensured." The helmsman never questions orders and with each mile traveled and each day sacrificed for the cause becomes more determined to continue plowing through life's waters undeterred. Storms are universally interpreted as confirmation that the battleship was the right choice for comfort, security, and survival. The battleships run in packs for the safety found in numbers, and delight in executing exact maneuvers for approval from their peer battleships. The helmsmen have their own coded language and regularly assure each other that they are God's elite warriors, and the only ones with God's truth. Any battleships that are abandoned, run aground, or sink are viewed as defective and unworthy, there is never a valid reason to abandon ship, to even consider such is evil. The helmsmen of the other types of sea-going vessels (Evangelical destroyers, Catholic PT boats, atheist tankers full of information, etc.) are going to be very sorry when Christ comes with his storm and their ships sink. The battleships are impervious to facts and information, and intentionally or unintentionally collide with and destroy whatever stands in its path, including family units. Somewhere, locked way down deep in the bowels of the battleship, is found a humane and loving authentic person, who cannot seem to contact the helmsman any more, but continues to try.

CHAPTER 13
BEING CHASED OUT

Whoever tells the truth is chased out of nine villages. –
Turkish proverb

*During times of universal deceit, telling the truth becomes
a revolutionary act. –* George Orwell

My primary concern while exiting the church was easing the pain of my loved ones, because they simply were not equipped to understand. I didn't see any reason why my mother would ever have to know that my records were removed. I could 'fly under the radar' with the local congregation, attending once in a while, and just sort of fade away. This would spare my wife and son any embarrassment or anguish. I had been assured by the Stake President that he would not tell anyone that I was no longer a member of the church.

At the conclusion of the disciplinary council, the Stake President said that I would receive a notice of the council's decision, and that would be the final stamp of completion. I thought it was over once and for all. Holy cow, was I ever wrong! I was surprised at what arrived (hand delivered) at my home. In addition to being notified of the decision to excommunicate me for apostasy, announcements were to be made to all the adults in not only my congregation, but in each of the 10 congregations in the Salt River Stake (immediate region). This letter is shown in Appendix A. This was a shock. I consider myself basically a private person. I did not think it appropriate that my exit from the church be broadcast to the world. This was a personal decision, and one that I did not make lightly. My reason for leaving was simple: I could not remain a member and remain intellectually honest with myself. Life is too short to live a lie. The real reason for my departure would not be conveyed in these announcements. There could be no balance, no objectivity, and no opportunity for my wife to be proud of me, no chance for my friends and neighbors to understand my heart. The more I considered it, the angrier I became.

It has been more than twenty years since I had heard an announcement made regarding a disciplinary church action. I thought the policy had been changed and that such announcements were no longer made, no exceptions. If such announcements were still made surely I would have heard about an announcement being made sometime in the last 20 years. To say that I was surprised at this tactic is an understatement. This possibility had not entered my mind as a potential outcome, and I was unprepared for it.

Once again, I was thrust into another dilemma, one that I had not asked for or anticipated. What to do? The letter mentioned an opportunity to appeal the judgment of the council to the First Presidency, which is similar in principle to an appeal to the supreme court. So I appealed. My appeal is shown in Appendix G. My motivation was to buy time until I could talk some sense into the Stake President to forestall the disaster of the announcements. I was actually pleased with the council's decision to excommunicate. I didn't want the church to have any power over me or any say in my actions. But more time meant more chance to have the announcements canceled. Plus, maybe a well-worded appeal would bring some heat down on the Stake President from his superiors, and they would order him to cancel the announcements. If I was going to get heat, I was determined to give as good as I got.

Another big negative with the announcements involved my mother. There were several people in the Stake who have family in Logan, Utah and know my mother and word would surely get back to her, probably within 24 hours. To forestall her hearing it through the grapevine, I would have to tell her. I would have to break the promise I made to my brothers. And I was powerless to do anything about it. The Stake President had forced yet another showdown. The nightmare became uglier and I became angry again at the church that simply would not let go. I asked for a quiet exit and it felt to me like the church wanted to broadcast it on CNN.

My appeal was denied, and the announcements were to take place on schedule, as promised. I was at the end of my rope. I was running out of options and running out of time. I turned to my on-line discussion group for advice. One member spoke up and suggested going public. Announcements of disciplinary actions in church were very rare and therefore might be newsworthy. Go to the mattresses. Take the fight to the people. With Mitt Romney running for President, and the recent PBS broadcast of "The Mormons", public interest in the machinations of Mormonism was at a peak. In the immortal words of Gene Wilder in the movie 'Young Frankenstein', I realized, as he did, that....

IT..... COULD....... WORK!!!!

Here was the opportunity to tell the story on my own terms, a chance for people to understand my heart, an opportunity for my wife to reap something more than guilt and shame from what would shortly become a very public exit from the church. At least her friends would see her husband as a rebel and an intellectual instead of the spawn of Satan. OK, granted, they still might think I was the spawn of Satan, but at least I would do the talking and tell my side of the story. This time the church was not going to be able to suppress the real information. For once the people would get the whole story, not a half-truth embroidered with venom and piety. It would be poetic justice: The Stake President wanted an announcement, then so be it. There would indeed be an announcement.

I sent e-mails to the Arizona Republic and the East Valley Tribune. I got no response from the Republic, but the spiritual living editor from the Tribune, Lawn Griffiths was mildly interested. We exchanged e-mails for a few days, and Lawn thought at first that it was not newsworthy at all. After all, people get excommunicated all the time. When I elaborated on the circumstances and the announcements he reconsidered and thought it might merit a position as the second or third story in the Saturday religion section and we scheduled an interview.

I went down to the Mesa Tribune offices, and talked with Lawn for about an hour. I provided him copies of my 'Search for Truth', my time-line, and the letter from the Stake President which promised the announcements. Lawn perked up as the interview went along, and our conversation seemed to gain momentum. The Mesa Tribune offices are coincidentally only a few blocks from the Mesa temple, so he took me down to the temple for a photo shoot after our interview.

Of course, balanced journalism involves hearing and presenting both sides. The newspaper phoned the local spokesperson for the church. The spokesperson was asked how often these announcements were made to congregations; the answer was rarely. He pressed, how rare? The spokesperson answered that is was extremely rare. This changed everything. It was like hitting the jackpot on a slot machine. Lawn called me and said that the story was certainly newsworthy and might be the lead story in the Saturday section.

During our interview, I asked Lawn to postpone the newspaper article until the Saturday after the announcements were to be made. I didn't want the newspaper article to affect the dynamics of the chess game being played out between me and the church. I didn't want to give the church the chance to change his colors and feign that the announcements were never going to be made; that I was making much ado about nothing.

Friday September 20, 2007   Winkelman, AZ

I was driving to the wedding of my niece in Henderson, Nevada, and my cell phone rang. It was Lawn Griffiths, the spiritual living editor of the Mesa Tribune. I pulled off the road to talk. Interest in the story was apparently escalating. One of the Tribune editors read the draft story slated for the Saturday newspaper and felt it was worthy of a more prominent spot in the Sunday paper, and Lawn and I discussed the final details. Running the story the same day as the announcements would have more impact for the readers. I was torn about running the story the same day, because I did not want the article to change the situational dynamics until after the announcement, but it felt right. It was entirely possible that the newspaper's phone call to the local church spokesperson had already changed the dynamic anyway, since chances that the church spokesperson had already contacted the Stake President were very high.

As I drove to Nevada, I realized that the newspaper article approach had changed a no-win situation into a no-lose situation. The story would be told on my terms. That was certain. It would take the sting out of the announcements. I really did not believe that the Stake President would back down on making the announcements, he had told me that the announcements were all set and in accordance with church policy. If the Stake President did an emergency stop to the announcements, then my wife would not have that additional embarrassment in church, which would please me immensely. The mere threat of the announcements caused more than enough mental anguish to justify the article.

Sunday September 23 2007 Mesa AZ

I drove down to the gas station early Sunday morning to get a copy of the East Valley Tribune. My article had made the front page of the Sunday paper. I never dreamed that it would be of that much interest, and thought maybe the East Valley Tribune had gone overboard with the front page approach. As it turned out, I was wrong. The article eventually broke all records for on-line reader comments, and merited two follow-up articles. The text of the first article may be found in Appendix H. The follow-up articles may be accessed on the Internet.[108]

I received two phone calls from strangers that day. One was from a local man who had left the church, along with his wife, some 15 years earlier, for the same reasons. We agreed to have dinner sometime in the near future. The other phone call was from a gentleman on the east coast that just wanted to congratulate me for my courage and honesty. He had reached the same conclusions from his research, but he was still a member.

I went to attend Sunday services for the last time that September day. I needed to hear the announcements, and I wanted to be there in person to make it more difficult for the person delivering the announcement, I wanted to make him squirm. In fact, I was toying with the idea of speaking up and elaborating on the proceeding for all those present. I was happy to see that the Stake President himself was in attendance in my congregation that day. The meeting ran its course, and no announcement was made. I cornered

---

[108] *East Valley Tribune* website, www.eastvalleytribune.com

the Stake President after the meeting and questioned him as to why the announcements were cancelled. He stated that the plan to make the announcements was tentative, and was never a sure thing. This of course, was not my understanding from his letter and subsequent correspondence to me. He went on to say that with the article in the paper, word would get out, and the announcements were not needed. I told him that I would have not gone forward with the article if I had known that the announcements were not going to be made, he simply shrugged. I took the shrug to mean that the water was over the dam now, and raging down the canyon under its own power. And water raging down the canyon is an apt description of my life for the next six weeks.

After being initially disappointed that the Stake President backed down (no announcements), after a day or two to reflect upon it, I realized that the events could not have turned out better. In fact, the more I thought about it, the more elated I became. It was clear to me that without the newspaper article, the announcements would have been made, with all the scorn and shame ladled upon my wife with no balance. Instead, the story was told on my terms, and the church was denied the opportunity to censure me and hide the reality of my intellectual disaffection with the restoration. In either scenario, I would have to make that dreaded phone call to my mother, which had been a 'fait accompli' once the Stake President made the decision to announce my excommunication to the stake and denied my appeal.

Looking back at the sequence of events leading up to article in the newspaper, the simplest explanation, and probably the correct one, is that the Stake President and I were engaged in an escalation of testosterone [conflict]. The Stake President makes no secret of the fact that during his teen years, he was known as something of a bully, never backing down from a challenge. I wanted to exit quietly, but because I had been sharing information with members the Stake President thought it appropriate to put me in front of a disciplinary council. Since I didn't want to go out with a whimper or just get a slap on the wrists and have to do it all over again, I carefully loaded and emptied both of my six-guns at the disciplinary council. Because I was probably way too happy about the verdict, and assertive in my description of the issues, which motivated the Stake President to use my fear of publicity against me by promising the announcements, ostensibly to shield the obedient sheep from the heretic. I made the final escalation by going to the paper.

I wasn't about to have an organization with more to hide than Jack the Ripper top me by going public.

My first phone calls that Sunday morning were to my older brothers. I also notified my on-line discussion group of the article in the paper and urged them to comment if they felt they wanted to add anything to the discussion. I then made the dreaded phone call to my mother. She seemed numbed by my description of the events that transpired. I did not get into any details, just that I simply could not be honest with myself and remain a member of the church. I expressed my wish that she respect my decision and try to be proud that I would be unashamed to stand and be counted for what I believe, even if it did not coincide with her beliefs. To make matters worse, the Stake President, earlier in his life, served as a missionary in the same mission in the West Indies as my parents, and was the first missionary transferred to the island of St. Kitts after my parents were there for a prolonged period. Therefore my mother knows and respects the Stake President and would not be apt to find fault with his actions. I am sure it was an added embarrassment to my mother that a missionary from her own mission, whom she and my father knew personally, was the one to preside over my excommunication. I missed the wisdom and stoicism of my father on this particular day (he died in July 2002). I like to think that he would have been supportive of me and helped the rest of the family respect my decision, he was that sort of a person.

How does my mother feel about my exit? Of course she feels sadness, which is the normal reaction for any parent that has a child leave the traditional family religion. But it seems to me that there are other emotions that play a role here. Perhaps the most surprising one is guilt. LDS parents are taught and reminded over and over again throughout their lives that it is their duty to teach their children to understand the doctrines, be baptized and "walk uprightly before the Lord" or "the sin be on the heads of the parents"[109]. Parents are promised that if a child is properly trained, he will always return to the fold[110]. If a child leaves the faith and does not return, then the parent must have failed and been a poor parent.

---

[109] *Doctrine and Covenants* 68:25,28
[110] Proverbs 22:6

There is no other possibility, because God never lies. The second one is fear. She fears that the other children, upon seeing my course of action, might follow suit. The last one is shame. For LDS parents, the degree to which their children adhere to the gospel (including holding important offices) in the church becomes the measuring stick of life success.

I have tried to explain to my mother that she has no reason to be sad, guilty, or shameful regarding my choices as an adult. I had the best mother in the whole world, as far as I can tell, and she has raised seven wonderful children, an amazing feat all by itself. My choices as an adult in no way reflect poorly on her mothering skills, but I think she has a difficult time believing that. In fact, I told her that she should be proud to have a son with the courage to take a decidedly unpopular position. I am afraid this idea fell on deaf ears, but I will keep trying.

The next six weeks are sort of a blur. Since the newspaper article had mentioned my lengthy 'Search for Truth' summary document, there were readers that wanted to know where they could get a copy of it. I obliged them by giving them my e-mail address and the requests came flooding in. I sent it and the timeline to approximately 150 people, including several in the United Kingdom and Canada. The story went national on MSNBC. The volume of comments accumulating on the first article was staggering[111]. No end seemed to be in sight. Most of the comments were supportive and complimentary.

In fact, overall, my departure experience since the newspaper article has been one of kindness, people reaching out to me with open arms, with no hidden agendas, and making new friends. I must have received at least twenty phone calls and countless e-mails applauding my courage, asking if I needed help or support in any way, and in general, people showing unconditional and unfeigned charity. My co-workers at Boeing have been among the most genteel and genuine. I will never forget the great kindnesses shown to me; these are treasures of inestimable value. I have made new friends, people that give every expectation of becoming

---

[111] The comments may be found at www.eastvalleytribune.com/story/98035

life-long friends. I can only hope my life is long enough to give back as much as I have received.

In stark contrast, my departure experience before the newspaper article was a freakish nightmare, accented by betrayal, exploitation of perceived weaknesses, attempts at character assassination, and vengeance. There is a lesson to be learned in my experience. Through all the years as a member of the church, I was convinced that the church was primarily a service organization, dedicated to blessing the lives of human beings. I naively assumed that this sort of treatment would extend to questioning members, and even those who abandon hope of finding satisfactory answers and ultimately leave the church. After all, I sat through many lessons describing the "court of love", which was the establishments' description for a disciplinary council. And I was aware of many people who had lost their membership and then returned to the fold. Obviously, it was in the best interest of the church to be nice to me – or so I thought, since I was a potential return member (with a good income).

The reality is that the church has little or no tolerance for the questioning member that openly challenges core beliefs. Nothing substantially has changed since Joseph Smith Jr. rallied his henchmen and illegally destroyed the printing press of the Nauvoo Expositor in the spring of 1844[112]. The truth is the mortal enemy of the lie. So long as the people can be insulated from the truth, the lie will prevail. Nothing strikes more fear into the heart of the perpetrator of deception than the truth teller. Joseph Smith felt this fear, and the church feels it today with similar trepidation. Therefore, the church carefully words the handbook of instructions with such terms as "protect the good name of the church" to justify breach of confidentiality, character assassination, or whatever tactic is needed to insulate the truth teller from the lay member. Instead of leaving the 'ninety and nine sheep in the fold and seeking out the one lost sheep', the LDS shepherd gets a high power rifle, climbs a tower, and shoots the lost sheep truth teller in the back of the head. I described this caricature to the Stake President during our last private meeting; we chuckled together.

---

[112] Fawn Brodie, *No Man Knows My History*, page 377

The church spends hundreds of thousands of dollars annually trying to provide plausible explanations for the deceptions of Joseph Smith and in general defending the lie.[113] The church recently sent a letter to local leaders around the world proclaiming that church headquarters will no longer respond to doctrinal or historical questions. Today the local leaders are left to cope with the questions as best they can. This insulates church headquarters from potentially damaging questions, and makes it more difficult for the lay member to get answers to tough questions. The church's hope, I expect, is that the lay member will simply give up and live with their cognitive dissonance. This probably works beautifully for the large majority of the membership.

I am personally surprised the church played the question-answering role as long as they did. Why? It is simply bad business. A deception becomes increasingly more difficult to defend to a membership that is thinking more and more like crime scene investigators every day. A tidal wave of immense information is sweeping the world, and the critical thinker must either sink or learn to swim through it. Consequently, the questions are getting tougher each day, and woefully inadequate answers from church headquarters broadcast to the entire membership expose the soft underbelly of the church to way too many offering-payers. Bad apologetics are infinitely worse than silence and amount to bad business. Thus the church has insulated itself from the onslaught of unanswerable questions, a return to good business practice.

Eventually, the East Valley Tribune on-line comments turned into a debate over the core issues and evidence that casts doubt on the claims of the church. The real reason that there were so many comments to my article was not the impact of the article or the issues surrounding my excommunication. The bulk of the comments amount to a point and counter-point debate of polygamy, historicity issues with The Book of Mormon, the origins of the Book of Abraham, the inconsistencies in the versions of the Joseph Smith story, the Kinderhook hoax/trap Smith fell into, and various other controversial religious issues. It was difficult to find time to read all the comments, let alone find time to respond to

---

[113] FAIR and FARMS websites; www.fairlds.org/ & www.farmsresearch.com/

many of the questions directed to me. Among those that were support-ing my position and applauding my efforts was a person with the pen-name Lincoln. I will discuss Lincoln later.

I will say that it was, above all, a rewarding time. I didn't really care for the spotlight per se, but having so many people out there read-ing and commenting and revealing that they had reached exactly the same conclusions that I had reached was comforting. On several oc-casions, I read a question or a misstatement by a commenter, and found that the misstatement or misconception had already been cor-rected or clarified by an ally before I had a chance to respond. It was gratifying to discover that I was not alone – in fact, I was far from being alone. I had been adopted by a new family, the post-Mormon family. They rushed to adopt me and the reception has been more than warm. As far as I can tell, the post-Mormon family is made up of the finest people on the planet. I feel more connected; more appreciated, more genuine, and have more in common with the post-Mormon community than I ever had with the Mormon community.

It was also nice to have my two daughters, Betsey and Megan, right there with me, reading and commenting. Betsey, my oldest child, had made an exit from Mormonism a few years prior. Religion never re-ally made any sense to her – especially the 'Christianity on Steroids' version of religion served up by the Mormon church. My second child Megan had thought for years that the church was true, but then life experiences revealed to her that the church simply wasn't all that it said it was. For example, she found that the church was not the only path to happiness. It didn't have all the answers; it was obvi-ously deficient in some ways. So, while I was aware that my daugh-ters were 'out' of Mormonism, their disaffection had nothing to do with my path of discovery, which revealed the pattern of deception of Joseph Smith Jr., and the continued suppression of information by the church today, which became the core issues for me.

Eventually, the comments to the East Valley Tribune articles slowed to a stop. I could breathe a little easier, and catch up on the rest of my life. A local radio talk show host, Darrell Ancarlo, was devoting 15 minutes of his show to my story, a friend at work clued me in on the morning of the show. I called in to the show, and I had a nice chat with him[114]. The others that called in were generally very supportive and positive. I was caught off guard by the unexpected question "are you the REAL Lyndon Lamborn?" I would run into this question a few more times, and it still surprises me. Who would want to impersonate me? As far as I know, no one wants to or has tried.

After my excommunication, I felt as if a great weight and burden had been lifted. I had always expected to become a mainstream Christian after leaving Mormonism. In fact, I had recently relished in the opportunity to visit the Holy Land in December 2005. However, as I settled into my new religious viewpoint, I became increasingly uncomfortable with orthodox Christianity. I wound up being a mainstream Christian for about one month before I realized that Christianity did not work for me, for reasons I will discuss later.

From the public exposure in the newspaper, I had three local people approach me by e-mail and ask to be included in my e-mail discussion circle. Before adding them to the discussion group, I met with them in person for lunch. It is always refreshing to meet disaffected members and non-members, because they are critical thinkers, people who steer their own ship, and are willing to discuss anything. One of these people had the pen-name 'Lincoln'. Surprisingly, Lincoln was a church member living in Mesa Arizona. After I introduced Lincoln to the group, group members recognized his penname and spoke up immediately and commended Lincoln for his wisdom and scholarship in various on-line forums they had frequented.

I was also astonished when I discovered that a family that I had known for many years, and visited regularly had been doing the same research and had reached the same conclusions as I had. We were mutually ignorant of the parallel secret lives we had been living for about two years. Needless to say, we spent more than a few hours discussing our discovery journeys, the emotions, the recovery, and the all-important family matters surrounding a departure from the faith.

---

[114] Darrell Ancarlo, KTAR 620 am

I was approached by many in various mainstream Christianity congregations with invitations to join with them. Of course, this was not unexpected, given the publicity surrounding my exit from Mormonism. I think I became something of a trophy fish for another religion to scoop out of the water and mount on their wall. Hey, look at us, we snared Lyndon Lamborn! It would make for great bragging rights. I guess I finally know what a woman with great legs feels like repelling those looking for a trophy wife. Many of these Christians claimed to have ex-Mormons in their congregations, which I never confirmed. I find it hard to believe that anyone could travel through the intellectual dismantling of Mormonism and then fall headlong into the myths of mainstream Christianity and accept these myths with their whole heart. On the other hand, I can readily understand those who want to continue their participation in a religious community for sake of family, especially if their spouse was already a member of another Christian church. I expect that, for the most part, ex-Mormons who join mainstream Christianity would tend to be moderates.

One invitation led to an interesting experience, and that came from a friend and co-worker. He invited me to lunch to discuss my exit from Mormonism. We had a lively discussion. As it came time to return to work, he extended to me an invitation to tell my story at Sunday school at the Red Mountain Community Church (RMCC). Once a month, they had a 'spotlight' on another religion, and he thought that having me as a guest speaker to discuss Mormonism and my experience would make for an interesting Sunday school. He added that many in the congregation already knew me and were curious about my experience. I accepted.

Sunday, November 18, 2007   Mesa, AZ   Red Mountain Community Church

I told my exit story and then the questions came pouring in. Eventually, the questions came around to what I believed now that my faith in Mormonism had been dismantled. I beat around the bush, and didn't feel prepared to tell them that my suspicions were that all organized religion was based on myth and not reality. I would need some better way to present the evolution of my beliefs in such a way that it would be understandable to them, and perhaps help them be a little less fanatic about their religion at the same time.

I did answer questions about my family and how my defection had affected them. I maintain a positive expectation that my wife and children will all eventually come to see that I made the right decisions, because I believe that I have. My daughters already applaud my decisions and actions, my son grappling with disappointment and confusion for about a year before he realized that the religion is a myth. I have been fortunate to have a tolerant wife that although being upset and disappointed with my choices, realizes that there is more to our relationship than just religious beliefs. Interestingly, since my exit from Mormonism, she is something of a folk hero when she attends church. She is seen as conquering an extremely difficult situation. In the eyes of the membership, she is sleeping with the enemy yet remains valiant and true to her belief in the church.

My chance to make a second presentation at the RMCC came. My friend invited me back for a second segment on Mormonism, and I spent a good portion of the hour allotment discussing uncertainty and the societal ills that are wrought when unreasonable fervor takes over. In fact, my preparation for this second installment of 'Spotlight on Mormonism" became the foundation for the writing of this book. Bob McCue saw my first 'Spotlight' on YouTube and provided me some valuable insights on how to approach and discuss the key topics for my second presentation, particularly with regard to human biases. Both of my presentations were recorded on digital video format, and are available for viewing on YouTube[115]. However, if you are reading this book, there is no reason to view the videos, because all the concepts and information are more thoroughly detailed in this book than in the video recordings. The only exception is a true story regarding Mormon magic underwear, which I now retell to close this chapter.

---

[115] The first video is at http://www.youtube.com/watch?v=ECjddl-jPwY, links to the others will appear

I related to the Sunday school group the historical basis and evolution of Mormon magic underwear, also known as the 'garment of the holy Priesthood'. I described how the garment was originally ankle length and long sleeve, like the Long Johns of the old west, with one-piece construction and a flap in the back and a fly in the front for men. The garment is worn by all temple-worthy members and is meant to be a reminder of their covenants to the Lord and is believed to be a form of protection from the evils of this earthly existence. The garment was shortened to knee length in the legs, and short sleeves sometime in the forties or fifties, but remained one-piece construction until the 1980's. This was the only type available to the members in the seventies when I first started wearing garments, beginning at age eighteen.

April 1   1986   Tempe, AZ

My co-worker returned to his desk, laughing uncontrollably. I turned around and asked what was so funny. As he gasped for breath, he said, "You know those convenient openings in your garments?" I said of course. "Well, he continued, I was just in the restroom, and was all set to use those openings, only to find out that my wife sewed them shut!" To this day, I have not heard of a more humorous April Fools day prank. Nobody can tell me that Mormons don't have a sense of humor.

August 20, 2008   Mesa, AZ

I received a letter today from a very grateful couple in Florida. Sometimes we don't realize how these seemingly little things can have a profound effect on others. The letter read:

Dear Mr. Lamborn,

I am so sure by now you have received countless amounts of mail from people going through a similar experience as you have recently. I hope you don't mind the letters including the one I'm writing now... I just have to. Thank you so much for everything you've said and done. It has been a lonely and painful journey for me...the memory of that pain is still very fresh in my heart. I've carried it with me for the past six years. Well a month ago I was browsing YouTube and came across a lecture you gave for a Christian group. I sobbed...but they were tears of relief that there was someone out there who knew what I felt! Also relief because I didn't even know about the "skeletons in the closet." Finally there was hardcore proof for the things I was feeling! It's not only the information you've provided me that is encouraging but it's your pure motive that has given me the courage to say...this isn't right (and feel confident Satan isn't influencing me). For the first time I had something to show my husband...with references (who doesn't love references?) Ha-ha. Now my husband is going through the "shock." He's said it was like being taught the world is flat your whole life and realizing it's round. Mr. Lamborn your courage and honesty are so appreciated. My life would not be the same if I had never heard your lecture. My husband and I have always lightly argued about how involved we would keep our two kids in the church. Of course I hardly wanted them involved at all but up until a month ago my husband still "knew" the church was true and therefore wanted them active. Now I look at my five month old daughter and relief runs through my body that I have spared her a life of guilt, dependency on "men of God", and lies! I am so relieved that now that my husband and I agree...I don't have to worry about my five year old son "serving the Lord" on a mission! Thank you! Thank you! A million times. I know how hard this must have been for you and your family. But again, thank you. I feel like I can now finally start to heal. I am at peace with what my gut has been telling me for the past six years. You rock:-)

Sincerely,

<name removed>
Orlando, FL

December 4, 2008   Mesa, AZ

I have now received a number of warm thank you letters, they seem to be fairly constant now, which confirms my reasoning for writing this book. The one today reads:

Dear Mr. Lamborn:

I would like to thank you for your work on searching for truth I found on www.mormonthink.com/lamborn.htm. I was amazed at how many of the same questions you stated that I had. Your list of Characteristics of a Mind Control Environment hit home so well. I have found a lot of information on this as I live with it each and every time I communicate with my Mother and Father. I also found on www.rickross.com/warningsigns.html by Rick Ross, Expert Consultant and Intervention Specialist; in his ten warning signs of a potentially unsafe group/leader.

My quest for the truth started on my mission in 1977-1978 with some very disturbing observations as with my whole life was believing as you stated in "making his own choices," when in fact I had been socially influenced to disconnect my own critical mind and decision-making capacity. I felt like my mission was like being in the SS in Hitler's Germany. The sad part was I was singled out as a bad elder for having my only two converts quit do to what they saw as abuse. I could go on and on yet do not wish to make this very long.

I wish to express how much I am glad you put this out to the world. I do not know what to do about the abuse I receive from my mother as she puts it "I will get my just desserts". I was told by the church to not talk to other members including my family about what I feel. I had the men in black come down to see me with a transcript of what I had talked about as an elders quorum teacher as well as talks I gave in sacrament meeting. I was threatened with ex-communication as well.

I would love to have a copy of your work searching for the truth. It has taken me a long time to de-program my mind and see the truth in how my family/ Church has manipulated me. It is still hard at times and say as little as possible about my life to my family.

My heart is with you and wish you all the best,

B.

CHAPTER 14
THE PRECIPICE

There will come a time when you believe everything is finished.
That will be the beginning. - Louis L'Amour

Mythology may be defined as other people's religious beliefs.
– Joseph Campbell (paraphrased)

Each human being, whether they realize it or not, are on a path of discovery. Each person's life is a series of events that cause us to think, to question, and to choose. Many of life's decisions are heavily weighted by events that happen early on in our childhood and teenage years. Most religions require some kind of formal religious training. Some religions you could go so far as to say the training is indoctrination. Many children go through years of Bible study, Sunday school, Parochial school etc. In some religions it can be very intensive. As the journey of life is traveled, many interpret the world through the lenses of their childhood religious indoctrination, our biases are initially fixed by our upbringing. Our biases determine how we will choose to see our surroundings; our "standard of measurement" on how we look at the world. It affects all our perceptions to some degree; how we view people of other faiths, government, natural laws, God, morality, sin, sex, salvation, how the universe was created, and often how life began and its purpose. Many people derive much meaning and comfort from their respective religious faiths. It is the guide and the light that governs much of what they do and think for their entire lives, a sort of users manual for mortal life.

A religious community can be a very cohesive group. It is also an environment in which the growth of some people will be nurtured and for others it will be impeded. There are no certain predictors of who will start to question certain religious dogmas in relation to what we can term the real world. Many people are driven by an intense desire to learn and to grow and to understand the world we live in as best they can. This for many can include religious studies. Experience indicates that IQ seems to play an insignificant role in whether or not one will question the religion of their upbringing. In fact, the most intelligent are often prone to have a strong and often impenetrable confirmation bias.

Questioning, if it is to happen, generally occurs very early in life or during the time of middle age. After middle age, most (but not all) people have arrived at the belief system of their choosing, and stop questioning, at least in our western culture. As a general rule the most logical and open-minded people will strain against growing subconscious disharmony at first, unconscious awareness of inconsistencies between religious belief and the real world they see around them. These inconsistencies begin to drain their energy and attention; until this awareness becomes oppressive. The dissonance is now cognitive, meaning that it is part of conscious thought processing, with the true beliefs of the person now in direct contradiction with his behavior.

The birth of this conflict can be likened to a filing problem. As people grow and learn though living their lives, more and more information has to be parsed and filed in one's brain. Each individual handles the information in a unique way. For some people, compartmentalization works. They can make and label files or compartments in their brain and segregate them; a file for science, a file for religion, a file for real life lessons learned, etc. They never mix the files and never pull two out at the same time. In fact, as I pointed out earlier, humans have evolved such that beliefs and data processing centers operate independently from each other. For many this relieves the cognitive dissonance of dealing with all the files all at once in one file folder. Others cannot do this, every file in their brain must agree and be consistent with every other file in their brain. The mind will do whatever it can to relieve dissonance discovered whilst on life's journey, they cannot ignore any conflicting information.

The problem for this person is as his life progresses and he finds more and more things to put on his dissonance shelf. The shelf tends to get very heavy and starts to sag if something is not done to relieve the growing weight. Humans innately prefer that their behavior, thoughts, and emotions be mutually consistent, and can only tolerate a certain amount of discrepancy between these three facets of their identity[116]. Some can stave off tragedy by taking each can of doubt off the shelf and addressing it before it turns to critical mass. This is a good way to approach the problem but can still lead to a complete loss of his world view and faith. If a person does not do this it can lead to a very dangerous phenomenon that can lead to putting this person's mental health and well being on a precipice. It is a tricky place to be, and can be viewed as standing on a cornice of snow and looking over it, taking one more step closer to the edge until that last step when the cornice collapses and an avalanche ensues.

Once the dissonance is strong enough, the individual resolves to dispel the mental discomfort regardless of the cost. This can be called an awakening, or even a crisis of faith. It is fueled by the need of many people to find consistency between their faith and the world picture which scientists and historians are unveiling. It can also be touched off by other factors, such as inconsistencies between life experiences and the groupthink, clergy corruption, discrimination, elitism, and other encroachments. This phenomenon happens to people in every faith based system, not just Mormonism. They have made up their mind to scale the wall of the faith corral and leave the herd, at least temporarily, in a quest to resolve the dissonance. The person realizes that he must stop fighting himself and continue his evolutionary process, finding harmony through change.

As the person considers his options while standing at the precipice, he realizes what is at stake. In order to find peace, he is compelled to step off the cliff, knowing full well that it will be impossible to climb back once he hurls himself off. Once committed, there is no way to know how far he will fall or where he will land. It is a terrifying experience. The person's entire belief system and part of his identity is at stake, and in all probability, it will be left in shambles, a pile of rubble in his mind. Everything a person ever thought they knew about life, his role in the

---

[116] Festinger, Rieken, & Schachhter, "When Prophesy Fails: A Social and Psychological Study of a Modern Group that Predicted the Destruction of the World", 1956

universe, his identity, and the nature of religion and God are thrown on the roulette table. They realize that nothing they knew for sure could be counted on to be true any longer. Truth takes on a whole new fearsome complexion. What is real truth and how can I find it? Is certainty impossible? The person realizes that he cannot remain on the precipice or return to the faith corral. The only option is to step off the edge. The deconstruction stage begins.

CHAPTER 15
THE PHOENIX

The further the spiritual evolution of mankind advances, the more certain it seems to me that the path to genuine religiosity does not lie through the fear of life, and the fear of death, and blind faith, but through striving after rational knowledge. – Albert Einstein

A man is accepted into a church for what he believes and he is turned out for what he knows. - Samuel Clemens (Mark Twain)

After I realized that Mormonism was just an illusion, the powerful fire of myth that had governed my life for 45 years had slowly burnt down, lost its fuel, and part of what used to be me turned to cold white ash. The world was out of focus for a while. It was like coming out of the darkness of a fog into the light. It took some time to get used to the idea that I had been so wrong for so long. I would no longer look at the world the same way. A new beginning was happening, I was being reborn, a Phoenix rising from the ashes and changing into something else.

I decided that attending Sunday services was not the proper thing to do. First of all, my objective to interject some real history and reason into the discussions would be frustrated because I had been labeled an apostate and nobody would listen to me. I had been demonized. Secondly, any time I set foot in the building, I would be condoning destructive mind control tactics and give the members the impression that I was repentant and desirous of returning to the fold. I resolved to only set foot in a church building for weddings, funerals, or family reunions.

Looking back, I realized that my adolescence had consisted of intense indoctrination and filling my mind with gospel ideals. There seemed to be so much to know about the gospel that I would never be able to absorb it all. It was like eating from a ten-foot tall Pez dispenser. I never really took time to decide what made sense to me. I spent all my time bringing my thinking into conformance with the group, because being with the group was a wonderful thing, a great big warm blanket and pacifier. So I continued to consume pill after pill from the Pez dispenser until I was completely assimilated.

Now my instruction manual for how to live life had been tossed into the trash. I felt like an authentic teenager for the first time. There was no warm blanket, no pacifier. Everything that I had been taught to believe, the very reason for my existence, was an illusion. My purpose for living, other than being a husband, father, aerospace engineer, and math professor was revoked. Without realizing it, I was transitioning from the deconstruction phase of faith into the reconstruction phase. For the first time in my life, I took personal responsibility for my faith. The locus of authority now resided with me.

After the collapse of my world view, I felt anger, betrayal, bewilderment, disillusionment, and great loss. While I considered counseling, I was successful in dealing with the aftermath by reading about the psychology of religion through on-line religious recovery websites. Until I was able to understand the psychology of what I was going through, it was difficult for me to recover and actually let go. Many people do need psychological counseling to deal with the aftermath, and I can readily understand why. The anger factor was a very powerful force and difficult to squelch. Prolonged anger is harmful. Working through anger is very messy and can take some time. There is a lot of sacrificing expected of members of the Mormon Church. The realization that one may have sacrificed much time and money for a lie is a very sobering and bitter pill to swallow. My disciplinary council was a big help in my healing, essentially a group therapy session for me.

This rebuilding process is a messy business and it cannot be avoided. I had discarded faith for rationality and now faced the uncertainty of a universe that seemed to be unknowable and incomprehensible. I felt alone, abandoned, and vulnerable. I was a bit depressed and discouraged, but only for a few days. While many who leave have family members who can be very intolerant about accepting a family member's intellectual or other distancing from the faith, my experience was generally positive and my family was generally accepting.

While my social transition was relatively easy and rewarding, painful social turmoil and upheaval can happen. Neighbors and friends can distance themselves putting life long relationships at risk. You feel that you are being ostracized instead of understood. How can that happen? All you were doing was looking for and holding onto the truth. The faithful member often believes that the disaffected has betrayed the group and must have a malfunctioning intellect and can no longer be trusted. It is just plain difficult on many levels for faithful members to deal with a loss of faith in a close friend.

I now had responsibility for my beliefs and had to confront all aspects of my character, my behavior, and decide what I valued. It was time to decide what was authentic and what was fantasy. Only two things were certain. I knew I existed and I was not going to be duped again. As the saying goes, once bitten twice shy. For the first time in my life, there was no more herd, no authority to turn to for expert advice, no opportunity to trust others to do my thinking for me. It was unsettling to say the least, and during times of uneasiness I entertained thoughts of returning to the faith corral and pretending nothing had happened. These thoughts never stayed long; I resolved to forge ahead.

I knew beyond any reasonable doubt that Mormonism was an illusion, but what about Jesus Christ? When I had heart to heart talks with the Stake President, he said that I was on the path to atheism. I disagreed. I told him we would have to agree to disagree on this point, because I never had any intention to become atheistic.

Virtually everyone I was acquainted with held Jesus Christ in high regard. So I decided to give mainstream Christianity a try. But I was not going to trust the group or experts. The decision as to whether Christ was divine or not was up to me, nobody else. The story of Christ, formally unquestioned was now subject to critical scrutiny. And so I immersed myself into the Christian school of thought. It lasted about 4 weeks.

For my Christian friends reading this work, what follows is a narrative illustrating why many Christians cannot participate fully and remain honest with themselves. There is uncertainty in all religion, and this narrative is given in the hope that the reader would be able to spend a few minutes looking objectively at Christianity and understand that uncertainty applies as much to Christianity as to any other school of religious thought. Increased tolerance and understanding is the end goal, no offense is intended. In order to make my story complete, describing my experience with mainstream Christianity is necessary. My conclusions regarding mainstream Christianity could be completely erroneous, but they could also be exactly correct.

My research into Mormonism included some critical examination of Old Testament events. The great flood and the story of Noah and the ark was one of the subjects I had studied. Most people I talk to do not believe there was a universal flood, that the story of Noah and ark is a bedtime story, part of Jewish folklore, meant to describe and give divine meaning about how mankind survived a catastrophic local flood.

Many faiths, including the LDS church require a literal belief in the worldwide flood of Noah.[117] As mentioned earlier, the LDS theology teaches that the earth is a living thing and required baptism by immersion[118] just like humans.

Belief in a literal flood that covered the entire earth (immersion) presents some fundamental obstacles for me. Here are my issues with the universal flood doctrine[119]:

---

[117] *The Book of Mormon*; Ether 6:7, 3 Nephi 22:9, *Doctrine and Covenants* 133:23-24, *Pearl of GP*; Moses 8:30

[118] *Ensign*, Jan 1998, p35: November 1981, Mormon Doctrine p 289

[119] DuWayne Anderson's *Farewell to Eden* contains an excellent discussion of the great flood improbabilities.

1. Ice. The ice sheets that cover Greenland and Antarctica predate the flood. If water covered the entire earth, why didn't the ice sheets float away or at least leave a record in the ice core?

2. Genetic Diversity. There is simply too much genetic diversity on the planet to be consistent with the idea that every land-based animal today descended from a few breeding pairs just a few thousand years ago. There are over 200,000 species of beetles and over 50,000 species of frogs – how could the ark have handled this number of species?

3. Worldwide distribution of species. It appears to me that some species evolve locally, and are necessarily geographically immobile. How could thousands of such species have become so widely distributed without any populations in between where they are today and where the ark supposedly landed? How, for example, did the duckbill platypus end up in Australia and nowhere else?

4. Fish and coral. Noah apparently did not take fish or coral on the ark. However, a worldwide flood would cause many fish types to be extinct and no coral would have survived. There are many coral reefs that are thousands of years older than the flood.

5. No room on the ark. Simple mathematics show that there was insufficient room on the ark to house all the animal species found on the earth, let alone the food required to sustain them.

6. No geological record. Vast floods have swept through regions of the earth, most recently after the last ice age. They occurred when huge ice dams broke, releasing stored water from impounded rivers. These floods left very clear and unambiguous signs in the soils, hills, canyons, and rocks. A universal worldwide flood would leave clear signs, but none exist.

7. Where did the water go? To the ancients, getting rid of the water must have seemed a trivial thing. After all, after seasonal floods the water just sort of disappeared, soaked into the ground or ran off to an unknown place. If water covered the earth at a depth to cover Mount Everest, there is simply nowhere for all that water to go. Ad hoc arguments about the continents sinking and the oceans getting temporarily shallower don't work either. We have

mapped the ocean sediments and they are much older than the flood.

8. How did the carnivores survive? There would not have been nearly enough herbivores to sustain the carnivores during the voyage and the months after the ark landed. For that matter, what would the herbivores eat after the flood subsided?

My view of the Old Testament changed at this point. I no longer believed in the literal historicity of the book. It was not long until I decided that the story of Adam and Eve is another bedtime story. The evidence contradicting a literal Adam and Eve as our first parents is conclusive:

1. The standard timeline places the fall of Adam somewhere between 4000[120] and 8000 BC[121]. Yet we have archeological evidence of intelligent, religious, and artistic peoples living at least 25,000 years ago with the Sumerians and cuneiform writings.[122] All major universities teach that ancient intelligent and religious civilizations pre-dated Adam and Eve.

2. DNA and population mapping of the human race indicate at least 150,000 years of human presence on earth and archeological evidence shows that human religious ritual and supernatural belief has been around for about 200,000 years.[123]

3. Anthropologists have geographically traced human ancestry to Africa.[124] Mormonism places the Garden of Eden in Missouri, and mainstream Christians typically picture Caucasian characters as Adam and Eve.

---

[120] "Old Testament Times at a Glance", LDS Church publication 00897, Intellectual Reserve, 2002

[121] http://pursiful.com/chronology/bib_timeline1.html, 5537 BC: Julius Africanus, d. 240, 5529 BC: Theophilus of Antioch, d. 181, 5508 BC: Date adopted by the Eastern Orthodox Church, 5500 BC: Hippolytus of Rome, d. ca. 236, and the Ethiopian Chronicle of Aksum, 5490 BC: Date adopted by the Syrian Orthodox Church, 5323 BC: Josephus, d. ca. 100.

[122] http://en.wikipedia.org/wiki/Civilization

[123] Joseph Campbell, Bill Moyer, The Power of Myth

[124] "African Origin of Modern Humans in East Asia: A Tale of 12,000 Y Chromosomes", *Science Magazine* 11 May 2001 Vol. 292. no. 5519, pp. 1151 - 1153

The conclusion regarding Adam was a life changing event for me. If there was no Adam, there was no original sin, no fall, and there was therefore no need for a rescuer (savior). Men are not inherently evil after all, and blood atonement was never required. One of the most destructive ideas ever presented in all of human intellectual history is the "rotten to the core" doctrine, in Mormonism it is commonly referred to as the "natural man is an enemy to God" doctrine[125]. Empirical data suggests just the opposite, the overwhelming majority of people are fundamentally honest and cooperative[126]. Letting go of the idea that mankind had fallen from a higher state into disrepair ever since the Garden of Eden was a great relief and comfort to me.

Without the fall of Adam, the basic doctrine requiring a savior of mankind falls apart and Jesus has been carrying a burden unjustly placed upon him. Then other evidences began pouring in, which for me cured the cement shoes on Christianity.

The recurring myth aspect of the life of a savior was particularly compelling for me. About sixteen different religions have a similar basic central savior story[127], some examples.

- In 1200 B.C, the Savior Virishna was:
  - Immaculately conceived and born of a spotless virgin "who had never known a man."
  - That the agent in the conception was a spirit or ghost.
  - That he was threatened in early infancy with death by the ruling tyrant, Cansa, who ordered the death of all male infants under the age of two.
  - That his parents had to flee to preserve the life of the infant.
  - That angels and shepherds attended his birth, with frankincense and myrrh.
  - That it occurred in accordance with previous prophecy.
  - He was saluted as the "Savior of men."

---

[125] *The Book of Mormon*, Mosiah 3:19
[126] Steven Levitt and Stephen Dubner, *Freakonomics*, Chapter 1 (What the Bagel Man saw)
[127] Graves Kelsey, *The World's Sixteen Crucified Saviors*

- He led a life of humility and practical moral usefulness.
- He wrought astounding miracles: healing the sick, gave sight to the blind, casting out devils, raising the dead, etc.
- That he was finally put to death upon a cross between two thieves.
- That he descended to hell, rose from the dead, and ascended back to heaven "in the sight of all men".

- In 1027 B.C., the Chinese God Beddou[128] was born of a virgin, narrowly escaped death (the same story of a King putting all male infants to death), was saved by shepherds, lived in the desert to age 30, at which time he began ministering, performed a litany of astonishing miracles and spent his life fasting.
- In 300 B.C., the Mexican God Quexalcote was born of a spotless virgin, led a life of the deepest humility and piety, retired to a wilderness, fasted forty days, was worshipped as a God, and was finally crucified between two thieves, after which he was buried and descended into hell, but rose again the third day.

There are other ancient parallel incidents throughout ancient history, and metaphoric ties to astrology are woven into the story. For example, December 25th is a special day in astrology. It is the day that the sun, after three days of being 'dead' in its excursion southward (for us in the northern hemisphere), is re-born as its rising position starts coming north again. Its position in the sky at the re-birth is attended by three stars, referred to as the 'three kings'. There are many other metaphoric parallels between astrology and the savior story. The simplest explanation is that the Jesus Christ version just happens to be the version of the myth popular today, largely due to the Nicene Creed and agreements made at that council. The French philosopher Bagin explains:

> The most ancient histories are those of Gods who became incarnate in order to govern mankind. All those fables are the same in spirit, and sprang up everywhere from confused ideas, which have universally prevailed among mankind, - that Gods formerly descended upon earth.

---

[128] S. Acharya, *Suns of God*

The last straw for me was the listing of all the historians who lived and recorded significant events during the time and environs of Christ that fail to mention him at all. The writings of these historians would fill a small library and go into great detail describing rulers, thieves, and basically everything and every one. The two that do mention Jesus (that are not forgeries), do not even come close to vaunting him as described by Christian religions[129]. It appears likely that Jesus was a relatively insignificant character in history until Paul and others began to write about him long after his death. The resurrection and virgin birth stories are not in any writings until 250 years after his death, and are not predicted in the Old Testament. And incidentally, virgin birth stories were common in the Mediterranean during this epoch[130]. A second-century Christian critic named Celsus articulated this concern when he wrote: *"Do you think all the other stories are legends, but that your story of Jesus alone is noble and convincing?"* If the Christ story had omitted the virgin birth and not relied on the fall of Adam to create a fallen state for mankind, then perhaps it would deserve serious consideration.

When this new way of thinking about the Old Testament is combined with other evidences casting doubt on the accounts of the virgin birth and resurrection, my short-lived tenure as a mainstream Christian came to an abrupt halt.

Interestingly, I have since spoken with several ex-Mormons who tried to embrace mainstream Christianity just as I had. They travelled the same path, with a similar outcome and timeline, an encounter of few weeks to a few months seems to be a typical experience. So, at least for me and a few others here in Arizona, it took about that long for reality to encroach and push the illusions aside. From the data I have been able to collect, less than ten percent of ex-Mormons wind up in conventional Christianity, so I seem to be more the rule than the exception. The whiskey analogy, which was applied to Mormonism is also readily applied to Christianity as shown in Appendix I. At this point, I was pretty disillusioned with organized religion as a whole. I had hit rock bottom. I

---

[129] **Tim C. Leedom**, *The Book Your Church Doesn't Want You to Read*
[130] John Shelby Spong, *Why Christianity Must Change or Die*, pp 80-81

came to appreciate this tongue-in-cheek definition of Christianity, again, no offense is intended:

> The belief that a cosmic Jewish zombie can make you live forever if you symbolically eat his flesh and drink his blood. That if you telepathically tell him you accept him as Master; he can remove evil from your soul, (the natural man) and won't kill you when he returns in glory. That this evil is present and inherent in humanity because a woman made from a rib was convinced by a talking snake to eat fruit from a magical tree.

Since the Bible and the church are obviously mistaken in telling us where we came from, how can we trust them to tell us where we are going? - Anon

I came to embrace the most simple and rational explanation for the origin for religion. Religion has been created and maintained by people having extraordinary experiences while wrestling with life's great problems and mysteries, and the false psychological feelings thereby associated. Philosopher kings, such as Plato, justified perpetuation of the myths, believing that chaos would result if the binding and comforting myths were discarded. Nietzsche labeled this the pious lie, based on the premise that since the masses were incapable of understanding what was in their best interest, they are better served through deceit. Therefore, the dishonesty, information suppression, and sometimes force became justifiable in the interest of the greater collective good.

So there I was, a pile of ashes sitting on bedrock, disillusioned with everybody and everything. Luckily, I did not stay in this zone for very long. Apparently, those that stay in this stage too long may become bitter, suspicious characters who trust nothing and no one. I came to appreciate this quote:

The truth will make you free; but first it will piss you off. - Gloria Steinem

It was at about this time I received an e-mail from a family member, when commenting on my departure from Mormonism, summed things up by saying "How convenient for you!" Wow. That comment really left me speechless. After pouring my heart and soul and life blood into a cause and then being forced to upset my wife, son, and mother, somebody really had the audacity to call the situation convenient. This was unexpected. Now that I have had time to think about it, this comment has begun to make sense to me. I think the typical member, after a number of years of running themselves ragged in the church, longs for a break and a change, some sort of relief from the constant pressure. They secretly or subconsciously want to check out of the game for a few years and let the chattering in their minds die out and get a chance to catch their breath. [In fact, millions do exactly that and never come back to church.] Thus it is understandable that a longtime member might view the painful and inconvenient deconstruction of a core belief system as somehow convenient while looking through the tinted lenses of Mormonism. And after a year or so of adjustment, it actually has been very convenient having Sundays off and more disposable income. However, at the time the question was asked, convenience was not really on the radar screen.

And speaking of convenience, many have lauded inquisitiveness as a valued quality. However, I often wonder if there a price attached to the questioning spirit quality. Is this one of those all important and hyper present unintended consequences of life? They are everywhere and not always intuitive. Sometimes when I feel compelled to connect the dots I wonder. There has been a price attached to the deconstruction of this nice, tidy religion I was raised in. Why can't I just play tennis, eat yogurt, ride a mountain bike or Harley, watch ESPN, and feel fulfilled like so many of the people I know? I need more substance to life, more issues to consider, and I wind up with more concerns than ever. Is this a happiness enhancer or detractor? Who knows? There is no one size fits all for human peace and happiness, but being inquisitive and connecting the dots seems the only course available to me. The evolution of a soul is something of Mandelbrot set[131], I guess, full of unpredicted twists and turns but each soul is ultimately beautiful in its own way.

So, I asked myself, are the teachings of the Bible, the Koran, Buddha, etc. worthless? No, of course not. In fact, now the teachings and symbols

---

[131] http://en.wikipedia.org/wiki/Mandelbrot_set

in religion are bathed in a new light, one that is not optically distorted through the lenses of organized religion. I came to see that even though some doors were slamming shut, new doors were swinging open. A highly defined theology, like Mormonism, is ideologically restrictive. Once the restrictions are removed, broader and deeper thinking is unleashed. The troublesome accounts of God-sanctioned murder and other troublesome issues in the Old Testament were set aside. Dogmatic belief, the "all-or-nothing" requirements typical of organized religion melted away. All of a sudden, raw teachings and enlightening metaphoric truth was exposed when the dogmatic literalism was stripped away. Flirting with ideological chaos was giving way to an explosion of growth and creative thinking.

I had entered the next stage of faith; I call it the reclamation stage. The Phoenix had begun to rise from the ashes of disillusionment. I decided that the world is far more complex than I expected, and now I could see more optimistic and positive solutions that were not previously possible for me to contemplate. Organized religion, I discovered, makes no sense at all and makes perfect sense, at the same time. Organized religion is counterproductive since it restricts, constrains, and ties ideas to myths while diverting wealth away from humanitarian causes. Organized religion makes perfect sense since it reinforces human biases, gives comfort, feeds the human craving for certainty, and fills a critical need to believe, belong, and lend meaning to life experiences.

I came to understand that spirituality transcends not just Mormonism, but all religiosity. I found the symbols in religious thought to be of tremendous value and power, but the groupthink to be worthless. I found that pious religiosity was the polar opposite of true spirituality. I found a new sense of peace in uncertainty, awe, and wonderment. I no longer felt compelled to understand everything in the universe, I realized that I had a whole lifetime to absorb as much and learn as much as I could and I would never comprehend it all, and that was in itself a revelation.

Then an unexpected thing happened. I began to see the prejudice and discrimination that were institutionalized through Mormonism. I always felt in my heart that all races were equal, but I was not going to go against what I thought God had said, so I adhered to the institutional doctrine. Even though I never thought ill of Blacks or Native Americans, up until my awakening I remained in the Mormon mindset, thinking that Blacks had been less valiant in the pre-earth life[132] and the ancestors of Native Americans had been lazy, wicked, and bloodthirsty[133]. Those thoughts were ever present. I never felt that the doctrine clouded my thinking or had any influence on how I treated people of these races, but I realized that the doctrines had affected my perception of their very existence. I always in my heart felt that women were equal to men, but went along with the groupthink with regard to women and their role. The final wall to come down was in respect to equality for gays and lesbians. Lawn Griffiths very effectively sums up my feelings on this issue[134]:

> I have grown weary covering the issue of gays in the church. That gays and lesbians deserve full acceptance and participation in the life and leadership of congregations is self-evident. That traditional marriage is threatened by gay marriage is no more valid than that adopting children will compromise the legitimacy of one's own natural children and the family unit. Or that blacks or Asians marrying whites would destroy traditional marriage. Bigotry is always an exercise in rationalization.

Now I could embrace fully what I felt deep down in my heart was correct, unencumbered by tainted perceptions of races, colors, or sexual orientation of fellow humans. A new sense of justice and equality emerged that was not tainted by the Mormon culture. The Phoenix was rising higher.

The new concepts and realizations were coming at such a rapid fire pace that my mind was struggling to keep up. It was becoming progressively easier to dispose of the ethnocentric and psychological baggage saddled on me and embrace the wonders of reality. With each step I took, I

---

[132] *Pearl of Great Price*, Abraham 1:21-27, 3:22-23, see also Speech of Elder Orson Hyde, delivered before the High Priests' Quorum, in Nauvoo, April 27, 1845, printed by John Taylor, p. 30

[133] *The Book of Mormon*, 1 Nephi 12:22-23, Alma 17:14-15,

[134] Lawn Griffiths, "Parting Thoughts about the Faith Beat", Mesa, AZ *East Valley Tribune*, 2 Jan 09

became more amazed, more overwhelmed, and more ecstatic about my newfound freedom from the doldrums of the groupthink.

My apprehensions began to dissolve; I now no longer harbored thoughts of returning to the faith corral. I seemed to have more energy. The peace and joy I felt were more profound than the peace and joy I had ever experienced when immersed in the illusions of Mormonism. I truly felt like a new person, a re-birth I had never experienced as a member of a church.

I found myself thinking and saying things that were unpredictable, even surprising myself at times. I was open to all information and concepts. My close-mindedness on many issues evaporated. For example, as a direct consequence, I changed my dietary habits. I found myself more willing to examine new and different ideas. I also realized that my journey of discovery would never end so long as I could think and reason. At age 50 I reckon I have reached about the mid-point in my path of discovery.

I learned that recovery from Mormonism includes deprogramming to shuck off years of indoctrination, it also includes letting go of many years of pent up emotions. Many people have large amounts of guilt for feeling that they never measured up to the enormous demands of the LDS church. It can take years to learn that you were never broken and to forgive yourself for being just human. Many Mormons never allow themselves to be human. According to LDS doctrine even a single bad thought makes one spiritually unworthy. There are tremendous psychological burdens placed on members of the LDS church and just because one has lost faith in the faith, letting go of the guilt can take a lot of time. In many cases the recovery from Mormonism requires grieving, for it is similar in scope to losing a family member. Each individual internalizes their faith system differently, and recovery will be as different as each individual.

My path was one of discovery and debunking the myth, which then automatically led to relief from residual guilt and self-loathing. Those who walk away from a religion without taking time to do the research remain at risk for unhealthful false guilt. Bob McCue explains:

Interestingly, many people leave Mormonism because it simply does not work for them without understanding of why that is the case. That is, their emotional experience within Mormonism does not justify the investment of time, effort etc. Mormonism requires. Sadly, people of this type often carry a burden of guilt with them because **they have not falsified the Mormon belief system.** All they know is that it does not work for them; that it does not feel right. Many of these people still hold Mormon beliefs, which ironically indict them. They believe they were not good enough to live by the Mormon rulebook. They feel guilty. And without the ability to **place their religious experience and beliefs in context,** it is difficult for them to shake these feelings. This is also often a function of not having abstract thinking skills at or above the level required to get out of the Mormon box. - Bob McCue

Now that my emotions were under control, the mental 'chattering' and clutter had dissipated, it was time to begin some core rebuilding. I knew what I did not believe in, but it was time to decide what I really did believe in.

When I had spoken to a lifelong friend about segregating reality from illusion, he mentioned the scientific method. Initially, this seemed cold and detached to me. But as I considered it objectively, I gradually warmed to the idea that the scientific method plays a vital and key role in what I believed. Virtually all the conveniences in our technological world and our understanding of the macroscopic and microscopic world and the cosmos we owe to the scientific method. The scientific method gave us medicine and disease control. Continual revision and acceptance of change is the 'stock in trade' for science, it takes no pride in itself, has no creed, no infallible spokesperson. It changes and adapts as new data and information and measurements are taken. In fact, it is the nature of science to continuously scrutinize, test, and disprove its own theories. I have little tolerance for those who enjoy the fruits of science and its methods yet criticize it as being fundamentally flawed. It has been and will continue to be our best tool in improving the quality of life for humans on the planet and deserves our attention and respect.

I decided that I still believed in natural spirituality and reverence for living things. There are many aspects to spirituality. Part of spirituality is conditioning the subconscious mind to work automatically to find innovative ways to increase harmony between oneself and his surroundings. It is taking time to focus the conscious mind to conjure and achieve life enhancement for the individual and the group. It is a yearning for harmony with self and with the universe. It is a heightened sensitivity to the needs of others and preparing oneself to assist others when the need arises. Much of the Buddhist tradition is evident in my synthesis of spirituality. It is forgiveness and authentic unrequited love. It is honing one's unique gifts and talents and sharing them with no expectation of reciprocity. Discrimination, organizational or personal, detracts from harmony and spirituality. I have people describe spiritual healing and renewal while running, riding a motorcycle, backpacking, river rafting, sailing, meditating, or walking in the park. They come away with a revised picture of themselves and new ideas and renewed resolve on ways to enhance life for themselves and others. I categorize these as spiritual experiences and believe they are completely natural. Spirituality begins and ends with the individual, having no need for group. In practice, religious groups tend to stifle many dimensions of human spirituality. Some cultures show reverence by apologizing to plants and animals that are sacrificed in order to feed the people. I found that after 45 years of intense church activity that I understood very little about true reverence. Reverence is about respect for all living things, conservation of resources, and finding harmony. I had believed that spirituality and reverence are mostly about praying, reading scripture, and being quiet in church. These activities have nothing to do with true spirituality and reverence. Truth and honesty also play roles in spirituality. Each time an individual believes a falsehood or rejects a truth, spirituality and honesty are diminished. Each time an individual rejects a falsehood or embraces a truth, spirituality and honesty are propelled forward.

Early in my discovery phase, I was discussing religion and its meaning in our lives with my younger brother Ed, and he said that the most important thing in life is how we treat other people. Religion is only beneficial if it helps people treat each other with kindness, respect, and equality. That conversation had a profound effect on me, and continues to influence me.

When Einstein developed the theory of quantum mechanics[135], it was a departure from the other theories of physics that were causal in nature.

---

[135] http://en.wikipedia.org/wiki/Quantum_mechanics

For example, we cannot accurately predict the location and velocity of particles from one moment to the next. They jump around and show up in unexpected places. Another outgrowth of the theory is that any time science measures something, the something is affected, which casts some doubt on what we are able to observe. While Einstein hoped for a better theory, after 60 years, the theory gives every indication of being the correct characterization of matter. It appears that uncertainty is part and parcel of the universe, that even if we knew the mass, location, and velocity of every particle in the universe today, we still could not predict the exact state of the universe and the exact location and velocity of each particle tomorrow. The uncertainty principle is here to stay, and being uncertain about things is not necessarily a bad thing. The world has uncertainty. If there is an organized higher power, that power has embraced uncertainty, and so should I.

I have decided that I believe in a non-zero probability of an afterlife. Since matter and energy cannot be created or destroyed, and the functioning human brain has energy, it stands to reason that the energy either goes somewhere or changes form when a human dies. The question is whether or not that energy transition results in survival of our intellect. So far, nobody has proven whether it does or it does not, so it is uncertain. But since I have embraced uncertainty, this is not an obstacle.

What about prayer? On the positive side, it can reinforce our human intentions to relate to the depths of life and love. It can help us become resolved to be an enhancer of life and reach the full measure of creation in our life experience. It can usher in positive thoughts and energy and give a person a positive focus. In a group setting, it can enhance trust, teamwork, and cooperation.

On the negative side, prayer can clutter the mind and increase 'chattering', the tendency to lose focus and lose touch with reality. Prayer, as taught by organized religion is fraught with hazard. First, prayer acknowledges that there is a personal God who listens and can change the outcome of events. This assumption runs against the body of evidence and brings with it a horde of dismal consequences regarding the nature of God, if such a being exists. It is in opposition to Occam's Razor and the scientific method. It can send unhealthy signals to the brain such as a desire to overcome the intellect and replace reason with blind faith. It can reinforce cultural and psychological boundaries, accentuating discrimination, tribalism, superiority, and arrogance. It can reinforce guilt and shame and other mind control tactics. It can readily lead to many unhealthful delusions such as the belief that the destiny of the individual is in God's hands and he needs not take responsibility for his own actions, which we call a cop-out in other forums. Therefore, prayer should come with a big warning label in red to be used with extreme care. Most of the negatives are eliminated if the person replaces prayer with meditation or self-talk, and focuses on positive, life-enhancing thoughts. In group settings, a moment of silence to focus and contemplate the group undertaking eliminates the negatives.

I have come to believe in Occam's Razor, which states that "The simplest explanation is usually the correct one." Religious apologists can do amazing mental contortionism, and I stand in awe of the clever mental masturbation they spew forth. I found almost all of the apologetic arguments to be insulting to my intellect, and really served to rub salt in my wounds rather than salve. No apologetics are better than bad apologetics by a wide margin. In the end, I have found that Occam was generally correct. I have found that it is best to look for the simplest explanation, I am reluctant to chart a crooked path or embrace convoluted reasoning.

I believe I know what Winston Churchill meant when he quoted Disraeli who said: "Sensible men (and women) are all of the same religion (and moral code)."[136]. Disraeli also said that "Sensible men never tell." Well, I am going to throw caution to the wind and attempt to tell. Most believers think that without religion, mankind would be devoid of a moral code and mayhem would ensue. The reality is that all sensible men and women are of the same religion and moral code, and remain sensible when placed in a religious vacuum. As evidence of this I have found that atheists and free-thinkers are among the most moral and ethical people I know, and far less likely to exhibit the prejudices, anger, propensity to violence, and ethnocentrism prevalent among religious affiliates. Experts agree that nature plays a strong role in formation of moral values[137]. The sensible person:

---

[136] http://en.wikiquote.org/wiki/Benjamin_Disraeli
[137] Steven Pinker, *The Blank State: The Modern Denial of Human Nature*

- Embraces uncertainty
- Realizes that religion is not about truth. Rather, it is about finding comfort, belonging to a community, and contributing to a service network
- Does not fall into mind control or unreasonable fervor
- Appreciates other faiths (they do not become preaching missionaries)
- Are naturalists/free-thinkers at heart
- Can be regular church-goers or unaffiliated atheists or anything in between

Do I believe in God? Well, a 'no' answer would be misleading, and a 'yes' answer would also be misleading. The question is insufficient, because the definition of God was not provided. Any attempt to define God diminishes God and attempts to bound what is boundless by definition. There is a Jewish saying that "Jehovah blasphemed himself by forgetting he was a metaphor[138]" which applies well to this paradoxical question.

I will go so far as to say that if there is an organized higher power of some sort, organized religions, as far as I can tell, have utterly failed to paint a box around it. The possibility that an organized higher power exists and that there is an afterlife are interesting thoughts, but ultimately are not important to me. This conclusion astounded me. I would have never expected that these paradoxical questions that have consumed philosophers through the ages would become trivial to me in only a matter of weeks.

Let me explain as best I can. The concept of a thinly-veiled parental figure as God that sits on a throne in the sky who controls the weather, earthquakes, tsunamis, has a chosen people, decides who lives and who dies every day, who can speak for him and who can't, etc. is out of a job and therefore does not exist as far as I am concerned. I have concluded that if there is some sort of organized higher power behind the workings of the universe, it is completely natural and definitely a hands-off entity and does not meddle in people's lives. Therefore, I am left to do the best I can on my own, which is exactly what I would do anyway if there is no organized higher power. Therefore, the question of the existence of said higher power is moot. It simply makes no difference in my life choices or decisions.

[138] Campbell and Moyer, *The Power of Myth*, p. 76

Similar logic applies for the possibility of an afterlife. The promise of a reward in the afterlife is the wrong motivation for doing nice things and being a nice person in this life. As I take my last breath in this life, I want to know and be satisfied that I have done my best to make a positive contribution and treated others as equals and accorded them kindness and respect. This is reward enough. A reward in the afterlife is not necessary to motivate me to be the best version of myself in the here and now. If there is an afterlife, that is a bonus. Once again, the existence of an afterlife plays no role in determining my actions in this life and is therefore unimportant.

My genetic makeup compels me to drive toward an answer if a significant unknown remains unresolved. This is commonly referred to as a cognitive imperative. However, now that these two issues have been swept off the table of significance, I have no cognitive imperative to continue the pursuit of these issues – and while I remain open to consider new information, these are now interesting chit-chat topics, but that is all. I find myself in agreement with Einstein, Spinoza, and many others that we, as an evolving people, no longer need the metaphor. The mystics, Buddhists, and affiliates of other traditions never needed it. I came to appreciate the bumper sticker which quips "Blasphemy is a victimless crime."

I consider myself a naturalist, with means there is a natural explanation for everything, there is no supernatural anything. Even though the naturalist is often painted as a pessimist, I have found the opposite to be true. The naturalist eliminates a vengeful, capricious, and judgmental God concept. The naturalist does away with the wrong motivations for treating other people well such as the promised rewards in heaven or to please God. The naturalist debunks the salvation for money schemes, and tends to motivate humanitarian donations in lieu of feeding church coffers. The naturalist dispels the environments of guilt and shame which can have devastating effects in teenagers and is a poor motivator for adults. The naturalist quells the anger, arrogance, and discrimination that seem to accompany organized religion. The naturalist forces alignment of science and ideology, eliminating cognitive dissonance issues between the two, and thus fosters better mental health. The naturalist dismisses the misconception that this life is relatively unimportant, helping the elderly live a more meaningful and contributory life.

For some reason, most people are drawn to the fantastic and the irrational. Humans seem predisposed to assume supernatural explanations for strange or unexplained life events. It is a popular social pathology. Consider the sales of Tarot cards, the profitability of psychic hotlines, popularity of horoscopes, astrology, and fortune telling. It permeates society around the globe. In Mormonism, each stake has a 'patriarch', and each adult member has the right to a 'patriarchal blessing', which is similar in nature to a detailed fortune telling. Members of the church prepare for this event with fasting and prayer. The patriarch lays his hands on the head of the member and pronounces the blessing. It is recorded and transcribed and becomes a permanent church record, so there is no need to try to remember what was said. The content of the blessing is essentially a complete life fortune as revealed by God for the individual. Forget Tarot card readings, calling the psychic hotline, or reading horoscopes – this is a custom God-revealed fortune told for each individual member. Of course, each blessing is contingent on the faithfulness and diligence of the member, which reinforces the environment of guilt and shame for any member who does not realize the full measure of their blessing. For some reason, it has been my observation that it is mostly the women who talk about and value these blessings more than the men. I think this is a way to fill the innate human desire to have their fortune told, to catch a glimpse of what God has in mind for them. Of course, just as any prophecy people believe in, the predictions and promises in the blessing tend to be self-fulfilling, but there are many exceptions – the accuracy of the blessings are hit and miss.

In these modern times, we tend to forget that magic was very much part of the world view just a generation or two ago. Beginning with the ancients, and continuing up to the present day, religion has been largely a vehicle to explain [what seems to be] magic[139].

Another manifestation of irrational superstition is teleology, which is the belief that everything exists for a purpose and every life event happens for a reason[140]. While this is most prevalent in children, many people

---

[139] D. Michael Quinn, *Early Mormonism and the Magic World View*
[140] Richard Dawkins, *The God Delusion*, pg 210

never grow out of it to embrace the innate randomness of the universe, which brings to each of us a potpourri of experiences and human associations.

For people who are drawn to the supernatural, the thinking goes something like this: because an event cannot be explained, it must be supernatural. If supernatural powers are real, then there must be a supernatural God directing it all. Since there is a supernatural God directing it all, there must be a system of rewards given to those who please Him and punishments for those who offend. And there must also be an afterlife, since it is too dismal to not expect one, so we better get busy finding somebody who can tell us what to do to obtain the best reward in the afterlife. Each step in the circular reasoning chain is as illogical as the others. I came to appreciate this quote:

Belief in the supernatural reflects a failure of the imagination. - Edward Abbey

The reality is that natural explanations could account for all life events, including those that seem to be inexplicable. Some possible natural explanations for seemingly supernatural events are statistical coincidence, the working of the subconscious mind, imagination, hallucinations, telepathy, influence of after-life entities (if such exist), or other unseen and as yet unexplained forces or influences. In the last 100 years we have split the atom, spliced the gene, mapped DNA, put a man on the moon, and beamed rock music into space. Much of what we consider commonplace today would seem like magic to a person living 100 years ago. What advances will occur in the next 100 years? We will undoubtedly uncover even more possible natural explanations for events and phenomena now generally thought to be supernatural or unexplainable. This is referred to as "gap filling" by Richard Dawkins[141]. Thomas Jefferson saw this clearly in his own day when he said:

The priests of the different religious sects... dread the advance of science as witches do the approach of daylight, and scowl on the

---

[141] Richard Dawkins, *The God Delusion*, Chapter 4

fatal harbinger announcing the subdivision of the duperies on which they live.

Many of you will have concluded that I am either an atheist or an agnostic by now. I prefer the naturalist label as a much superior descriptor. What is an atheist anyway? The Wiktionary says that an atheist is "A person who does not believe that deities exist; one who lacks belief in gods". Throughout history, atheists were simply people who did not believe in the prevalent God of the day. For the sun-worshippers, the Jewish people were atheists. For Jewish people, Christians were atheists. Whoever does not believe in your God is by definition, an atheist. I can categorically state that I do not believe in any version of God defined by current mainstream religions, which puts me squarely in the atheist camp for most of the readers. With all the countless Gods concocted by man, I claim that my Christian friends and I have something in common. We are all atheists, I just believe in one less God than they. Throughout history, the atheist label denotes a course change in thought, and is a badge of honor.

Another reason that I prefer the term 'naturalist' to describe my beliefs is that the terms 'agnostic' and 'atheist' presume to attach significance to the organized higher power and afterlife questions. In my case, they are not. Therefore, these descriptors are both inadequate and misleading; they do not apply to me as a naturalist.

It should be pointed out the naturalist viewpoint does NOT preclude a belief in the possibility of a higher power and/or an afterlife. I predict that the potential <u>natural</u> explanations for a higher power and an afterlife will ultimately bring more comfort to a majority of humans than the Adam and Eve story, the flood, the story of the cosmic Jewish zombie born of a virgin, the prophets of Islam, etc., as science and true history erode the foundational tenets of organized religion. It may not occur in my lifetime, but I believe it will happen.

About this time I received a phone call from a member of church with whom I had been acquainted for years. I described what I had discovered about the 'restoration' of the gospel and that I could no longer be honest with myself and participate. He asked what my beliefs were now, so I described my naturalist viewpoint. He exclaimed, "I can understand about Joseph Smith, but God and Jesus too?" I replied, "Brace yourself, it gets worse. Wait 'til I tell you about the Easter Bunny."

Finally, I realized that growing up in Mormonism and being part of an ethnocentric society had certain positive effects on me. I had a strong desire to be self-sufficient and obtain a solid education. Perhaps this was as much family influence as cultural, but the LDS faith does emphasize learning and education, and that is laudable. I had good friends, a loving and nurturing home, and have retained wonderful family relationships throughout my life. To some degree, the Mormon culture contributed positively in these arenas. Resentment left me. The Phoenix had taken flight.

...the word God is for me nothing more than the expression and product of human weaknesses, the Bible a collection of honorable but still primitive legends which are nevertheless pretty childish. If something is in me that can be called religious, then it is the unbounded admiration for the structure of the world so far as science can reveal it. – Albert Einstein

The religion of one age is the literary entertainment of the next. – Ralph Waldo Emerson

Using religion to control the masses is probably the world's second oldest profession, is just as honorable as the first, and is driven by the same kind of primal forces. – Bob McCue

Most religions prophecy the end of the world and then consistently work together to ensure that these prophecies come true. - Anon

Atheism leaves a man to sense, to philosophy, to natural piety, to laws, to reputation; all of which may be guides to an outward moral virtue, even if religion vanished; but religious superstition dismounts all these and erects an absolute monarchy in the minds of men. - Francis Bacon

CHAPTER 16
A HOUSE DIVIDED

Resentment is like taking poison and waiting for the other person to die. - Malachy McCourt

Husbands and wives become comfortable with the Mormon identity of their spouse, which we must remember is not the authentic version of their partner. The depth of this issue is particularly profound for life-long members like me. My wife only ever knew the Mormon Lyndon identity, not the authentic Lyndon. [In reality, I only knew the Mormon Lyndon identity, and discovering the authentic Lyndon has been as traumatic for me as it has been for other family members.] It has to be disconcerting that within a matter of months, she finds herself living with a relative stranger, the emerging authentic version of Lyndon. Thus the feelings of confusion and betrayal, with their associated emotions, are completely understandable. There is no way around it.

Religious divisions in families are nothing new to society. However, the consequences and ramifications are particularly traumatic in Mormonism. While the most harrowing schism is when the rift is between husband and wife, other divisions can also be devastating to family relationships. First, let us examine the marital relationship and the consequences of a disagreement in theology.

While many couples find that religious beliefs play a minor role in the marital relationship, this is generally not the case when one is LDS and the other has been LDS and leaves the fold. While it is always best to attempt to make any change together as a couple, circumstances do not always allow this to occur. The result is a house divided by faith.

From a doctrinal viewpoint, the church teaches that the highest degree of heaven is reserved for husband-wife partners who are both faithful and endure to the end[142]. Eternal procreation and eternal sexual activity are prime motivators in attaining this goal. All members aspire to the highest degree of heaven, so if ones partner leaves the church, the plan is frustrated. From the standpoint of the faithful member, the choice is simple; stay with the infidel and hope that he/she comes back to the church, or get a divorce and try to find a new partner who will be true to the church for life. The doctrinal viewpoint is myopic and one-sided with no flexibility.

Expectations play a huge role in human living, and Mormons expect other Mormons to remain loyal to the church for life. Couples who are married in the LDS temple enter into a covenant that includes faithfulness to the church in addition to faithfulness to their spouse. It is natural and understandable that when one decides to leave the church, the other feels betrayed. The marriage ceremony is short and sweet. The officiator says:

"Brother _____, do you take Sister _____ by the right hand and receive her unto yourself to be your lawful and wedded wife for time and all eternity, with a covenant and promise that you will observe and keep all the laws, rites, and ordinances pertaining to this Holy Order of Matrimony in the New and Everlasting Covenant, and this you do in the presence of God, angels, and these witnesses of your own free will and choice?"

The groom then says, "yes". The officiator then turns to the bride and says:

"Sister _____ do you take brother _____ by the right hand and give yourself to him to be his lawful and wedded wife, and for him to be your lawful and wedded husband, for time and all eternity, with a covenant and promise that you will observe and keep all the laws, rites and ordinances pertaining to this Holy Order of Matrimony in the New and

---

[142] Rulon T. Burton, *We Believe: Doctrines and Principles of the Church of Jesus Christ of Latter Day Saints*, p D-208

Everlasting Covenant, and this you do in the presence of God, angels, and these witnesses of your own free will and choice?"

The bride says "yes".

The officiator then says:

"By virtue of the Holy Priesthood and the authority vested in me, I pronounce you _____, and you _____, legally and lawfully husband and wife for time and all eternity, and I seal upon you the blessings of the holy resurrection with power to come forth in the morning of the first resurrection clothed in glory, immortality and eternal lives, and I seal upon you the blessings of kingdoms, thrones, principalities, powers, dominions and exaltations, with all the blessings of Abraham, Isaac and Jacob and say unto you: be fruitful and multiply and replenish the earth that you may have joy and rejoicing in the day of our Lord Jesus Christ."

It is also interesting that the husband receives the bride, and the bride gives herself to the husband, another manifestation of the patriarchal order, and the tradition of viewing women as property. The New and Everlasting Covenant means, among other things, polygamy. Mormons are taught that polygamy will be the law of the Celestial Kingdom, and by marrying in a Mormon temple the couple is presumed to have agreed to this, though few understand the implications of the ceremony in this regard. A famous quote from Gordon B. Hinckley underscores this:

> Husbands, love and treasure your wives. They are your most precious *possessions*[143].

Those of us who have been married for a prolonged period realize that marriage is not what Hollywood portrays to be a lifelong love affair. Campbell writes[144]:

> What is marriage? The myth tells you what it is. It's the reunion of the separated duad. Originally you were one. You are now two in the

---

[143] General Conference, April 2007
[144] *The Power of Myth*, p 5, 7

world, but the recognition of the spiritual identity is what marriage is. It's different from a love affair. It has nothing to do with that. It's another mythological plane of experience. When people get married because they think it's a long-time love affair, they'll be divorced very soon, because all love affairs end in disappointment. But marriage is recognition of a spirituality identity. If we live a proper life, if our minds are on the right qualities in regarding the person of the opposite sex, we will find our proper male or female counterpart. But if we are distracted by certain sensuous interests, we'll marry the wrong person. By marrying the right person, we reconstruct the image of the incarnate God, and that's what marriage is. … Marriage is a relationship. When you make the sacrifice in marriage, you're not sacrificing to each other but to unity in a relationship. Marriage is not a simple love affair, it's an ordeal, and the ordeal is the sacrifice of ego to a relationship in which two have become one.

When one leaves the faith and the other remains, spiritual unity virtually dissolves. A large portion of what were common life goals and aspirations are no longer shared. The only thing left is the bedrock of the relationship. Only the basic marital commitment, sharing of property, unity in parenting, and temporal life goals remain communal.

The children, depending on their ages and level of activity in the church, may have many different emotions to deal with about the parental division. Younger children are often confused. Faithful adolescents, with their black and white worldview, may tend to feel anger and betrayal. Doubting adolescents usually feel great relief and a dissipation of pressure when another viewpoint is endorsed by a parent. The world becomes a bigger place for them.

Many adults remain active members solely to spare their families the strife and pain associated with a faith change. They feel that 'going along to get along' is the best choice. For some, this course of action is palatable, and acting the role does not present a problem, at least not in the beginning. Often, the disaffected role-player finds himself/herself speaking up more and more in church discussions and pointing out unorthodox views and little known facts that contradict the groupthink. Some can continue in this role for their lifetime, believing that more good can be done from within the herd than can be done from without. For the spouse who has determined that remaining an active member can no longer be endured and cannot seem to interest their spouse in any kind of objective review of their faith, the choices are grim. One avenue is to simply stop attending and stop participating in any way, leaving the family and the rest of the congregation to wonder about motives. The other is to leave the church and explain the motives, publicly renouncing the faith. Those remaining affiliated with the church see this as a betrayal, a show of weakness, a manifestation of hidden sin, and/or a threat to their lifestyle.

Let us take a moment and consider the pain that is sure to be felt by immediate and extended family members. Is this a valid reason for a non-believer to pretend to believe? What are the long-term effects of the anguish caused by departure of a loved one? First, let us consider the effect of the turmoil on lifelong faithful parents, grandparents, and extended family adults.

In our Western culture, the elderly are viewed as fragile and worn out, rigid in their ways, and deserving of rest and repose. Very little is expected of them, except perhaps an occasional consultation. Their life contributions have been made, the elderly are put out to pasture to enjoy the autumn of their used-up lives. What we fail to realize is that taking this view of the elderly does them a grave disservice. Our Western culture can learn much from other cultures which have a radically different expectation of their elderly, and get radically different results. Many cultures expect the elderly to be the most important contributors to society, and they are. Siblings fight over the opportunity to care for their parents and grandparents in their old age, due to the coveted opportunity to learn from them on a daily basis. The elderly in these cultures regularly live to be over 100 years old[145] and generally retain sharp minds and disease-free bodies well into their nineties and even to the century mark and beyond. Nature teaches us that living things are strengthened and revitalized through struggle and change. Living things that are not challenged become diseased and wither and die. Experienced parents

---

[145] John Robbins, *Healthy at 100*

also realize that humans tend to live up to expectations. Isolating our elderly from life challenges and expecting them to be incapable of adapting to change sentences them to a mundane and foreshortened existence. Challenging them is an example of what many have referred to as "tough love", which may seem hurtful at first, but in the long run is the most loving and humane.

Pretending to remain a faithful and believing member of any church in order to spare family members pain, while being a noble desire, ultimately robs the family the opportunity to grow and learn. The 11th Article of Faith, a foundational tenet adhered to by church members, and penned by Joseph Smith states:

> We claim the privilege of worshiping Almighty God according to the dictates of our own conscience, and allow all men the same privilege, let them worship how, where, or what they may.

Upon the departure from the faith of a family member, other family members are forced to embrace this belief with their whole hearts, often for the first time. According this courtesy to strangers is automatic, but tolerance for a close family member defection is an entirely different matter. This type of growth and development has to be considered a life experience enhancer, as it makes all persons involved more tolerant and accepting of others. It also gives family members the opportunity to see first hand an example of a free-thinker, which may help them think 'outside the box' as they break out of similar adverse circumstances, whether they be societal, professional, or personal/familial. This is another example of tough love that can ultimately pay huge dividends.

The disaffected member, at one point or another during their research phase, invites their spouse and adult family members to do research and desires to discuss his findings with them. Since the church has pre-conditioned everyone to beware of anti-Mormon literature, such invitations to objectively examine core beliefs are often rejected and the spouse and faithful family members go into self-defense mode, and their minds, at least initially, shut tighter than ever. They often feel that more church activity, prayer, and scripture study will provide the needed spiritual power to overcome this life trial, and perhaps influence the defector to see the 'error of his or her ways'. Interestingly, in a showing of group strength and tribalism, the congregation rallies around the faithful spouse and heralds him/her as a hero, heaping attention and accolades at every occasion. After all, the faithful spouse is sleeping with the enemy and is overcoming great adversity in their life and is in need of extra support. The walls separating the divided household are thus built higher and stronger. Only time can weaken them.

Upon rejection of the invitation to investigate the church, the skeptic feels insulted that the family lacks trust in his or her judgment. While the Mormon church emphasizes a 'family first' motto, when the skeptic wants to discuss the deep issues openly, the faithful portion of the family immediately puts 'church first' and refuses to examine the issues. Since the skeptic has been an integral part of the family decision making, the insult goes even deeper. From the skeptic's viewpoint, the family has trusted his/her judgment and has relied on this judgment for key family decisions, including in many instances, their sustenance. A relationship of mutual trust has been built. The failure of family members to read anything at all or do any investigating is interpreted as disrespect, a lack of trust, betrayal, ingratitude, or a combination of these feelings. As one skeptic breadwinner puts it; "My family has relied on me and accepted my decisions on my profession, what house to buy, where to live, for daily food and shelter, for retirement planning, for medical and heath advice, what schools to attend, which careers to pursue, and more. I have done more research into religion than all my other endeavors combined, yet my family will not pick up a single book and read for a few hours to become informed and prepare for perhaps the single most important decision of their lives."

Another 'house divided' situation is where the parents leave the church and the children remain immersed. When the parents present a united front, the children usually are amenable to an objective examination and are less likely to completely shut down and revert to self-defense mode. We usually don't give children the credit they deserve in their capacity to detect falsehoods, even very young children. Many couples have had excellent success 'deprogramming' their children by simply gently presenting both sides of every issue during family discussions and allowing the children to choose whether to continue to attend church, seminary, etc.

Others have found success in combining this approach with attendance at other more open and tolerant religious services, such as Unitarian/ Universalist congregations. Some report that the children begin voluntarily distancing themselves from the church in as little as six months, but it can take up to several years, especially for the older children who have more invested.

The final house divided by faith scenario is when one or more of the children leave the faith, and the rest of the family remains faithful, including the parents. The parents generally dismiss the actions of the child as simple rebellion. The faithful siblings usually look to parents and church leaders to reconcile the actions of their wayward brother or sister. The usual reasons which are generally presented, which may have no basis in fact, are rebellion, weakness, sin, Satanism, etc. When the disaffected child attempts to explain to their siblings the real reasons for their departure, some parents panic. The thought that the wayward child might convince the others to leave is too much of a threat. They feel they have to drive the wayward child from the home to prevent the spread of the anti-Mormon information. Thus families are shattered, trust and love and tolerance are replaced with anger, segregation, and betrayal. At church, the parents are counseled to hold onto the hope that the lost sheep will one day return to the fold, and are promised that if they remain faithful, that this will happen one day. It is yet another manipulation to reinforce the environment of guilt and shame, because if the child never comes back to the church, then the blame falls on the parents because they lacked faith. Although not supported from a doctrinal standpoint, some hold onto the hope that if they remain faithful to the end, their wayward family members will repent in the afterlife. Humans will go to great extremes to fabricate a safety net of hope.

The eternal family doctrine plays a pivotal role in homes divided by faith. Some faithful parents and siblings, convinced that they will never see or associate with the wayward family members in the afterlife, lose hope and simply give up on the defectors. The logic goes something like this: since I will not be able to see them in the afterlife, there is no reason to pursue a healthy relationship with them now. It is better to just cut bait now and save the emotional investment. Thus, ironically, the eternal family doctrine often torpedoes family relationships in homes divided by faith.

Conclusion

In a house divided by faith, the stakes are high and emotions run even higher. The decision to publicly leave the faith is a difficult one. Pretending to remain faithful for the sake of family ultimately does them a disservice. Although each situation is different, taking the tough love approach is generally the appropriate course of action, because it results in the most benefit for loved ones in the long run.

Initially, faithful family members may feel betrayed and go into self-defense mode, turning off all critical thinking skills. Only time and loving patience will restore objectivity and open-mindedness, although there are no guarantees. Church doctrines tend to strengthen the resolve of the faithful to build walls and withdraw from relationships, which often frustrates healing and reconciliation efforts.

CHAPTER 17
STANDING FOR SOMETHING MORE

Bringing out the best in us does not require the worst in us; our love of human beings does not need to be nurtured by delusion. – Sam Harris

Always try to leave things in better condition than you found them. – Reuel Lamborn

With the recent passing of Gordon B. Hinckley, the 15th president of the LDS church, I have been reflecting on his life's work. He wrote a book called <u>Standing for Something</u>. His life's work and legacy may be summed up by recounting some revealing moments in his life. The reader is left to draw his/her own conclusion.

Hinckley on discerning truth and error and having nothing to hide:

Here is a document that will never again see the light of day.

Hinckley allegedly made this statement as he completed a transaction purchasing a document from Mark Hofmann, a dealer in historical documents. The document was a forgery that contained fabricated information that might have become an embarrassment to the church. Hofmann would eventually peddle 48 forgeries to the church, either through direct sales or indirectly through 'purchase-donate' beneficiaries.

Hinckley regarding the financial interests of the church[146]:

---

[146] Gordon B. Hinckley, *Ensign*, Nov 1999

We have a few business interests. Not many. Most of these were begun in very early days when the Church was the only organization that could provide the capital that was needed to start certain business interests designed to serve the people in this remote area. We have divested ourselves long since of some of these where it was felt there was no longer a need. Included in these divestitures, for instance, was the old Consolidated Wagon and Machine Company, which did well in the days of wagons and horse-drawn farm machinery. The company outlived its usefulness.

The Church sold the banks which it once held. As good banking services developed in the community, there was no longer any need for Church-owned banks.

In 1991, the Arizona Republic printed an extensive list of the Church's US corporations. TIME magazine reported in August 1997 that independent investigators had "been able to quantify the church's extraordinary financial vibrancy. Its current assets total a minimum of $30 billion. If it were a corporation, its estimated $5.9 billion in annual gross income would place it midway through the FORTUNE 500, a little below Union Carbide and the Paine Webber Group but bigger than Nike and the Gap." In the meantime, the Deseret News reports[147] that during Hinckley's tenure, Utah has ranked number one in per capita bankruptcy filings in the 50 states from 2001 through 2004, displacing the previous champion, Tennessee, for this distinction.

Hinckley comments on a key doctrinal question[148]:

Q: There are some significant differences in your beliefs. For instance, don't Mormons believe that God was once a man?

A: I wouldn't say that. There was a couplet coined, "As man is, God once was. As God is, man may become." Now that's more of a cou-

---

[147] Dave Anderton, *Deseret News*, Mar 26, 2004

[148] President Gordon B. Hinckley with Don Lattin, the *San Francisco Chronicle* religion writer, Sunday, April 13, 1997. *Time* magazine of August 4, 1997, in an article titled "Kingdom Come," page 56

plet than anything else. That gets into some pretty deep theology that we don't know very much about.

Q: Just another related question that comes up is the statements in the King Follet discourse by the Prophet.

A: Yeah

Q: God the Father was once a man as we were. This is something that Christian writers are always addressing. Is this the teaching of the church today, that God the Father was once a man like we are?

A: I don't know that we teach it. I don't know that we emphasize it. I haven't heard it discussed for a long time in public discourse. I don't know. I don't know all the circumstances under which that statement was made. I understand the philosophical background behind it. But I don't know a lot about it and I don't know that others know a lot about it.

Compare these responses to the actual teachings of Joseph Smith Jr.[149]:

I will go back to the beginning before the world was, to show what kind of being God is. What sort of being was God in the beginning? Open your ears and hear, all ye ends of the earth, for I am going to prove it to you by the Bible, and to tell you the designs of God in relation to the human race, and why he interferes with the affairs of men.

God himself was once as we are now, and is an exalted man, and sits enthroned in yonder heavens! That is the great secret. If the veil were rent today, and the great God who holds this world in its orbit, and who upholds all worlds and all things by his power, was to make himself visible, — I say, if you were to see him today, you would see him like a man in form — like yourselves in all the person, image and very form as a man . . .

---

[149] *History of the Church*, vol. 6, pp. 304-306

... I am going to tell you how God came to be God. We have imagined and supposed that God was God from all eternity. I will refute that idea, and take away the veil, so that you may see.

... he was once a man like us; yea, that God himself, the Father of us all, dwelt on an earth, the same as Jesus Christ himself did; and I will show it from the Bible.

Here, then, is eternal life — to know the only wise and true God; and you have got to learn how to be Gods yourselves, and to be kings and priests to God, the same as all Gods have done before you.

It is also clear that this doctrine is still taught today. The first chapter of the 1992 edition of the Latter-day Saint teaching manual, Gospel Principles page 9 quotes directly from the above passage.

We should not forget that, in addition to the explosion in bankruptcies in Utah during Hinckley's tenure, the so-called "Plan of Happiness" taught by Hinckley was accompanied by the following societal phenomena:

In November of 2007, Forbes reported that Salt Lake City is America's leader in per-capita plastic surgery[150], a symptom of a society that emphasizes community acceptance through appearance. The Deseret News[151] and ABC news[152] report that Utah is America's most depressed state, with the highest per-capita anti-depressant use, especially in women. Studies done at Utah State University[153] suggest the pressures of Mormonism contribute to the problem. Utah has a consistently high suicide rate[154] among men aged 15 to 24, has the most per-capita fraud in America[155], and is the nation's leader in mortgage fraud[156]. Since 1991, Utah's

---

[150] Rebecca Ruiz, "America's Vainest Cities", *Forbes Magazine*, 11/29/07

[151] James Thalman, *Deseret News*, Nov 28, 2007

[152] R. Goldman, "Two Studies Find Depression Widespread in Utah, Study Calling Utah Most Depressed, Renews Debate on Root Causes", March 7, 2008

[153] http://www.usu.edu/psycho101/lectures/chp2methods/study.html

[154] http://health.utah.gov/opha/publications/hsu/9903suicide.pdf

[155] Consumer Fraud and Identity Theft Complaint Data, 2006, Federal Trade Commission, 2/07, page 18

[156] *Deseret News*, 26 July 2005

rape rate has inched higher than the national rate. By 2002, Utah ranked 14th[157]. Studies done on key word searches indicate that pornography is especially insidious in Utah[158], a symptom of sexual repression.

In one of his final addresses to the Church before his death[159], Hinckley stated:

> First came Moroni with the plates from which was translated <u>The Book of Mormon</u>. What a singular and remarkable thing this was. Joseph's story of the gold plates was fantastic. It was hard to believe and easy to challenge. Could he have written it of his own capacity? It is here, my brothers and sisters, for everyone to see, to handle, to read. Every attempt to explain its origin, other than that which he gave, has fallen of its own weight.

Compare this assertion to three well-documented possible explanations for the origin of <u>The Book of Mormon</u>, each one having a probability far greater than the story of the angel Moroni and the gold plates, none of which has fallen of its own weight:

1. Plagiarism of Solomon Spaulding's <u>Manuscript Found</u>, mingled with religious additions answering the popular theological questions of the day. Spaulding and Sidney Rigdon frequented the same printing house in Pittsburgh where Spaulding had submitted his book Manuscript Found for printing, and Rigdon took interest. Spaulding's widow accused Rigdon of stealing the manuscript after Solomon's death. Eight people made statements[160] that <u>The Book of Mormon</u> was largely the same story they had read in Manuscript Found, with religious sections added. The two works shared several common names, and both used the phrase "it came to pass" frequently. It was common knowledge among Rigdon's descendants that Sidney was a principle contributor to <u>The Book of Mormon</u>[161].

---

[157] Geoffrey Fattah, "Utah rape rate rising", *Deseret News*, Apr 12, 2005

[158] "Porn Pervasive in Utah", *Deseret News*, 20 Jan 2007, , "Utah is No. 1-for Online Pornography Consumption ", 3 Mar 2009, *Salt Lake Tribune*

[159] Gordon B. Hinckley, "The Stone Cut Out of the Mountain", *Ensign*, November 2007

[160] Fawn M. Brodie, *No Man Knows My History: The Life of Joseph Smith*, p. 443

[161] Howard A. Davis, *Who Really Wrote The Book of Mormon?* 1977

2. Plagiarism of Ethan Smith's <u>A View of the Hebrews</u>, mingled with religious additions answering the popular theological questions of the day. <u>A View of the Hebrews</u> was published in a neighboring county seven years prior to <u>The Book of Mormon</u> and was a very popular book in the region. Church historian BH Roberts felt this theory was very plausible due to 18 parallels he found significant and went so far as to brief his findings to Church officials[162] in 1922. Additional discussion of these parallels and evidence of plagiarism between the two works may be found in a detailed book report in Appendix E.

3. Automatic writing. The dictation of <u>The Book of Mormon</u> fits very comfortably into the category of 'automatic writing' that is well-documented[163]. Automatic writers have routinely produced very lengthy works in a very short time, picking up where they left off, even in mid-sentence, hours or days after having interrupted the dictation. Some automatic writers have actually been able to pen a letter to a friend while earnestly dictating. Other automatic writers have found their gift is heightened by gazing into a crystal or translucent stone. The book <u>Jane Eyre</u> was produced via automatic writing, as well as <u>The Urantia Book</u>. Automatic writers often feel their gift is of God and their works are inspired, which could have led Joseph to believe that he was called of God. This explanation fits with the method of dictation: Joseph peering into his hat through a peep stone with no gold plates required.

Was Hinckley unaware of these other well-known theories, or was he acutely aware of them and attempting to mislead the membership of the church? I don't know. The reader is left to decide which is more likely, but he was either guilty of unforgivable ignorance, irrationality, or deception. I use the term unforgivable not to grind an axe but because he held a position of trust, and therefore has a moral duty to be informed regarding that which he is discussing and also be truthful. Several other

---

[162] <u>Brigham D. Madsen</u>, <u>Brigham H. Roberts</u>, <u>Sterling M. McMurrin</u>, *Studies of The Book of Mormon*

[163] Dan Vogel and Brent Metcalfe, *American Apocrypha, Essays on The Book of Mormon*

examples showing that Hinckley was either woefully misinformed or dishonest may be found at the website of Richard Packham[164]. [Interestingly, honesty is one of the ten virtues cited in Hinckley's book <u>Standing for Something</u>.]

So what did Gordon B. Hinckley stand for during his lifetime? What have been the short-term effects of his life? What will the long-term effects be? What does his legacy leave behind? Is this a person whom we should aspire to emulate?

My friend Mr. Chad Spjut, who had been a member of the church for 34 years, visited Hinckley's grave site and offers his opinion on the matter:

> As I stood there on Hinckley's grave, I made a point to stand on the spot where I imagined his head to be located under the earth. It felt strange standing on the location of his head, as I imagined his body deep beneath the soil, clothed in his temple garb, awaiting the Mormon resurrection. Standing on his head, looking down at the ground and thinking about who this man was, why he did the things he did, and how his choices directly affected my life and the lives of countless others.
>
> I was angry. Angry at this man who knew the secrets, the lies and deceptions, going as far as being a participant in the lies and cover-ups himself. Why? He knew; there was no escaping that. He knew that he was lying, stealing and misleading millions who followed him, and for what? Power? Position? Fame? Did the thought ever cross his mind that he was doing more harm through his deceptions than he was in bolstering the good aspects of Mormonism? Did he notice the blood on his hands of those who took their own lives in desperation in not being able to live up to the lies and impossible standards of his fraudulent organization? Did he recognize the epidemic of depression which burdens and tears at the lives of many within his organization due to the overwhelming burden of work and guilt so easily heaped upon them? Did he care to think about the tens of

---

[164] http://packham.n4m.org/lying.htm

thousands of families torn apart as member after member discovers the truth and then parted ways from his organization? The divorce, the pain, the bitter tears, suffering and anguish caused by his continual support of the deception he furthered?

No, I don't think he really did. I don't think these concerns were ever on the mind of Gordon Hinckley.

As I continued to stare down at this spot of grass and earth, a sense of sadness and pity was followed by disdain which filled my heart toward this man. Here was someone who could have righted the wrongs of Mormonism's past and its despicable founder Smith. He could have told the truth, he could have counseled and directed a new path for Mormonism, free of the fraud and deceptions of its past. He could have put his religion on a new footing of truth and integrity, something which they so openly tout in public, yet so blatantly ignore in practice. He had his chance to change it all, yet he did nothing.

To be fair, Hinckley was a very talented public speaker and intelligent enough to realize that the way of the future was to push the LDS boat out into the waters of mainstream Christianity. He did his best to do just that, downplaying the weird doctrines and getting in front of cameras. But, like so many of us humans, and this includes me, his accomplishments were well short of his potential.

LDS members will say that they loved President Hinckley and are totally happy living the gospel plan. They do not see the societal ills reported by the press, so they imagine they must be fabrications and should be ignored. How can they be so content in the midst of such serious social problems? The only logical response is:

It is no measure of health to be well adjusted to a profoundly sick society. - Jiddu Krishnamurti

I seriously considered simply setting aside the weird doctrinal baggage and look for the good and continue to believe in some portions of the religion. I asked myself, why not? On the surface this seemed innocuous and perhaps even beneficial. But I found that in addition to the dangers, it is simply not the best approach to long term human happiness and fulfillment. Some Indian tribes, when faced with a difficult decision, would consult the eldest tribal women who would then base the choice on the projected effect of the decision on the sixth generation. The tribe was interested in the long view (sixth generation) and the humanitarian view (asking the opinion of the eldest women).

If I were to remain a member, my descendants, at the sixth generation, would be in high risk groups for:

- Suicide
- Depression, use of anti-depressants, and mental illness
- Financial woes (keep up with the Jones', giving up retirement $, etc.)
- Becoming victims of fraud, especially affiliation fraud
- Having their lives governed by guilt and shame

To illustrate the gravity of this decision, consider a young man, being brought up in a faithful LDS or Christian fundamentalist home, who finds himself sexually attracted to men or children or guilty of masturbation. He has been taught that homosexuality is a sin against God and nature (Lev 20:13). He has been taught that abstinence from sexual relations outside the bonds of marriage is a strict requirement for salvation and has been obedient. He is also familiar with Matthew 18:6, which states: "But whoso shall offend one of these little ones which believe in me, it were better for him that a millstone were hanged around his neck and that he were drowned in the depths of the sea." He has been taught that masturbation is a grievous sin, like unto murder. The combination of raging hormones, despair, guilt, and shame are too much and he commits suicide, confident that he has done the right thing to take his own life according to the clear teaching of scripture and God's emissaries. Religious indoctrination, combined with the black and white world of the adolescent is at the foundation of this tragedy. Some have speculated that this scenario is played out to its grim conclusion as often as once a week [or even more] here in the Western United States. It is tragedy of immense proportions. Since I would never want this to happen to my descendants I am compelled to take action. I am convinced that

Mormonism, as currently practiced, is something that the vast majority of humanity is better off without. Similar case studies could be offered for depression, financial ills, fraud victims, and the long term ill effects of guilt and shame. I also have a fundamental aversion to seeing my posterity become beasts of burden for a multi-billion dollar corporation.

In addition to the long term ill effects on my descendants, for me personally, the desire to know the truth about religion was stronger than the desire to believe and belong. I decided that there is no shame in being true to myself, and that the unexamined life is not worth living. Since the truth has nothing to fear from examination, neither should I refrain from research due to fear of the unknown. The truth was truly liberating, even though the journey to the truth was terrifying. I expected the discovery process to be lonely, but it was not. I also was apprehensive that the truth might lead to despair and depression, but I was wrong. I found that life is too short to live a lie, to feel compelled to feign belief in order to go along with the group.

For the faithful, life as part of a religious group is usually mostly about social interaction and helping the other members of the group cope with life. However, I found that danger lurks in the potential for the member to become fanatical and fundamental. For example, members of the LDS church, by virtue of their membership, are endorsing the following doctrines:

- All Christian ministers were corrupt in 1820[165].
- God chose a man who admittedly preyed on the superstitions of the people for gain as His oracle.
- Polygamy is an eternal truth and divine principle.
- That God would send an angel with a sword to strike down his prophet if he did not take additional wives.
- There is no punishment for marrying women already married to another man if God commands it. Keeping it a secret from the first husband is also OK.

---

[165] *Pearl of Great Price*, Joseph Smith History; 1:19

- The laws of God trump the laws of the land, making it OK to destroy a printing press and conspire to commit murder.
- That God is a racist, and discriminates against people based on skin color and lineage.
- God chooses not to warn his people regarding impending calamities (World Trade Center attack, tsunami, hurricanes).

Those who believe that the Bible is the literal word of God endorse the following:

- Foreign wives should be divorced. Ezra 9 & 10
- Slavery. Col 3:22, 4:1
- Homosexuals are to be executed. Lev 20:13
- Disobedient children are to be stoned. Duet 21:18-21
- False God worshippers are to be executed. Duet 6:14-15, 8:19, 30:17
- Sickness is often due to demonic possession or sin. Mark 2:1-12, Matt 9:2
- Women are not to speak in church. 1 Cor 14:34-35
- Sexuality: The Bible condemns intercourse during menstruation, celibacy, marriage to non-Jews, naming sexual organs, nudity, masturbation, and birth control. The Bible permits prostitution, polygamy, sex with slaves, concubinage, treatment of women as property, and marriage to girls age 11-13.
- Adherence to the ten commandments includes treating women as property. Exodus 20
- Planar earth concept. Job 38:13-14, Isaiah 40:21,22, Daniel 4:10-11, Matt 4:8, Rev 7:1
- Discrimination. Gen 9:18-25

The Bible has been quoted in the past to uphold slavery, condone genocide, justify race and sex discrimination, prevent distribution of medicines, and many other inhumane practices. We seem to forget that the proponents of these inhumanities all claimed to be acting according to the "clear teaching of scripture". Using the Bible and other books heralded as containing God's will continues to find widespread use throughout the world in justifying inhumanity. Not many years ago, religionists quoted scripture and recommended against distribution of the smallpox vaccine[166], claiming that the vaccine frustrated God's plan for cleansing the earth. I personally heard similar arguments, among LDS members, denouncing AIDS research in the eighties. Now some religionists are opposed to stem cell research. Others justify terrorism by quoting their scripture. So long as there are humans who believe in one true God, they will continue to justify inhumanity in His name.

Belief in most current mainstream religions brings with it additional troublesome issues unrelated to the canon:

- God values belief in the absence of evidence (faith) as the most important attribute a man can posses. In other forums we call this gullibility.
- God favors those who are born in a particular geographical region. Since virtually all religions teach that the path to salvation lies only with their religion, and despite missionary efforts, religious allegiance is predicated mostly by geography, then God must have geological favorites.
- God only wants a small percentage of humans to obtain salvation. Once again, since the major mainstream religions teach that it is their way or the highway, and this must be acceptable to the all-powerful God, then losing a large percentage of us to the adversary must not bother him.
- God favors those who are able to suppress their intelligence and ignore science and emerging true history.
- God prefers building churches and supporting clergy over humanitarian aid.

It is interesting that religious faith enjoys automatic respect in today's society, and when one examines history objectively, that respect has not been earned. The teachings of 'moderate' religion, though mild by themselves, are an open invitation to extremism.

I took a step back and took a hard look at core values and realized I was not supporting what I knew in my heart to be good and correct. I found

---

[166] Christopher Hitchens, *God is not Great: How Religion Poisons Everything,*
  Chapter 4

that the definitions of good and evil given to me were lacking and tortu-
ously complicated. I decided that behaviors that enhance life are good
and those that diminish life are evil. It is that simple.

The classical concepts of sin and punishment and a capricious God to
administer the whole thing were growing small in my rear view mirror.
The sin concept puts one in a state of conflict, which is the opposite of
harmony and therefore the antithesis of spirituality. Sin puts one in a
servile condition throughout one's life[167]. The sin concept robs mankind
of the opportunity of adopting correct behavior voluntarily and the innate satisfaction derived thereby. Identifying with the positive aspects
of life and choosing to embrace life enhancing behavior on a want-to,
choose-to basis was a big boost for me. Of course, choosing to enhance
life (good) will tend to have positive long term effects on the individual
and group, and choosing to diminish life (evil) will tend to have negative
long term effects on the individual and the group. The consequences are
all natural, none are supernatural.

I believe that the religious faithful who do not believe that they can overcome the apparent despair and turmoil of leaving the faith community
are selling themselves short. The human psyche has resilience beyond
our capacity to imagine. Ask a first time marathon runner, he will tell
you. He has faced down despair and found a way to overcome. Just
like children who are reluctant to have dad remove the security of the
training wheels, many fear going without the warm fuzzy blanket and
pacifier of organized religion. But how much more fun did we have with
the more agile bicycle without those restrictive training wheels? Here
is something else to consider. Most of the hundreds of thousands of
people who are now ex-Mormons, ex-Christians, etc., at one time or another in their life, also felt they could not cope with a loss of their faith.
But they did it. And they are generally happy, well-balanced people enjoying a fulfilling life experience. Some of the nicest people you will
ever know are ex-Mormons and ex-Christians. Caterpillars undergo a
metamorphosis to become butterflies. You will have to go into a cocoon
for a while, but it is worth the wings.

---

[167] Campbell and Moyer, *The Power of Myth*, p. 66

After I was jolted out of my slumber, I reevaluated my life contribution. Twenty years after I die, what will my children and grandchildren believe my life has stood for? Did I leave them a demon-haunted world and an environment of guilt and shame? Do I want to be remembered for perpetuating illusions and telling of half-truths? Will I have left things better than I found them, or made them worse? Will I be counted among those who believed that mankind is inherently evil, that charity and goodwill are only achieved through delusion? Or will I be among those who raised their arms and cried out to the world: "The age of reason has dawned. The time to droop and stoop in delusion has passed."

I believe that there is hope that religious strife and unreasonable fervor will subside as the voice of reason is sounded, as men and women find new joy in taking responsibility for their own lives. It has been my observation that religious zeal leads to one of two end states. The first end state is an escalation of self-perceived righteousness and arrogance. The religious zealot never intends this to be the end state, but it is inevitable because he values his code of righteous behavior, and by default is compelled to think less of those who cannot attain it. The second end state is a self-deprecating condition as the person realizes he can never measure up, and never will. Neither circumstance is healthy or beneficial.

In the popular television series "Heroes", young men and women with supernatural powers become heroes to protect mankind in the struggle of good versus evil. In the fantasy world, heroes and villains are readily distinguished, as are the battle lines of good an evil. In the real world, heroes do not have super powers and often go unrecognized, villains pose as saints, and the battle lines are seldom if ever clearly delineated. Who are the heroes in the real world? They are generally not superstar athletes or movie stars.

A hero is a person who is precisely aware of his/her knowledge limits, is never afraid to admit it, and strives continuously for deeper understanding with an open mind.

A hero is a person who, despite crushing peer or family pressure, refuses to prostitute his/her intellect to unreasonable beliefs.

A hero is a person who consistently leaves conditions better than he or she found them.

A hero is one who can shed the delusion that they are the center of the universe, that an external deity would protect or rescue them – and take possession of their own soul and destiny.

A hero is one who seeks to advance the cause of understanding, doing good by stealth and teaching by example.

A hero is one who develops his talents and gifts and accepts the call to action when life figuratively taps him on the shoulder requesting use of his unique skills to help another human being.

I do not have all the answers. However, I believe that I have begun to ask the right questions. One of those questions is not whether we have religious faith, it is whether religious faith has us. I refuse to walk in fear and regress to an age of unreason. I have found that regardless of the religious beliefs of my ancestors, I am not descended from fearful men and women. My forefathers were not afraid to write, not afraid to associate, not afraid to speak, and not afraid to align themselves with causes that were, at the time, decidedly unpopular. I am cut from that same mold.

This is not a time for me to remain silent, to excuse myself from the arena of public opinion. I cannot absolve myself from the potential results of my inaction. I have learned that silence implies consent, and participation gives implicit sanction. I find that I cannot champion humanitarianism abroad by deserting it at home. It is clear to me that the time to break the chain of faith abuse is now. I assert that we no longer need to resort to the worst in humanity to bring out the best in humanity. I have resolved to exalt the virtues of new ideas and new ideals, rise above the delusions, and stand for something more.

In the second verse of the song, "The Man's Too Strong", Dire Straits accurately portrays corporate religion in general and Joseph Smith Jr. in particular as follows:

I have legalized robbery, called it a belief.

I have run with the money, and hid like a thief.
I have rewritten history with my armies and my crooks.
Invented memories, I did burn all the books.
And I can still hear his laughter, I can still hear his song;
The man's too big, the man's too strong.

To amplify this excellent montage of how humanity justifies its conduct using religion (which I will refer to as "faith" in this poem), I add the following:

An Ode to Dire Straits

We have legalized robbery and called it faith, but that is not all;
We have exalted gullibility and called it faith.
We have censored the voice of reason, embraced delusions, and called it faith.
We have granted power to demons, feared the imaginary, and called it faith.
We have sanctioned discrimination and called it faith.
We have numbed our intellect with conformity and called it faith.
We have justified suppression of information and perpetuated lies and called it faith.
We have condoned inhumanity and called it faith.
Our elderly have abandoned life in preference for death and we called it faith.
We have surrendered our free will and called it faith.
We have declared ourselves the Chosen Ones and spat on our neighbor and called it faith.
We have apologized for reality and called it faith.
We have traded sanity for security and called it faith.
We have abused our children with guilt and shame and unbridled fear and called it faith.
We have demeaned our women, esteemed them as property, and called it faith.
We have laid waste to families and called it faith.
I sit on the sand and feel the rhythm of the waves.
I lay down my burden and watch it dissolve with the tide.
The water and the sand and the sky become one.
I will study faith no more.

CHAPTER 18
BOMB'S AWAY!

Question with boldness even the existence of a God; because, if there be one, he must more approve of the homage of reason, than that of blind-folded fear. - Thomas Jefferson

Those who can make you believe absurdities can make you commit atrocities. – Voltaire

August 19ᵗʰ, 2007   Salt River Stake High Council Room Mesa, AZ 7:00 am

A ccording to what I have been taught over my lifetime, a typical disciplinary council involves a humble and contrite offender, pleading for leniency and begging for mercy from the council. Often tears are shed and the dialog is intended to tug at the heartstrings of those present. The fifteen judges are painted as benevolent dispensers of God's love and make every effort to put themselves into the shoes of the wrongdoer. My disciplinary council session bore no semblance to that standard portrayal.

Looking back at 35 years of speaking to church groups, this opportunity to teach was my favorite. There is no greater gift than the gift of knowledge. In summary, I attempted to convey the following concepts to the men in attendance:

1. The most important thing in life is how we treat other people.
2. Organizations that suppress information ultimately cause disillusionment and loss of trust among its members, and is immoral.

3. There is no rational justification for suppression of information.

4. The 'truth test' taught to church members is illogical (based on circular reasoning) and is at best unreliable, and has been described as a recipe for self-deception.

5. Religious beliefs should never be confused with truth and sure knowledge. The free association of these distinctly different entities and 'bearing testimony' of religious beliefs is actually bearing false witness, and is rampant in the church.

6. Intentionally misrepresenting religious beliefs as sure knowledge should be avoided in order to remain innocent of bearing false witness.

I hoped that the men in the room left that day with a few things to think about, and the unreasonable religious fervor in Mesa, Arizona was decreased a little bit after our discussion. I knew most of the men in the room, and enjoyed speaking to them. It was therapeutic for me and I got what I wanted - excommunication. Interestingly, one of the men present smiled and nodded during my talk and seemed in complete agreement with what I was saying. It would not surprise me if he was a closet intellectual and a reasonable person, left the faith corral a long time ago, and is a complete non-fanatic. I know they are out there, and occupy high offices in the church. I suspect at least one of them was in attendance at my disciplinary council that day.

A nearly perfect transcript of the disciplinary council may be found in Appendix F in its entirety, and is available for listening on YouTube. Apparently, somebody in the room actually recorded the proceeding. Fancy that!

There is one incredibly ironic portion of the dialog in my disciplinary council that merits special mention. During the dialogue, I bring up the subject of suppression of information, and the Stake President attempts to censure me (suppress me from discussing the issue) not once, not twice, but three times. Looking back at it, I have to laugh at the irony. True life is stranger than fiction in so many ways.

During the course of the dialog, the Stake President valiantly attempted to justify the LDS faithful history policy, which includes non-disclosure of certain facts and events. This policy was the key issue that sent me on a path of discovery that ended with my excommunication. An excellent discussion of these so-called justifications has been documented by Bob McCue[168], which I will summarize.

The LDS church feels the faithful history policy is warranted, with members offering the following arguments:

- Milk before meat
- The Church never hid anything
- Disclosure would do more harm than good
- The Church is no worse than other religions respecting misleading disclosure
- The Church is at war with evil and combat rules apply

The milk before meat premise is that teaching some things which are true, prematurely or at the wrong time, can damage the student and kill his joy in learning. Well, after 25 years of being a priesthood leader in the church, serving two years as a missionary, obtaining two university degrees, and attending church for 45 years, I was never served any meat. When I discovered the meat on my own and wanted to discuss it, I was chased away from the dinner table. Thus the policy of milk before meat goes way beyond the loving and protective teacher persona. For these reasons, the milk before meat argument is baseless and therefore invalid.

The idea that the Church never overtly hid anything, and that if the member is unaware of certain church history aspects it is his own fault was the primary argument presented to me by my Stake President during my disciplinary council. Of course, the Church does hide things. The Church archives are inaccessible to member and non-member alike. Sterling McMurrin adds: "When the Church refuses its own historians access to the materials in its archives, it obviously has something to

---

[168] Bob McCue, "Out of My Faith", pp 96-114 http://www.mccue.cc/bob/spirituality. htm

hide."[169] The LDS Church is the only major religion based in the USA that does not disclose complete financial data[170]. In the early 1970s the Church effectively dismantled its official historian's department[171] to further distance itself from real history. The idea that not knowing the real history is the fault of the member is a feeble excuse and morally bankrupt position. The church actively teaches its members to only study from approved sources. Then, if the member goes outside approved sources and learns the real history he has been disobedient and is also at fault! Either way, the Church manages, incredibly, to serve up a guilt trip.

The idea that disclosure would do more harm than good presupposes two things: the Church is true at its foundation and is also the best path to happiness for humans. I have heard this argument quite often, which is articulated something like "Since the Church is true, why does the history and the contradictory information matter?" Well, first of all, the chance that the church is true is actually quite small (see probability estimate in Appendix E), and the aforementioned societal ills associated with Mormonism introduce enough doubt about the happiness claim. English philosopher John Stuart Mill said that any attempt to withhold information is a peculiar evil. If the information is correct but withheld, we are robbed of the opportunity of exchanging error for truth. If it is wrong and withheld from us, we are deprived of a deeper understanding of the truth in its collision with error. Thus there can be no objection to full disclosure, and there is a well-founded moral objection to selective storytelling.

That the LDS Church meets the same standard of disclosure met by other religions is not accurate. Since the founding of Mormonism is relatively recent, much of its history and tangibles are available for scrutiny. Other denominations in this category are the Seventh Day Adventists and the Reorganized LDS Church (now called Community of Christ), both of which have admitted that there are cracks in their foundations and have transitioned their faith basis to something more durable. The LDS church falls way short of the standard set by its contemporaries.

---

[169] *The Mormon Corporate Empire*, pg 211
[170] *Time Magazine*, August 1997
[171] Leonard Arrington, *Adventures of a Church Historian*

The idea that the Church is at war with the forces of evil and thus there are no set rules of engagement is an interesting argument. To be at war, there needs to be a real enemy and threat. Boyd K. Packer has defined the threat as "gays, intellectuals, and feminists"[172]. Two of these groups are only seeking emancipation and an end to institutionalized discrimination, same as blacks were seeking in the 50s and 60s. The intellectuals are seeking honesty and full disclosure. The truth should have nothing to fear from examination. The Church is currently enjoying unprecedented fair press coverage (The PBS documentary "The Mormons", Hinckley on 60 Minutes, Larry King, etc.). It seems to me that the Church is using inflammatory language to fabricate a false crisis to justify wartime tactics. If there is a real threat to the Church, it is emerging information, which the Church is powerless to arrest anyway.

And speaking of war, in the life before this life, according to Church doctrine, we all took part in a war in pre-earth life heaven. Two plans were presented there which created the conflict; Christ's plan included agency and choice, Satan's plan took away agency and would force everyone to be obedient. Two-thirds of the heavenly host accepted the plan of Christ and followed him. The remaining one third of the heavenly beings gave up their agency and followed Satan. McCue points out:

> The position that the Church has adopted is, essentially, this: The Church routinely withholds information that might incline us to do things that the Church is sure would not be right for us, thereby manipulating us toward doing the things it thinks are right. Whose plan does this sound like? [Christ or Satan? The Church suggests that] we don't need to discuss the public lying Joseph Smith and others engaged in, since it could be written off as the mistakes of a few people. The "faithful history" concept and general restriction of information is far broader than that. It is an institutional characteristic, and one that Karen Armstrong[173] points out we share with other fundamentalist organizations. Fundamentalist organizations, she says, tend to be anti-historical because they are fighting a war

---

[172] Documented in the PBS Documentary *The Mormons*
[173] Karen Armstrong, *The Battle for God*

with the scientific community, and the less they have to explain to their members in that regard, the better that war goes for them.

Returning to my disciplinary council discussion, I told the men that the selective storytelling that I received my whole life in the church was simply unacceptable. Knowing only one side of the story put me in a weak and embarrassing position and was ultimately a disservice to me. My hope was that the Stake President would relay this information to the higher ups and if somebody was keeping score, they would record that one more member was lost due to their faithful history policy.

I made certain that the council understood that I wanted to continue to attend Sunday meetings and discuss true history and continue to inject some reality into the group discussions. I told them that it boils down to two choices, either welcome me as a member, or get a court order to keep me out of the church. This comment was made to ensure that I was excommunicated, and it worked.

I think if I had to do the disciplinary council sermon again, I would have been more forceful, more in command, and more insistent that I have a chance to discuss whatever I wanted for as long as I wanted. I should have taken 30 minutes and outlined all the historicity problems of <u>The Book of Mormon</u>, the obvious fraud associated with the <u>Book of Abraham</u> and the Kinderhook hoax. I would have distributed the timeline and read every entry to them, pointing out the trends, and the patterns of deception. I should have challenged all of them to wake up, examine the very real possibility that a charlatan had power over them, stop bearing false witness, and take ownership of their lives. I would have felt better knowing that I had given them all just cause to do some research and critical thinking of their own.

In any case, it was a relief to have it over. I had what I wanted – I was no longer a member. I was elated and had no residual anger. It felt good to air the issues, it was free therapy for me and helped me quell the anger and disappointment I harbored in the church leadership. Best of all, I would never again have to answer in the affirmative to that awful question "Are you a Mormon?"

APPENDIX A
EXCOMMUNICATION
CONFIRMATION &
ANNOUNCEMENT NOTICE

THE CHURCH OF
JESUS CHRIST
OF LATTER-DAY SAINTS

MESA ARIZONA SALT RIVER STAKE   September 2, 2007

Lyndon Lamborn
8238 E. Mawson
Mesa, Arizona 85207
(480) 380-5075

Dear Brother Lamborn:

This is notice that at the Disciplinary Council of the Mesa Arizona Salt River Stake, on
August 19, 2007, at which you were in attendance, you were excommunicated from the Church
of Jesus Christ of Latter Day Saints.

As a result of your excommunication, you are no longer a member of the Church and cannot
enjoy any membership privileges, including the wearing of temple garments and the payment of
tithes and offerings. You may attend public meetings of the Church if your conduct is orderly,
but you may not give a talk, offer a public prayer, partake of the sacrament, or vote in the
sustaining of Church officers.

If you disagree with the decision of the Disciplinary Council, you have a right to appeal to the
First Presidency. An appeal should be in writing and should specify the errors or unfairness you
would claim in the procedure or decision. This appeal should be presented to me within 30 days.
It will then be forwarded to the First Presidency.

Because of the nature of your excommunication and your involvement with the people of this
area, an announcement will be delivered to the Melchizedek Priesthood quorums and Relief
Society in each of the wards in our stake. The announcement will be delivered by the bishop on
Sunday September 23, 2007 that you have been excommunicated for apostasy.

Lyndon, I hope and pray that your heart will be softened and search out the spiritual aspects of
life. I invite you to worship with us and ask you to respect our rights of worship.

I love and care for you and your family and hope the very best for you.

Sincerely,

R. James Molina, Stake President
Mesa Arizona Salt River Stake

APPENDIX B
REFLECTIONS ON POLYGAMY

Children have a tough enough time growing up in a normal society with normal parents and expectations. Growing up in a polygamous community is a nightmare for both young women and young men. The young women are doomed to be placed in an arranged marriage with more than likely an older man, the young men mostly get ousted to eliminate competition. It is a distasteful form of child abuse, and I am ashamed that it goes on in our great state of Arizona. I do not have the statistics on this, but I have heard that the occurrence of birth defects in polygamous communities is higher than the national average due to in-breeding. If true, this is a tragedy of immense proportion.

The LDS officials want to have people stop associating LDS and Fundamentalist LDS, but it will not happen as long as the LDS ascribe to polygamous doctrine. Polygamy is at the heart of LDS doctrine, the patriarchal order, and has only been temporarily suspended from active practice (see additional info below). If the LDS church really wanted to eliminate this association, they would have to declare Smith a fallen prophet, renounce all his revelations from polygamy on, etc. Until this happens, the LDS church continues to foster the doctrine of polygamy. Of course, that will never happen, because it would cast too much doubt on the teachings of Smith and subsequent prophets. Successful organized religion is never about doing the right thing, it is always about doing what is necessary to continue the deceptions and accumulate wealth and power.

More on this point: It is important to understand that in The Church of Jesus Christ of Latter-Day Saints (LDS), Polygamy is doctrinal and taught as eternal truth taught by its founder, Joseph Smith and successors, it is scriptural (found in Doctrine and Covenants Section 132), and is still practiced today in Mormon temples (men can be sealed to multiple eternal wives, women get only one eternal spouse). From the much-heralded book "Mormon Doctrine", second edition, Bruce R McConkie, sustained as a prophet seer and revelator, said this about polygamy.... "Obviously the holy practice will commence again after the Second Coming of the Son of Man and the ushering in of the millennium."

It is crystal clear that polygamy is an eternal core teaching of Mormonism, and is not "behind us" as Gordon B. Hinckley claimed. It is dead center in front of mainstream Mormonism, and an integral part of its dreamed-of future.

Virtually all polygamy in the western United States traces to Joseph Smith. The irony is that there is overwhelming evidence that Smith was a fraud, a master at preying upon the superstitions and guilt of the people. Anybody who undertakes an objective investigation will discover this and realize that polygamy was an invention by Smith to justify his womanizing. The fact that so many remain deceived and ignorant of the readily available information and evidence is mind-boggling for those who embrace the information age. His deception becomes very transparent when one considers his approach to seduce his victims using the tale of the angel and sword. Every member of the church, at a minimum, should read either Todd Compton's "In Sacred Loneliness" or Newell-Tippetts "Mormon Enigma" to understand the real facts and events and how polygamy was ushered into our day and age. Both of these books are told from the faithful believer point of view and have won awards. The facts and events are well established in these books. In addition, many non-members with an interest in polygamy have thoroughly enjoyed reading these works.

The welfare monies collected by the FLDS communities represents a burden for the middle class taxpayers like me and is dishonest at its foundation.

In addition to the child abuse, taxpayer burden, and the increasing occurrences of birth defects in these communities due to in-breeding, polygamy bothers me because it is prejudicial at its foundation - men can have more than one wife for eternity, but no such opportunity is afforded the woman? And this is the worst kind of prejudice, the God-sanctioned variety. It leads the male down the path of treating women as property, a tradition as old as the ten commandments, and something that we as a human race need to put behind us forever.

The general population of the LDS church still believes less than 2% of the men in the 19th century church practiced polygamy, and when they did it was to care for widows with children, or to allow poor women who couldn't find husbands in a church where women vastly outnumbered men the blessings of marriage. The members are never told the population dynamics were actually over-balanced with men, and more like 30-40% of the men were polygamists. I have polygamists on both sides of my family tree, including a great-grandfather that spent time in prison for violation of polygamy statutes. LDS members don't realize that sister-wives referred to their husbands as "Mr. Smith, Mr. Young, Mr. Snow," etc., that the husband generally brought home a new wife without asking for approval from the others, same as he wouldn't ask permission to acquire a new horse or a wagon. Many polygamist children never had a loving relationship with their fathers. In fact it was just the very opposite. Few bedtime stories read, few to no trips to the park, seldom were there happy families gathered around the dinner table each night to bond after a tough day, no dads to help kids with their homework. Very few LDS church members know that polygamy continued to be practiced well into the 20th Century by church authorities and others who sneaked off to be married in Mexico and Canada where laws were more forgiving.

Naturalists and economists point out that polygamy is found in many cultures, and it is a wonderful institution for propagating the seed of the dominant alpha male and is economically progressive. Polygamy may have actually played an important role in the strengthening of the human species and completely natural. My opinion is that the era when polygamy benefits mankind is long over. I find that the negatives far outweigh the positives.

APPENDIX C
LETTER TO BISHOP

This is my letter to the bishop after he allegedly contacted all of my brothers' bishops, allegedly calling into question their convictions and motives.

Dear Bishop,   October 3, 2005

I have spent the weekend listening to conference and trying to understand your actions. I also read the two articles you sent from the brethren. I always enjoy what they have to say, just as you do. I remain, unfortunately, stupefied with regard to your decision to contact the Bishops of my brothers.

First off, a few clarifications on our conversation. I know that such a startling revelation will bring with it some high emotions and things become easily distorted, and this is understandable.

I mentioned that the discussion group were all church-going members and sincere, (even a bishopbric member) to get the point across that we are NOT a bunch of apostates with axes to grind. I also never said that I did not believe in the restoration, only that I had doubts about it. Your interpretation was that I did not believe – these are your words, not mine. I never said that everybody in the discussion group had the same doubts or the same beliefs, only that we shared knowledge and discussed points of doctrine and history in an open forum.

With regard to my lessons in High Priests group meeting, I said that YOU probably would consider some of the things I bring up inappropriate. I think that discussion of real facts and events is TOTALLY appropriate in a truth-telling forum like High Priests meeting. If I did not believe such discussions were appropriate I would not have carried them to my ward brothers. Do we fear the truth in this church? I hope not. We should be lovers of truth and follow the admonition of

Paul with regard to seeking the truth of all things. Everything I shared with the group over the last several months are well known, well-documented facts and events that most church historians could discuss without even any crib notes. The information on the wives of Joseph Smith is available through the church genealogy website, including the information on Helen Mar Kimball and Zina Diantha Huntington. The information I shared on the papyri and the Book of Abraham was printed off the "I have a Question" link from the LDS website. Even the book A View of the Hebrews has been reprinted by the BYU Center for Religious Research, and the preface discusses the presentation of the facts and paradoxical questions presented to the Council of the 12 by BH Roberts in 1922. If I have mis-stated any fact or related any untruth I will happily write a letter of apology to all my brothers in the ward. I think you will find that I have only been truthful, nothing can be construed to be classified as apostate doctrine in any way, shape, or form.

At what point have I been labeled as an apostate? At what point did you think that my "discussion group" was an apostate group? If you can find a definition of "apostate" that fits me I would like to see it. I am seeking learning and truth, and I make my personal study at matter of prayer. I seek the spirit. As a result of my study, I am having isolated doubts about the restoration. How this puts me into the apostasy category is a real head-scratcher. The stake president went so far as to call me an instrument in the hands of Satan, which is another puzzler.

In the 1960s, President Hugh B. Brown, a Counselor in the LDS Presidency, said the following. "I admire men and women who have developed a questing spirit, who are unafraid of new ideas as steppingstones to progress. We should of course respect the opinions of others, but we should also be unafraid to dissent-if we are informed. Thoughts and expressions compete in the marketplace of thought and in that competition, truth emerges triumphant. [....] Only error fears freedom of expression. [....] This free exchange of ideas is not to be deplored as long as men and women remain humble and teachable. Neither fear of consequence or any kind of coercion should ever be used to secure uniformity of thought in the church. People should express their problems and opinions and be unafraid to think without fear of ill consequences. [....] We must preserve freedom of the mind in the church and resist all efforts to suppress it."

Joseph Smith said something very similar about welcoming people with differing viewpoints into the brotherhood of the church. I will find that quote for you if you like. I believe I remain humble and teachable. You suggested I spend more time reading The Book of Mormon and praying. I readily agreed, and promise to strive to do that. (Side note: Since we spoke, my discussion group has suggested that I consider buying An Ancient American Setting for the Book of Mormon by BYU Prof John L Sorenson. This might help with some of my questions.)

Church policy mentions protecting the innocents. Under what scenario could your actions NOT hurt innocents? Every possible outcome I can imagine hurts innocents.

This begs another question: what are you trying to protect the innocents FROM? Is the truth about church history so damning that it should be concealed and censored? Are truth and facts going to somehow harm the good name of the church? I remain as baffled and puzzled regarding your actions as ever. In fact, the more I consider it, the more I am convinced that your actions were unwarranted and misguided, regardless of your good intentions.

I feel I am an innocent, and I have been hurt. I consider my brothers and their families to be in the same category. This action will certainly harm Nancy and Joe, and I am positive that you believe them to be innocents. If this action is truly in harmony with church policy, my ethical standards require that I refrain from active participation in such an organization. I will never confide in a Priesthood leader again, since I now know that confidentiality is a myth. I might continue to attend for the sake of Nancy and Joe, but all joy and interest in the Church for me will be lost.

I am truly sorry to say this, because I hold you in high esteem, but your actions remind me of the witch hunts in Salem and the story line from Fahrenheit 451. Maybe I am missing something, but I see no possibility that such actions would be condoned by the Master. After donating

$100,000+ in offerings and giving two years of my life, I would have thought that I merited better treatment than this.

Your brother in the faith,

-Lyndon

APPENDIX D
MODERN TRUE HISTORY
TIMELINE OF THE LDS CHURCH

12/23/1805   Joseph Smith is born in Sharon Vermont

1823, 1825:   Ethan Smith, Poultney Vermont, publishes <u>A View of the Hebrews</u> proposing a Semitic origin for the American Indian, a dark skin race annihilating the whites, and quotes Isaiah.

1826:   Joseph Smith stands trial for fraud. He admits deception for gain, and that he could discern nothing with peep stones.

1830:   <u>Book of Mormon</u> first edition published

1834:   51 people sign an affidavit asserting that Joseph Smith Jr. and Sr. were "destitute of moral character". Printed in <u>Mormonism Unvailed</u> by ED Howe.

1842:   To fulfill prophesy, Joseph Smith directs Porter Rockwell to assassinate Gov Lilburn Boggs. Porter misses. Taking a cue from Joseph, 'bloody' Brigham Young would later use Porter, Bill Hickman, and others to commit various crimes, including murder, when he felt it necessary.

4/5/1843:   Joseph Smith prophesies that those in the rising generation would see, while still in the flesh, the second coming of Christ. Generally accepted cutoff date (Bruce McKonkie): 2000 AD.

Spring 1844: Not satisfied with only 22 wives, Joseph Smith makes overtures to Jane Law, wife of William Law. Jane refuses, an argument ensues, and the Laws are excommunicated. William Law, determined to expose polygamy and polyandry to the world, buys a printing press and publishes the first and only edition of the "Nauvoo Expositor". Faced with losing everything, Joseph Smith leads a raid on and illegally destroys the free press, setting off a series of events that would culminate in his death and that of his brother, Hyrum, in a gunfight on June 27, 1944.

1844-45: Following the death of Joseph Smith, James J. Strang professes to be the successor to Joseph Smith, translates characters from metal plates, produces a book, and 11 witnesses, none of whom ever denied their testimonies. Three of the Whitmers, Martin Harris, Hiram Page, William Smith, and Lucy Smith all followed Strang's leadership from 1846 to 1847. Emma is unable to reconcile polygamy/polyandry and distances herself from Brigham Young. Brigham introduces blood atonement oaths in the Temple ceremony swearing vengeance on the killers of Joseph and Hyrum. An oath swearing revenge on the US Government would also be added to the Temple rites.

Sep 1857: Approximately 120 innocents of the Baker-Fancher wagon train are massacred at Mountain Meadow. A week before, Young promises the Indians all the cattle in the wagon train if they would do away with the entire company. 3 weeks after, Young distributes $3500 in goods to the Indians in the region. Stake Pres. Isaac Haight and Bishops William Dame and Philip Klingensmith participate in the massacre. All told, 40-60 LDS members participate. John Lee, the only participant showing remorse, is ironically selected as the patsy. He is executed by firing squad on March 23, 1877, at Mountain Meadow.

1890:	Faced with confiscation of church property, W. Woodruff produces the 'Manifesto', the beginning of the end for polygamy. Plural marriages actually increase in 1891-93.
1904:	Bill Hickman publishes <u>Brighams Destroying Angel</u>, his involvement in crimes and murders ordered by bloody Brigham. The Congressional Smoot hearings bring intense pressure to enforce the provisions of the Manifesto and polygamists finally begin to be excommunicated.
1906:	Substantial changes are made to the temple ceremony. A more politically correct ceremony emerges. The blood oaths of vengeance for the killers of Joseph and Hyrum and oaths against Government are removed.
1922:	BH Roberts presents <u>Book of Mormon</u> historicity problems to Quorum of Twelve & First Presidency - no explanations are offered by the Brethren.
1947:	Fawn Brodie publishes <u>No Man Knows My History</u>, setting the standard for subsequent modern LDS history authors.
1952:	Thomas Stuart Fergeson founds 'The New World Archeology Association' for the express purpose of bolstering evidence supporting the <u>Book of Mormon</u>.
1967:	<u>Book of Abraham</u> original papyri are discovered in NY museum
1969:	<u>Book of Abraham</u> papyri are found to contain ordinary funerary papers and 'book of breathings'. Papyri have nothing to do with Abraham and post-date Abraham by 600 yr. Joseph Smiths' Egyptian 'alphabet' established as nonsensical.

1970: Church opens archives to free examination by historians. It is a brief renaissance for church historians.

1975: A disillusioned Thomas Stuart Fergeson reports that zero forensic evidence can be found that supports the Book of Mormon as a real history. The church quietly halts all archeology efforts.

1978: Faced with external criticisms, threats of closing whole countries to missionary work, anguish over faithful Brazilian members denied blessings, Spencer Kimball announces that Blacks can have the Priesthood.

1979: Missionary lesson plan eliminates the 'Truth' discussion.

1980: Church archives are closed, the renaissance is over, overt obfuscation begins.

1981: Signature Books is founded, in direct response to the cancellation of Leonard Arrington's 16 volume History of the Church project.

1981: Boyd K. Packer gives landmark talk requesting that members limit historical research to faith-promoting approved source materials. Packer will go on to say in later years that the Church "has little use for the truth" and that "gays, intellectuals, and feminists are the biggest threats to the Church."

1984-1986: Mark Hofmann sells forged documents to the church. Dallin Oaks publicly describes the Holy Ghost /Salamander incident (a fabrication). Other documents are purchased and hidden.

1990: Substantial changes are made to the temple ceremony. A more politically correct ceremony emerges yet again.

The penalty of death symbologies and evil minister episodes are removed.

1998, 1999:   FAIR and FARMS websites step up to 'combat' true history and other doctrinal critiques. Apologist arguments often leave the questioning member thinking: "Is this the best we got?"

Sept 1993:   Six prominent scholars who were deemed too liberal are either dis-fellowshipped or excommunicated. The 'September Six' are now folk heroes to many disaffected members who view their intellectual honesty as higher moral ground than church orthodoxy and 'faithful history' ignorance.

1995:   Recovery from Mormonism message board launched, boasting 1000's of hits daily.

1996-1998:   In a valiant attempt to mainstream the Mormon church, Hinckley goes on television, including 60 minutes & Larry King Live. Attempt to mainstream? Polygamy remains a boat anchor.

2001:   The Reorganized LDS Church de-emphasizes Joseph Smith, the <u>Book of Mormon</u>, and the "inspired translation" of the King James Bible, and becomes "The Community of Christ. Membership drops by 75%.

2001:   Utah displaces Tennessee as the state with the highest bankruptcy rate. Utah teen suicide rate is double the national average in 1992,96,98.

2002:   Grant Palmer, 34-yr CES instructor, publishes <u>An Insiders View of Mormon Origins</u>, a purely factual book. He is disfellowshipped 12/4/04 & instantly becomes a folk hero among LDS and ex-LDS truth seekers. The Los Angeles Times reports that Utah ranks #1 in antidepressant and narcotic drug usage.

2004:   Simon Southerton publishes <u>Losing a Lost Tribe</u>. Requests for membership record removal exceed 100,000 per year. Church buys 88,000 acres in Nebraska, making it the 2nd largest landowner in that state with 228,000 acres. Church assets are ~40 billion, with 925,000 acres in N. America, and the largest foreign landowner in Great Britian. The church is rumored to be the largest beef producer in the USA, and easily the richest per capita religion in the world.

10/22/2005:   First Ex-Mormon Foundation Conference held.

2006:   Turner-Bergera award for Best Biography goes to <u>Mormon Enigma</u> biography of Emma Hale Smith.

2007:   Salt Lake Tribune establishes zero real growth for the world wide church. PBS produces "The Mormons", shining a light into the dark corners of LDS history. The program concludes with a profound question: Can the Mormon church survive its own history? On the heels of "The Mormons" comes "September Dawn", a romance movie using the Mountain Meadow Massacre as part of the storyline.

APPENDIX E
SEARCH FOR TRUTH SUMMARY
(ABRIDGED)

<u>Foreword</u>

My purpose in writing this document is to succinctly express thoughts, concerns, and track progress in my search for the truth with regard to the LDS church. This is a work in progress.

Of course, the first question is "why question?" Haven't I already found the truth and now all is needed is to "endure to the end?" Well, for the past 30 years (since age 17) this is what I have thought. Recent events and feelings have changed my mind. To whit: (1) Several of my non-member friends seem to know more about aspects of church history than I, which is troubling to a four-year seminary grad, returned missionary, and life-long member; (2) An apparent reluctance of church officials to discuss and address questions arising from scrutiny of LDS origins; (3) We are counseled to search for and discover truth (see quotes below); (4) It is only in the past 25 years that any of this information has been available to the general public, and deserves (in fact demands) attention.

1 Thess 5:19-21: *Quench not the spirit. Despise not prophecyings. Prove all things; hold fast that which is good.*

The truth will cut its own way. (Joseph Smith Jr.)

To Latter-day Saints there can be no objection to the careful and critical study of the scriptures, ancient or modern, provided only that it be an honest study – a search for truth. (John A. Widtsoe)

This book [The Book of Mormon] is entitled to the most thorough and impartial examination. Not only does [The Book of Mormon] merit such consideration, it claims, even demands the same. (James E. Talmage, *The Articles of Faith*)

James E. Talmage on closed mindedness:

The man who cannot listen to an argument which opposes his views either has a weak position...

Brigham Young on science and religion:

Religious teachers... advance many ideas and notions for the truth which are in opposition to and contradict facts demonstrated by science, and which are generally understood. In these respects we differ from the Christian world, for our religion will not clash with or contradict the facts of science in any particular. (Discourses of Brigham Young, 397-98)

If we have the truth, [it] cannot be harmed by investigation. If we have not the truth, it ought to be harmed. (J. Reuben Clark, counselor in the First Presidency)

We are grateful in the Church and in this great university that the freedom, dignity and integrity of the individual is basic in Church doctrine as well as in democracy. Here we are free to think and express our opinions. *Fear will not stifle thought, as is the case in some areas which have not yet emerged from the dark ages. God himself refuses to trammel man's free agency even though its exercise sometimes teaches painful lessons. Both creative science and revealed religion find their fullest and truest expression in the climate of freedom.*

I admire men and women who have developed the questioning spirit, who are unafraid of new ideas and stepping stones to progress. We should, of course, respect the opinions of others, but we should also be unafraid to dissent – if we are informed. Thoughts and expressions compete in the marketplace of thought, and in that competition truth emerges triumphant. Only error fears freedom of expression... This free exchange of ideas is not to be deplored as long as men and women remain humble and teachable. Neither fear of consequence nor any kind of coercion should ever be used to secure uniformity of thought in the church. People should express their problems and opinions and be unafraid to think without fear of ill consequences. We must preserve freedom of the mind in the church and resist all efforts to suppress it. (Hugh B. Brown, counselor in First Presidency, Speech at BYU, March 29, 1958)

Thomas Jefferson taught that however discomfiting a free exchange may be, truth will ultimately emerge the victor. English philosopher John Stuart Mill said that any attempt to resist another opinion is a "peculiar evil." If the opinion is right, we are robbed of the opportunity of exchanging error for truth. If it is wrong, we are deprived of a deeper understanding of the truth in its collision with error.

If a faith will not bear to be investigated: if its preachers and professors are afraid to have it examined, their foundation must be very weak. (George Albert Smith, Journal Of Discourses, v 14, page 216)

These issues are deeply important to me. I do not treat them lightly, whatever the shortcomings of my prose. The shortest path to the point is sometimes very blunt. Such bluntness should not be interpreted as making light, cheapening, or detracting from the seriousness and importance of the issue being discussed.

The Book of Mormon

Here are some questions about The Book of Mormon that I continue to struggle with.

1. The numerous domesticated and other animals (horses, cattle, sheep, elephants) cited in The Book of Mormon were not present upon arrival of the Europeans and are not found in the fossil record. None of the glyphs that I have personally encountered on this continent show domesticated animals – only deer and birds and such. Also, silk and wheat cited in The Book of Mormon were not present upon arrival of the Europeans. If The Book of Mormon is a true and accurate historical record, how is this possible?

2. The wide use of steel and wheels in The Book of Mormon does not square with the stone age level of the natives, and not a single steel artifact, steel mine, wheel, axle, or smeltering implement has been unearthed in the archeological digs on this continent. According to the huge battles, there would have been literally hundreds of thousands of steel swords and shields. A visit to the Native American history museum in Washington, DC also indicates that steel and horses were only part of native American culture after Europeans introduced them. How does a civilization forget how to make and use wheels? A somewhat lame attempt to answer these questions is found on the lds.org "I have a Question" forum, but falls about a mile short of an adequate explanation. If The Book of Mormon is a true and accurate historical record, how is this possible? For that matter, how did Nephi obtain a bow of "fine steel" in 600 B.C.? How did Shule, the Jaredite Prince, make swords of steel to overthrow his brother Corihor in 1900 B.C.? Refinement processes and carbonization techniques for producing spring steel would not be invented until about 300 B.C.

3. Linguists agree that the variety of languages found among the native Americans suggest thousands or tens of thousands of years in development/isolation and a non-Hebrew origin. It is just not logically plausible that at least some Indian tribes were speaking Hebrew at 421 AD as asserted by The Book of Mormon. If The Book of Mormon is a true and accurate historical record, how is this rapid confusion of languages, with no Hebrew similarities, possible?

4. Lehi's group of immigrants consisted of 17 adults and 3 of them were probably too old to have children (Lehi, his wife and the wife of Ishmael). In addition, the Mulekites also migrated a few years later, but when they joined the Nephites in the year 120 BC it says that they outnumbered the Nephites but those two groups together totaled less than half the number of Lamanites - so assume there were half as many Mulekites as Lehi had in his group - if population growth rates were similar for the two groups. The rapid growth rates of human populations are a relatively recent occurrence in human history. Prior to 1650,

the average annual global human population growth rate was at best .04% per year. By 1650 it jumped to .4%. By 1850 it hit .8%, by 1950 it jumped to 1.8 % due to advances in medical care. Examining the continual records of battles and numbers of people killed in <u>The Book of Mormon</u>, reconciling the reported population with the growth rates it would have taken to achieve it becomes virtually impossible. A couple of examples, 2 Nephi 5:34 says the Nephites and Lamanites had already waged wars against each other by the year 560 BC. If they had been multiplying at the unheard of rate of 2% a year since they arrived, the total number of adults would have been 55. If half of them were women and some men too old to fight, or too young, or too infirm. There would have been a total of about 20 'combatants' counting both sides in this war. Skip ahead to 187 BC in which 3043 Lamanites and 279 of Zenifs people were slain in a single day (Mosiah 9:18-19). If that many were killed, then think how many were not killed. Women, children, battle survivors, etc. But just to produce the total number reported killed (3322 people) in this one day, it would have required a population growth rate 1.2% continually for the preceding four centuries! To put this in perspective, a growth rate of 1.2% was never achieved on a global basis or even in industrialized regions until 1950. This Nephite growth rate is 30 times the .04% growth rate that existed in the world as a whole during the same era. This is just to account for the number reported killed in a single battle in the book. Consider the required population growth rates if you were to estimate only 10% of the entire population was killed (account for women, children, old people, survivors of the battle, injured survivors of the battle, and just adults that didn't participate in the battle). So jack the growth rate up to produce 10 times more people. And this is for a single battle in their history. The book is filled with battles killing thousands of people. If <u>The Book of Mormon</u> is a true and accurate historical record, how can the population growth inconsistencies be reconciled?

5. The account of Ammon cutting off arms of his assailants does not square with my experiences with butchery. Cutting off a limb is difficult, even when the joint can be exactly located and

the tendons and muscles cut. Cutting through the large bones found in the human arm is simply not possible in a single stroke, or even multiple strokes. It requires a saw or the combination of an axe with a rigid chopping block. (Due apologies for the graphic nature of the wording, as well as Monte Python/Holy Grail fans.) If <u>The Book of Mormon</u> is a true and accurate record, and God follows his own physical laws, how is this account possible?

6. In 3rd Nephi there are passages that mimic the King James translation of the Bible exactly, but differ from the Joseph Smith translation of the Bible. Examples:

<u>Matthew 6:13</u>: And lead us not into temptation, but deliver us from evil: For thine is the kingdom, and the power, and the glory, for ever. Amen.

<u>JST, Matthew 6:14</u>: And suffer us not to be led into temptation, but deliver us from...

<u>3 Nephi 13:12-13</u>: And lead us not into temptation, but deliver us from evil. For thine is the kingdom, and the power, and the glory, forever. Amen.

We have been told that plain and precious things have been taken out of the bible. However, <u>The Book of Mormon</u> is purported to be the word of God, being pure and hidden away from the evil and/or ignorant men who changed the bible over the centuries. ("We believe the bible to be the word of God as far as it is translated correctly; we also believe <u>The Book of Mormon</u> to be the word of God.") This was obviously a case of a mistranslation or deliberate change. If the Lord thought it was important enough to reveal to Joseph the change in meaning (God doesn't lead us into temptation, but we can ask for his help to avoid temptation) as he translated the bible, why didn't this meaning become obvious in 3rd Nephi?

<u>Mathew 6:22</u>: The light of the body is the eye: if therefore thine eye be single, thy whole body shall be full of light.

JST, Matthew 6:22: The light of the body is the eye; if therefore thine eye be single to the glory of God, thy whole body shall be full of light.

3 Nephi 13:22: The light of the body is the eye; if, therefore, thine eye be single, thy whole body shall be full of light.

> Again, the JST does a great job clarifying the verse. However, the same question remains. Why is the 3rd Nephi verse exactly the same as the mistranslated or changed King James Bible version?

7. When Jesus spoke to the Jews, he taught a very piercing lesson when he said "if any man compel thee to walk with him a mile, walk with him twain" as recorded in the New Testament. This lesson refers to Roman law during the occupation that stated if a Roman soldier asked, the Jew had to carry his pack and walk with him for a mile. The Jewish audience could immediately relate and understand. Jesus said the same thing to the Nephites who were NOT under Roman occupation and would have no idea what lesson was being taught. A similar problem exists with using the phrase "whoever shall say to his brother Raca (a curse and term of hatred), shall be in danger of the council" in 3 Ne 12:22. Committing 'raca' in Palestine resulted in being brought before the Jewish Sanhedrin or "council". As an Aramaic word, 'raca' would have no meaning to the Nephites, and the 'council' reference would also be meaningless. If The Book of Mormon is a literal translation and the most correct of any book, how is this possible?

8. The native American people did not use a 7-day week calendar, observe a Sabbath tradition, or even have a Sabbath legend. It seems implausible to me that a people of Semitic origin would abandon this tradition. It is also implausible that a people converted to Christianity and having worked metals that no artifact depicting the life of the Savior would survive. Not a single one. How is this possible?

9. When Nephi went back to get the plates from Laban, he explains that they needed the record to help them keep the law of Moses. If they were living "strictly" in accordance with the law of Moses, where in the book are the references to the Passover,

the Feast of the Tabernacles, sabbatical years, jubilees, thank offerings, unleavened bread, ephods, usury, purification, circumcision, or unclean animals? And since all of the people were of the tribe of Joseph, where are the Levites who alone had the authority to administer the rites?

10. Nephi's account has the heavily laden family leaving Jerusalem and travelling in the wilderness for three days, then camping on the shore of the Red Sea, a distance of 170 miles, through rugged and desolate terrain. The Grand Canyon of the Middle East would have to be traversed, and they would still have to average more than 60 miles a day. How is this possible?

11. The account of the Jaredite submarines presents a horde of extreme difficulties. I shall single out one. The discussion of glass windows which could be "dashed to pieces" ignores the fact that the Romans would not invent glass-making for another 2000 years. The phrase "The thought make reason stare" comes to mind.

12. Michael Marquardt and other scholars have found over 300 quotations in the BoM that apparently came from prophets and apostles who lived after 600 B.C. when Lehi and his family left on their migration to the New World. Most of these quotations appear in the King James wording, including the mistakes that were later corrected by Bible scholars. How could the writers of the BoM obtain this information? Why would their wording mimic all the KJV Bible errors? For that matter, how did the writers of the BoM get such terms as "church", "synagogue", "gentile", "baptism", "Bible" and "Jesus Christ"? None of these terms were defined or used prior to 600 B.C.

13. The Mayas of Central America were an amazing civilization, that has only been recently (last 30 years) well understood and documented. Experts have deciphered their 800 hieroglyphic signs, including an amazingly accurate calendar. Their language has no resemblance to Hebrew or Egyptian, and neither do the languages of the Incas, Aztecs, Toltecs, or other New World peoples. The Mayas used a base 20 mathematics system, and did their math vertically. Their calendar began in 3114 B.C. and their civilization did not crumble until about 900 A.D. In their

peak, they numbered in the millions, with strongholds in the 'narrow neck of land' which responsible archaeologists suggest as the only (remotely) possible site for events in the BoM. How is it possible that the Nephites felt they came to an uninhabited continent and never met the Mayas? "Most LDS literature on archaeology and The Book of Mormon ranges from factually and logically unreliable to kooky. In general, it appears that the worse the book, the more it sells." - John L. Sorenson, BYU professor and Mormon anthropologist.

14. Even without DNA test results, the evidence that the American Indians are not of Hebrew origin is overwhelming (language, skeletal structure, customs, stone-age technology). Every serious, unemotional, and unbiased investigator I know concludes that the origin of the American Indian is eastern Asia. The Church has taken the position that the actual origin of the American Indian does not invalidate The Book of Mormon or undermine the teachings of Joseph Smith. This position raises even more questions regarding prophecies and commandments in the D&C and teachings of virtually every prophet from Joseph Smith to Hinckley. Since they all taught that the principal ancestors of the American Indian is the Lamanite, and such is not the case, then we should follow the counsel of Duet 18:22 and disregard their warnings? When church members refer to Native Americans as Lamanites, this is commensurate to calling a black man a "nigger", and is of great offense to informed Native Americans. How should I use my influence to lovingly but assertively bring this bad habit to an end among church members?

15. Apologists have set forth a limited geography theory with DNA being swallowed up by the other indigenous tribes. These theories fall apart when you read, 2 Nephi 1:8 which explains that Lehi told his children that God had kept and preserved the land from "other nations" so the land would not be overrun, leaving them with no place for an "inheritance." Since this theory contradicts doctrine, it must be discarded.

16. Parallels between Ethan Smith's A View of the Hebrews and The Book of Mormon appear too numerous to be a coincidence.

A View of the Hebrews was published some 7 years prior to The Book of Mormon, and Joseph Smith almost certainly had access to a copy of the book (it was published only 30 miles away from his home. In fact, many believe Oliver Cowdery helped with the printing). Plagiarism cannot be proven, but circumstantial evidence for plagiarism is strong. If The Book of Mormon is indeed an original work, how is it possible that there are so many parallels and similarities? (As a teacher, my experience has been that shared inaccuracies indicate plagiarism beyond reasonable doubt, and that is the case here.) I have read the book A View of the Hebrews and attached my book report for reference. A more lengthy comparison of the works was done by BH Roberts, General Authority of the church, and is available for review at <<http://home.comcast.net/~zarahemla/BOM/parallel.html>>.

17. BH. Roberts lists parallels between Book of Mormon stories and Bible stories. I will not take time to reiterate them, the reader is referred to Brother Roberts book Studies of The Book of Mormon and www.mormonstudies.com for a complete discussion. One example is the similarity between the story of Alma the Younger and Paul in the New Testament. Consider the similarities and identical sequences of events: Both were wicked and on missions of persecution on their day of conversion. Both fell to the earth and had manifestations that were not understood by their traveling companions. Both were asked by the Lord why they were fighting against Him. Both became helpless: Paul was struck blind, Alma was struck dumb. Both went without food for two or three days, then immediately converted and began preaching. Both healed a cripple, both were cast into prison. Both prayed for deliverance and the Lord loosed their bands and caused an earthquake to open the prisons and allow their miraculous escapes. Since Joseph generally had an open King James version of the Bible next to his hat and peep stone, the evidence for plagiarism becomes more than strong. The similarities between Lehi's dream and a dream recorded in the journal of Joseph Smith Sr. is more than striking (see attached excerpt from the journal of Smith Sr.) Roberts also points out the common

phraseology between the Bible and The Book of Mormon, and several individuals have compiled listings of common phrases. Roberts goes on to point out the fantastic nature of the stories of The Book of Mormon, as compared to the Bible. While it obviously pained him to say it, he was obligated to state what would be obvious to later generations: The Book of Mormon, when read by a Bible scholar, reads like a series of fairy tales, almost to the point of insulting the intellect of an informed reader. Given all the evidence, how can an informed member ignore the apparent plagiarism of the Bible and the fantastic nature of the stories as being simply a combination of fiction and plagiarism?

18. I have been presented several articles that are so-called evidences for the truthfulness of The Book of Mormon. Since many church members have cited them as iron-clad evidence, it is appropriate to address them with unbiased scrutiny. The first is the story of the Egyptian fellow that translated The Book of Mormon from English into Egyptian. He noted that many of the awkward English phrases translated beautifully into Egyptian, which was a confirmation that the original text must have been written in Egyptian. Also, several words, such as 'ziff' have meaning in Egyptian and no meaning in English. Proof positive, right? Well, I noticed in 1977 as I read The Book of Mormon in French how many of the awkward English phrases translated beautifully into French. Also, there is the unmistakable French word 'adieu' in The Book of Mormon that has no English meaning. Applying identical logic, we should therefore also conclude that the original Book of Mormon must have been written in French. In reality, the English language, especially old English, is awkward and translating a work such as The Book of Mormon into any language is going to find ample phraseology improvements. Finally, given the number of unusual terms in The Book of Mormon, just about any language is going to find a word or two that are identical or have similarities. It should also be pointed out that The Book of Mormon was supposedly written in Reformed Egyptian taught to single individuals by non-native Egyptians over many generations in complete isolation from Egyptian people. Given normal language evolution, the phrase-

ology used to record The Book of Mormon would bear no resemblance to modern day Egyptian anyway. Reformed Egyptian (if such a thing ever really existed) must have nothing in common with standard Egyptian characters since Joseph Smith had zero luck translating the Egyptian papyri that eventually became the Book of Abraham (see Book of Abraham section).

19. The second evidence for The Book of Mormon has to do with the different writing styles found therein. Since the Book of Alma has a different writing style than the Book of Helaman (for example), according to some expert somewhere (no peer corroboration), The Book of Mormon could not have been concocted by a single person (Joseph Smith). Assuming that there are indeed significantly different writing styles present in The Book of Mormon, an argument could be made that this is a confirmation that Joseph Smith was using plagiarism and the writing styles and phraseologies changed as he changed source material documents. The source materials could have been the Bible, Ethan Smith's A View of the Hebrews, the Spaulding Manuscript, and material Joseph gleaned from sermons he had heard. Some have suggested that Sidney Rigdon submitted complete sections of The Book of Mormon from the Spaulding Manuscript Found, and the circumstantial evidence is compelling. It was common knowledge among Rigdon's descendants that Sidney was a principle contributor to The Book of Mormon. Spaulding's widow was convinced that Rigdon stole the manuscript, and those that had read the manuscript were struck by the oft-repeated phrase "And it came to pass", which is a trademark of The Book of Mormon. Another consideration is the evolution of the young Joseph Smith over the 7 year period from whence sprang The Book of Mormon. I believe, based on my life experience, that anyone's writing style changes most dramatically between ages 17 to age 24, and is strongly influenced by what that person is reading. A common misconception among LDS is that each book in The Book of Mormon was written by the person the book is named after, which is not true. Most of The Book of Mormon was supposed to have been written by Mormon, with Moroni writing 13 pages, Nephi writing 117, and others contributing only a few

pages each. Helaman and Alma were supposedly written by a single man, Mormon. The presence of different writing styles, if such exist, could easily be interpreted as evidence of plagiarism and against the truthfulness of the work.

20. Another evidence for the truthfulness of <u>The Book of Mormon</u> is the apparent miracle of the translation. The rapid dictation, how Joseph was able to restart exactly where he left off in the narrative, and spelling words with which he was unfamiliar. The simplest explanation is that Smith was tucking portions of the Spaulding manuscript into his hat. It also turns out that the dictation of <u>The Book of Mormon</u> fits very comfortably into the category of 'automatic writing' that is well-documented. Automatic writers have routinely produced very lengthy works in a very short time, picking up where they left off, even in mid-sentence, hours or days after having interrupted the dictation. Some automatic writers have actually been able to pen a letter to a friend while earnestly dictating. Other automatic writers have found their gift is heightened by gazing into a crystal or translucent stone. The book <u>Jane Eyre</u> was produced via automatic writing, as well as <u>The Urantia Book</u>. Automatic writers often feel their gift is of God and their works are inspired, which could have led Joseph to believe that he was called of God. This explanation fits with the method of dictation: Joseph peering into his hat through a peep stone and no golden plates required. It also fits with his inability to decipher Egyptian characters on the papyri 12 years later.

Ten centuries ago a handful of Norse sailors slipped into Newfoundland, established small colonies, traded with local natives, then sailed back into the fog of history. In spite of the small scale of their settlements and the brevity of their stay, unequivocal evidence of their presence has been found, including metalwork, buildings, and Norse inscriptions. Just six centuries earlier, <u>The Book of Mormon</u> tells us, a climactic battle between fair-skinned Nephites and dark-skinned Lamanites ended a millennial dominion by a literate, Christian, Bronze Age civilization with a population numbering in the millions. Decades of serious honest scholarship have failed to uncover credible evidence that these Book of Mormon civilizations ever existed. No

Semitic languages, no Israelites speaking these languages, no wheeled chariots or horses to pull them, no swords or steel to make them. They remain a great civilization vanished without a trace, the people along with their genes. - Simon Southerton, Losing a Lost tribe, p. 199

If instead of containing only the ideas very typical of nineteenth century people, The Book of Mormon instead contained references to something yet unknown in Mesoamerica – for example, the ballgames or bloodletting ceremonies – then certainly the book would demand a second look. Instead, not only does The Book of Mormon fail to provide any such new, post 19th Century information, but it contains context that is anachronistic to ancient Mesoamerica, both materially and socially, that utterly fail the "if... then" line of questioning.

How can an honest and informed person logically dismiss this evidence and continue to pretend that the civilizations and conditions presented in The Book of Mormon refer to a real people?

Witnesses to The Book of Mormon

Most church members lend credence to the powerful testimonies of the "three witnesses" and "eight witnesses". I have been among those, as was my father, Reuel Lamborn. I was surprised to find out that the experiences of the witnesses were all through what was referred to as 'second sight' in the terminology of the day. The seeing of the angel, seeing the plates, and even handling of the plates were not actual physical events for any of the witnesses. It was only while they were carried away in vision did they experience anything. The Whitmers were staunch believers in second sight and their visions and experiences smack of one-upmanship as I read the accounts. Many of the witnesses were reluctant to sign the witness documents prepared by Joseph Smith due to the literal and physical tenor of the documents. Martin Harris testified publicly that none of the signatories to The Book of Mormon saw or handled the physical records. Stephen Burnett wrote the following in a letter dated 15 April 1838 to Lyman Johnson:

> ...I came to hear Martin Harris state in public that he never saw the plates with his natural eyes, only in vision or imagination, neither

Oliver or David & also that the eight witnesses never saw them and hesitated to sign that instrument for that reason, but were persuaded to do so.

On August 11 1838, Warren Parrish wrote: "Martin Harris, one of the subscribing witnesses, has come out at last, and says that he never saw the plates, from which the book is purported to have been translated, except in vision and he further says that any man who says he has seen them in any other way is a liar, Joseph [Smith] not excepted."

To me, this is a denial of the testimony text as written in the preface to The Book of Mormon. When instructors and church leaders assert that none of the witnesses ever denied what they had seen/heard, this seems to be telling a half-truth at best. I need to discuss this with a church leader as to the appropriate manner and forum in which the whole truth should be told. Remaining silent on something so plain and important is interpreted by many as accord, which makes me uncomfortable, since I am not in agreement with what is being taught.

I was also surprised to find out that after Smith was killed, a man named James J. Strang professed to be the successor to Joseph Smith, translating characters from metal plates. Strang showed these plates to hundreds of people, produced 11 witnesses, and translated them, producing the "Book of the Law of the Lord". There is no direct evidence that any of the men ever denied their testimonies, which were similar to those in the preface to The Book of Mormon. Three of the Whitmers, Martin Harris, Hiram Page, William Smith, and Lucy Smith all followed Strang's leadership from 1846 to 1847. This replication of an earlier pattern of belief gives us an idea that it may not have been as difficult as we might imagine having the witnesses accept Joseph's claim of having gold plates as an ancient record. Axiom: WHAT ONE MAN CAN DO ANOTHER MAN CAN DO.

And while we are on the subject of witnesses, 51 people willingly signed the following affidavit:

We, the undersigned, have been acquainted with the Smith family, for a number of years, while they resided near this place, and we have no hesitation in saying, that we consider them destitute of that moral character, which ought to entitle them to the confidence of any community. They were particularly famous for visionary projects, spent much of their time in digging for money which they pretended was hidden in the earth; and to this day, large excavation may be seen in the earth, not far from their residence, where they used to spend their time in digging for hidden treasures. Joseph Smith, Senior, and his son Joseph, were in particular, considered entirely destitute of moral character....

When the account of the 3 and 8 reluctant witnesses to The Book of Mormon is mentioned in the Church, why do we ignore the statement of these willing and adamant witnesses?

The Book of Abraham

The original papyrus scrolls that Joseph Smith translated into the Book of Abraham were found in 1967 and authenticated by LDS and independent scholars. Over a half dozen Egyptologists, including the expert hired by the Church, verified that the scrolls are Egyptian funerary documents typically found buried with mummies, and post-date the time of Abraham by 1500 years. The information contained on these scrolls bears no resemblance to the Book of Abraham and could not have been "in Abraham's own hand" as asserted by Joseph Smith. Joseph's own cross-reference showing the characters and the corresponding meanings is complete nonsense, according to every Egyptologist who has examined the documents, some of which are in Joseph Smith Jr.'s own hand, according to handwriting analysts. With the Urim and Thummin and Joseph's expertise developed during The Book of Mormon translation, the translation of the papyri should have been a two or three day effort. The fact that it took three men about 8 months to 'decipher' raises a question regarding authenticity. All of the participant diaries indicate that the work was a literal translation, not a revelation inspired by funerary documents and vignettes as some LDS apologists suggest. None of the participants mention anything about funerary documents or excerpts from the Book of Breathings which are actually found on the papyri. An attempt to answer this question is found in the "I have a Question" forum on lds.org, but the explanation is insufficient. After examining all the facts, the serious investigator can only conclude that Joseph Smith was NOT capable of translating Egyptian. And furthermore, the alphabet and grammar that Joseph took great pride in and quoted later in life were obviously contrived gibberish. If Joseph Smith was indeed a Seer, had the Urim and Thummim, and God's blessing to translate, plus a load of experience in translating The Book of Mormon, how is it possible that the papyrus scrolls could not be translated? If the Pearl of Great Price is indeed a literal translation, in Abrahams' own hand, as claimed by Joseph Smith and others in diary accounts, and noted in the Preface, how does one explain this dichotomy?

With regard to the translation of the Book of Abraham, since Moroni kept the gold plates that were the purported source of The Book of Mormon, the translation of the Book of Abraham is the only opportunity that we have to judge whether Joseph Smith really could interpret Egyptian characters by the "gift and power of God". If Joseph Smith could not translate these documents that yielded 11 pages of English text in 8 months (1.4 pages per month) with help, then how is it possible that he translated the 531 pages of The Book of Mormon in 19 months (28 pages per month) without help?

The Book of Abraham contains lengthy descriptions of astronomy and physics. Some examples:

Explanation of facsimile #2, Fig. 5 we read; "... this is one of the governing planets also, and is said by the Egyptians to be the Sun, and to borrow its light from Kolob through the medium of Kae-e-vanrash, which is the grand Key, or, in other words, the governing power, which governs fifteen other fixed planets or stars, as also Floese or the Moon, the Earth, and the Sun in their annual revolutions. This planet receives its power through the medium of Kli-flo-is-es, or Ha-ko-kau-beam, the stars represented by numbers 22 and 23, receiving light from the revolutions of Kolob."

Abraham 3:1-9 there is a lengthy description of the reckoning of time. The scripture states that "the set time of the lesser light which is set to rule the night."

The idea that some stars borrow their light from other stars was a short-lived theory among scientists in the 1830 timeframe. The theory that there was some medium in space that transmitted power and conducted gravitational forces was prevalent until about 1920. Now we know there is no medium. The laws governing relativity and time have nothing to do with the night or day or proximity to a particular star, only relative velocity as a percentage of the speed of light. This has been proven using atomic clocks and satellites. Planet or star rotation does not create light, light is emitted from the thermonuclear fusion process in active stars. None of the <u>Book of Abraham</u> theories on astro-physics match what has been discovered using the scientific method. Latter-Day prophets have taught that true religion and true science will always agree, yet with the <u>Book of Abraham</u> there is direct contradiction. How is this possible?

Overwhelmed by evidence against the authenticity of the <u>Book of Abraham</u> and the <u>Book of Moses</u>, the RLDS Church (Community of Christ) no longer considers these works to be part of its canon of scripture. When will the LDS Church face the music and follow suit?

<u>Joseph Smith History</u>

The account of the first vision is not readily reconcilable with historical information. The body of evidence indicates that Joseph experienced an epiphany or second sight experience, which was common and sort of an expected prerequisite for Protestant ministers of the day. Neither Joseph Smith nor anyone else prior to 1838 referred to the vision as authority to act as God's agent of the restoration. No one, friend or foe, remembers any persecution or even a claim to have experienced a vision prior to 1827. The persecution that began in 1827 was tied to money-digging and treasure hunting, not associated with a claim to have seen God. Had Joseph's mother Lucy heard her son say that Jesus Christ had personally instructed him to "to go not after them" and to not "join any" church because "all" of the ministers, creeds, and churches were "an abomination in His sight," she and her several children certainly would not have joined the Presbyterians and worshipped with them from 1825 to 1828. Historians agree that the ("great excitement") revivals occurred in 1824-1825, citing fifteen documented sources. No source can be found for an 1820 revival or any religious excitement that year. Having a young man claim to have seen God and Jesus Christ would surely have been the talk of the town and found its way into local papers, letters of local inhabitants, diaries, especially the diaries of the Smith family. There are no such accounts from that time period, not from friends, family, or enemies. Such a lack of third-party evidence defies all logic and reason. Early portrayals of the Godhead as a single entity in the The Book of Mormon would surely have brought forth questions in Josephs mind and not found their way into The Book of Mormon, and there would not have been any need for corrections to The Book of Mormon text after the first manuscript was drafted. How can an honest and informed member of the church accept the Joseph Smith history as accurate in light of the surrounding circumstances: lack of third party corroboration, and contrary evidence?

One of the many things that drew me to the Joseph Smith story was the unusual sequence of events that led up to obtaining the gold plates. I thought the story of the multiple visions, waiting periods, etc. much too odd to be contrived by a young man. Recent information [see Grant Palmer's An Insiders View of Mormon Origins for a detailed discussion] now points to an uncanny number of parallels between the Joseph Smith History account and a series of folk tales written by ETA Hoffmann (ETAH). A listing of each parallel would take pages to enumerate. Not only are individual events paralleled, sequences of events are shared between the two works. One example is that the plates could only be delivered on the day of the fall equinox. ETA Hoffmanns' tale has the treasure also being delivered on the day of the fall equinox. While it remains possible that the folk tales of ETAH merely influenced the fuzzy recollections of Joseph, or that ETAH had inspiration regarding the restoration of the true gospel, such is implausible (giant leap of faith at best). How can an honest and informed member of the church accept the Joseph Smith history, especially the story of the coming forth of the golden plates, as an original work?

In the trial of 1826, Joseph Smith was brought before the court on charges of fraud (money digging for profit). While apologists are quick to assert that Joseph was never convicted of any crime, whether or not there was a conviction is beside the point. At this trial, Joseph freely admits, under oath, that he was incapable of locating buried treasures using either his peep stone or while being carried away in vision. Anyone who objectively studies the trial of 1826 will reach one sure conclusion: At this time of his life, Joseph Smith was in the business of making money by preying on the superstitions of the people. Bear in mind that this is 6 years after the reported date of the 'First Vision'. Does it make logical sense that a young man of 19 years who had experienced a visitation from God would find his way into this line of business? The money digging went on for years, this was not just a one-time foible or lark. Objective historians agree that this early modus operandi set a pattern that lasted his whole life, while apologists dismiss this as just being a temporary weakness that Joseph was able to work through and put behind him. Which is it? In order for the members of the church to objectively examine the history of Joseph Smith, should not this information be brought up during church discussions on the subject? If not, why?

Joseph Smith produced three versions of his history, the official history of Joseph Smith that is accepted as part of scripture was the third and last attempt. The first two written histories made no mention of two personages in the vision. It was only after other prominent church members began claiming that they had had visitations from heavenly beings did Joseph Smith 'remember' that he had experienced a visitation from God and Jesus Christ, and that he had received a special directive to be the leader of the restoration. Any trial lawyer or judge will tell you that a witness that changes his story with each telling is an unreliable witness and his testimony is always set aside. For what possible reason would a rational and reasonable person place credence in such flimsy story-telling?

In summary, the Joseph Smith story fails all the truth tests – and rather miserably. There is no third-party corroboration of any of the facts or events. The story, if true, has people doing unreasonable and illogical things. The highly questionable metamorphosis of the account and evidence of plagiarism really removes any doubt to an objective investigator: the story is contrived.

It should also be mentioned that the stories that Joseph relates regarding baptism, restoration of the Priesthood, and other visitations from heavenly messengers follow the same pattern. The memory and the recording of the event happens well after the supposed occurrence, and each event morphs from the metaphysical to the physical, and becomes more embellished with each telling. In a court of law, testimony from such a source is set aside.

Kinderhook 'Translation' Hoax

I insert fac-similes of the six brass plates found near Kinderhook... I have translated a portion of them, and find they contain the history of the person with whom they were found. He was a descendant of Ham, through the loins of Pharaoh, King of Egypt, and that he received his Kingdom from the ruler of heaven and earth. - Prophet Joseph Smith, Jr., *History of the Church*, v. 5, p. 372

The six brass plates were actually fabricated out of copper by Wilber Fugate. Fugate admitted having used acid to burn the engravings into the copper and make them look old, then placing them where they were sure to be found. Smith fell headlong into this trap and was caught in a lie. How can a reasonable member dismiss this behavior and accept other 'translations' by Smith in good faith?

Polygamy

Since I have polygamist ancestors on both my father's and mother's sides of the family, this is not a trivial question or issue for me. I was taught that the reasons for polygamy were to build up the kingdom rapidly and to take care of women whose husbands had been killed.

1. Why did Joseph and other General Authorities marry young girls?
Helen Mar Kimball, born 20 Aug 1828, married Joseph Smith May 1843
  (14 years old)
Lucy Walker, born 30 Apr 1826, married Joseph Smith 1 May 1843
  (17 years old)
Sarah Lawrence, born 13 May 1826, married Joseph Smith abt 11 May
  1843 (nearly 17 years old)
Sarah Ann Whitney, born 22 Mar 1825, married Joseph Smith 27 Jul
  1842 (17 years old)

Nancy Mariah Winchester, born 10 Aug 1828, married Heber C. Kimball 10 Oct 1844 (16 years old)

This seems to serve no practical purpose. Fourteen-year-old girls are barely able to take care of themselves, let alone raise a family with a husband who is sharing time with 20 other women and their kids. I need clarification on this one.

2. Why did Joseph marry women that were already married?

Example: Zina Diantha Huntington born 31 Jan 1821. Married Henry Bailey Jacobs on 7 March 1841. Married Joseph Smith on 27 Oct 1841 while still married to Henry. After Joseph's martyrdom, married Brigham Young on 2 Feb 1846. (Source: Official church family history web site: http://www.familysearch.org/Eng/Search/frameset_search .asp) This seems contradictory to D&C 132: 61, which says that to be justified in taking more than one wife, the woman must not be vowed to any other man.

3. It is a documented fact (multiple accounts diaries, personal histories, and the LDS family search website) that Joseph Smith Jr. took multiple plural wives without the knowledge or consent of Emma. He was also caught in adultery with Fanny Alger. He persuaded women who were already married to marry him. Most (or all) of these marriages were performed outside of the temple, also verifiable using the same sources and documented Church history of the temples. Five different people (Joseph Smith, Joseph F. Smith, Benjamin F. Johnson, Mary Lighter, and Lorenzo Snow) assert that an angel of God with a sword commanded Joseph to institute polygamy or the angel would slay him. This event goes contrary to everything I have come to believe regarding agency, angels, and the nature of God. I can only conclude that this is a contrived vision to convince young women to marry him, which worked wonderfully well. The scriptures tell us that in the mouths of two or three witnesses all things are established, so I (as will any sincere investigator) accept these marriages and the so-called threatening angel story as fact. This presents a dilemma for me. How do I explain this to an investigator of the church? The progression from adultery to spiritual wifery to polygamy to polyandry casts a large shadow of doubt over the revela-

tions Joseph Smith Jr. received during the latter years of his life. We are reminded frequently in the church that iniquity drives away the spirit and we lose any right to revelation. How would it be possible for Joseph to continue to receive revelation from God if he was not keeping God's commandments himself?

4. From Mormon Doctrine, page 578, second edition, Bruce R. McConkie, sustained as a prophet, seer, and revelator: "Obviously the practice will commence again after the Second Coming of the Son of Man and the ushering in of the millennium." This statement runs counter to the Gordon B. Hinckley assertion that polygamy is in the LDS past. Which is it? Is polygamy a practice never to be reinstated in this life, or only put on hold because it is against the current laws of the land?

5. Jesus practiced polygamy. (Brigham Young, Journal of Discourses, Vol 1, pg 119-120) True or false? If false, do I also discount other doctrines taught by Brigham Young? If true, may I bring this up in Gospel Doctrine when discussing the life of Jesus? After the movie "The DaVinci Code", Hinckley asserted that Jesus was never married and did not have children. Whom shall I ignore, Gordon B. Hinckley or Brigham Young?

6. Brigham Young, JoD, Volume 11, pg 269 "The only men who become Gods, even the Sons of God, are those who enter into polygamy." What is to be made of this doctrine?

7. Why was Wilford Woodruff sealed to 267 women? Mar 1, 1877 - Wilford Woodruff describes his 70th birthday celebrations: "I was there Surrounded with one hundred and fifty four virgins, Maidens Daughters and Mothers in Zion from the age of fourteen to the Aged Mother leaning upon her Staff. All had assembled for the purpose of Entering into the Temple of the Lord to make me a birth day Present by being washed And Anointed and receiving their Endowments for and behalf of One hundred and Thirty of my wives who were dead and in the spirit world . . ." After the temple ceremonies are completed Woodruff attends a party in his honor where "their was presented before me a present of a birth day Bridal Cake three Stories high . . ." A poem composed and read for the occasion includes the lines "We meet to day with Joy to act

A proxy for thy dead,/ And Give thee scores of wives who'll be Like Crowns upon thy head" On Woodruff's next two birthdays women go to the St. George Temple and act as proxies in sealing plural wives to him. In 1879 he writes that it "makes 267 in all of the dead single women who have been sealed to me in the Endowment House in Salt Lake City, and in the St George Temple."

Worthy of note: The fact that temple marriage and polygamy stand or fall together was made very clear by Charles Penrose who was a counselor in the First Presidency of the Church. Elder Penrose showed that the revelation (DC 132) was the only one published on Celestial Marriage and if the doctrine of plural marriage was repudiated so must the glorious principle of marriage for eternity, the two being indissoluble interwoven with each other. (Millemial Star, Vol 45, page 454.) Polygamy is an integral part of LDS doctrine and attempts to distance the church from it are lip service. For that matter, why doesn't the church allow polygamy to be practiced today in countries where it is legal?

Seer Stones

Every eyewitness account of the translation of The Book of Mormon describes Joseph Smith peering into a hat through a peep stone. Russell M. Nelson, Dallin Oaks, and other church leaders have confirmed this modus operandi. Various figures in the Old Testament possessed implements with divine powers, rods being the most common. Another passage in the Old Testament condemns use of such items (Leviticus 20:27; Deuteronomy 18:11; 1 Samuel 28:7; 1 Chronicles 10:13). Many have associated the use of such stones with the occult, and the debate rages on. The debate is of no real importance to me. What is important is that the use of peep stones was part of the mystical and magical environment that enveloped the people living in the early 1800's. Virtually all persons having a belief in 'second sight', visions, etc. also believed implicitly in the power and use of peep stones. It permeated the society. Every man who lived on the earth," Joseph said to them, "was entitled to a seer stone, and should have one, but they are kept from them in consequence of their wickedness, and most of those who do find one make evil use of it." (Brigham Young's journal, as quoted in Latter-day Millennial Star, 26:118,119)

On three occasions, Joseph Smith admitted that, in reality, he could see nothing through the peep stones; twice while under oath in a court of law, and the third time was to his father-in-law Isaac Hale. One has to judge when a human being be more prone to tell the truth; (1) Under oath in a court of law and to one's father-in-law while assuring him that his daughter was in good hands, or, (2) while telling stories to a wealthy and superstitious Martin Harris. You be the judge, but I am inclined to believe that Joseph Smith was telling the truth in court and to Isaac Hale and he could not, in fact, discern anything with the peep stones. The stone and hat were simply props to give the appearance of a mystical translation/revelation process. Joseph also used the stones for other revelations, not just the so-called translation of The Book of Mormon. If revelation through seer stones is the proper method revealed by God for his 'prophets, seers, and revelators', why aren't they still in use today? Why does the church of today distance itself from this practice if it is a divine conduit to reveal the will of God? Since Smith taught that all righteous men were entitled to a peep stone, does one conclude that the men of the LDS faith today are all wicked?

And what should be made of the attempt to sell the copyright of The Book of Mormon in Toronto, Canada? Joseph peered into his hat using the stone and purportedly received a revelation that this endeavor would succeed. Hiram Page and Oliver Cowdery went on this mission and failed. Upon their return, Joseph inquired of the Lord regarding this failed attempt, and the following revelation came through the stone: "Some revelation are of God; some revelations are of man; and some revelations are of the devil." If the method of revelation is unreliable (by Smiths' own admission), how can we be sure of any of Smiths' so-called 'revelations'?

Mathematical Viewpoint

It may seem cold and harsh to apply mathematical theory to examine the claims of the church. However, the work of Galileo and other pioneers of truth, in the face of adversity, have historically borne fruit. Mathematical truth is one facet of the scientific method, and is unique in that there can be no debate regarding correct results. There is no opinion, no bias, and no room for discussion. This is the unique beauty of mathematics: it stands on its own. Granted, an assigned probability or an estimated probability is only an opinion, but in engineering analysis, generous assumptions are routinely used as tools to obtain irrefutable results. This method is tried and true and will be employed in this section.

Another mathematical certainty has to do with cumulative probability. When two experiments or items are required to be positive, their probabilities are multiplied together to determine the probability of both experiment A and experiment B being positive. For example, if the chance of rain is 10% today and 25% tomorrow, the chance of getting rain on both days is $0.10*0.25 = 0.025$, or only 2.5%. Simply stated, events that are unlikely become much more unlikely if they are connected to other events which must also have a positive outcome.

Hypothesis: In order for the claims of Joseph Smith to be factual, three key items must be positively true:

1. The events of the first vision as written in Joseph Smith history must be factual.
2. The Book of Mormon must be an actual translation of a history and not conjured.
3. The Book of Abraham must be an actual translation of papyri or actual revelation from God.

The Joseph Smith story fails all truth tests quite miserably (see Joseph Smith History section). But I will be very generous and say that there is a 10% chance that his story is true, or $p_1 = 0.10$. If this seems unfair to the reader, factor in the actions of Joseph Smith family members and lack of corroborating testimony of persecution, etc. I assert that this probability is very generous in light of all the evidence at hand.

The Book of Mormon has eight references to days of the month. They are as follows:

Day	Month	Year	Verse	Circumstances
1	1	66 BC	Alma 52:1	Assassination of Amalickiah
2	1	62 BC	Alma 56:1	Helaman sends an epistle to Moroni
4	1	34 AD	3 Ne 8:5	Destruction before Jesus visits the Nephites
5	2	81 BC	Alma 16:1	Lamanites begin a war against the Nephites
3	7	Abt 64 BC	Alma 56:42	Account of a war between Nephites and Lamanites
4	7	81 BC	Alma 10:6	Alma the younger is converted
12	10	81 BC	Alma 14:3	Alma the younger is freed from prison
10	11	72 BC	Alma 49:1	Lamanites march on the city
41	(Sum)			

There is nothing in the circumstances of the events to expect that they would be biased toward the first part of the month. In other words, we would expect these events to be randomly distributed throughout the days of the months. For 8 random month dates, the mean of the sum would be about 8*15.5 = 124. For the sum of 8 random month dates to be as low as 41 is relatively improbable. It is relatively simple to quantify the probability using a random number generator (in EXCEL 'randbetween') and repeat the experiment, counting the times that the sum of 8 random numbers between 1 and 30 is less than or equal to 41. I performed this experiment 1 million times, and got 139 positives, a statistically significant experiment. The probability of 139/1000000 is p_2 = 0.000139 or about 1 positive every 7200 tries. There is therefore a 1/7200 chance that these dates describe randomly distributed events in history, and there is a 7199/7200 chance that the work is fiction and the writer of the book had a tendency to favor dates close to the first of the month for some reason. (See also Duwayne R. Anderson, "Farewell to Eden" pp 330-340) This is a very generous probability, since we are ignoring all the other incongruities associated with the book.

The probability that the <u>Book of Abraham</u> is an actual translation of the papyri or a revelation from God is probably the most remote of the three. Nobody who has honestly researched this matter (who I know) has reached the conclusion that the <u>Book of Abraham</u> is an actual translation, and this includes many devout church members, including General Authorities. Therefore, the only remaining possibility for the believer is that the book is a pure revelation inspired by the papyri, and Joseph Smith misrepresented the revelation as a translation and cooked up the alphabet to justify the purchase of the papyri to the destitute saints to avoid their ire.

Therefore, the most fair approach in evaluating the truth of the <u>Book of Abraham</u> is to ignore the obvious deception regarding the purported "by his own hand" claim and assume that the book was pure revelation. Remember, the <u>Book of Abraham</u> is where we are told that God wanted to withhold the rights of the priesthood to the black-skinned people (Abraham 1:26-27) Is this an eternal truth? In addition, we must ask ourselves what the probability is that the astro-physics revealed in the book constitute eternal truths. That lesser stars "borrow" light from greater stars, that there is a medium of energy transference in space, and that somehow light emissions are tied to planet or star rotation, and that time reckoning has something to do with the night and/or proximity to a particular star or planet. Any physicist would assign a probability of zero to the possibility that these phenomena are eternal truths. I will assign what I consider a generous probability of one in ten thousand. My justification is that there are at least 10,000 expert physicists in the world today that would assign a lower probability than this, and I believe in the scientific method and cumulative results of science in this arena over the last 90 years. A one in ten thousand probability is $p_3 = 0.0.0001$.

The cumulative probability that the restoration is an eternal truth and not contrived is therefore the product of the three:

$$P_{cumulative} = p_1 * p_2 * p_3 = 0.10 * 0.000139 * 0.0001 = 1.39 * 10^{-9}$$ or about one in a billion.

Mathematically, this is a low enough probability to safely ignore the hypothesis. The great mathematician Pascal, the co-inventor of statistics, wrote that no matter how small the probability that religion is true, it makes sense to follow it, because the reward is infinite. This is commonly referred to as Pascal's Wager. Pascal realized that the probability of any religion being true is small. Pascal actually embraced Jansenism and gave up doing math and focused on religion. Now Jansenism is an insignificant footnote in religious history and all but forgotten. On the other hand, Pascal's mathematics will live on and will benefit mankind forever. Pascal, due to religious pressures, only gave mankind perhaps 1/100 of the math that he was capable of giving. What a waste of a wonderful intellect. I submit that it is more important to learn from Pascal's mistake than follow his advice. [Pascal's argument also illogically assumes that God would reward a pretended belief.]

How can the informed and logical church member be expected to supplant mathematical evidence with the nebulous and unreliable 'whisperings of the spirit"?

In Conclusion

I believe that many things can be established as truth beyond any reasonable doubt using the truth tests described and the scientific method. Unfortunately, the existence of God and knowing His will are not among those things that can be established beyond any reasonable doubt. Any who assert otherwise have been deceived or are delusional by definition and should not be trusted. In theology, the bare truth is that certain key tenets are unknowable.

Humility has been defined as nothing more than consistently recognizing truth and accepting the truth with all its consequences. To cling to a myth despite overwhelming contradictory evidence, denying the possibility that one has been deceived, and then purporting to occupy the higher moral ground is false pride at its ugliest and a manifestation of sociopathic behavior.

My entire research experience can be summed up in a conclusion reached by Hippocrates in 400 BC: "There are, in effect, two things: to know and to believe one knows. To know is science. To believe one knows is ignorance."

I believe that organized religion is beneficial only to the extent it helps its members be kind to other people and tolerant of others with different belief systems. Unfortunately, organized religion has a less than stellar track record in this regard. I do see this improving with time, and hope this trend will continue. I also hope that those who have read this document will adopt a more tolerant view of religion, abandon fanatical and ethnocentric tendencies, and resolve to treat all humans with kindness and respect, including friends and family who adjust their belief systems to align more closely with reality.

To me, trying to mix obvious illusions with spirituality is more frustrating than comforting. "All that the human race has achieved, spiritually, and materially, it owes to the destroyers of illusions and the seekers of reality." – Erich Fromm. I am resolved to abandon illusion and seek reality.

-Lyndon Lamborn, June 2007

Recommended reading:

Studies of The Book of Mormon	B.H. Roberts
An Insiders View of Mormon Origins	Grant Palmer
The Keystone of Mormonism	Arza Evans
Mormon Enigma, Emma Hale Smith	Newell and Tippetts
Farewell to Eden	Duwayne Anderson
No Man Knows My History	Fawn Brodie
By His Own Hand Upon Papyrus	Charles M. Larson

Book Report: A View of the Hebrews 1825 2nd Edition, Ethan Smith
(First edition was published in 1823)
Republished by Religious Studies Center, BYU, First Printing, 1996
With an introduction by Charles D. Tate Jr.

Tate's introduction indicates the huge variation in conclusions reached by historians regarding this books' influence on Joseph Smith. It all boils down to frame of mind and maintaining an objective viewpoint. The famous incident with BH Roberts and the Quorum of the 12 in 1922 (p ix)* and his letter to Heber J. Grant (p xvii) are mentioned. Tate also mentions that Oliver Cowdery was a printer in the town that first printed the book and may have actually helped with the first printing (<u>A View of the Hebrews</u> p xviii). What the introduction fails to mention that I believe is key to setting the stage is that the origin of the Native American was front page news as Joseph Smith was growing up. Someone who could explain where these people came from would be **Batman** (Ref BH Roberts, <u>Studies of the The Book of Mormon</u>).

The basic premise and thrust of <u>A View of the Hebrews</u> is that Native Americans are actually descendants of the lost 10 tribes of Israel. The 10 tribes departed into the north country and then went east and north, and eventually traversed the Bering Strait to the Americas. Much of the book is devoted to studying the customs, traditions, ceremonies, legends, etc. of the American Indian and pointing out similarities to Hebrew traditions, ceremonies, holidays, etc.

There are stark differences between <u>A View of the Hebrews</u> and <u>The Book of Mormon</u>, which apologists are quick to point out. <u>A View of the Hebrews</u> has the migration over the Bering Strait, which could have been frozen and not involved ships, whereas <u>The Book of Mormon</u> has a great sea voyage. The <u>A View of the Hebrews</u> work focuses on the 10 tribes aspect, whereas <u>The Book of Mormon</u> has only the families of Lehi and Ishmael. <u>A View of the Hebrews</u> quotes 775 BC as the date of the destruction of Jerusalem, <u>The Book of Mormon</u> starts at 621 BC with the event to follow. <u>A View of the Hebrews</u> discusses pyramid building at length (p 154-155), <u>The Book of Mormon</u> has virtually nothing on pyramids. <u>A View of the Hebrews</u> discusses parchments (p 168-169), <u>The Book of Mormon</u> has gold plates. Tate mentions a book that points out 84 "un-parallels" that could be added to these main ones (p xvii).

The most damning evidence FOR plagiarism is shared inaccuracy. This is primarily what I was looking for as I read. The shared inaccuracies, as I see them are as follows:

1. The use of iron and mastery of working with iron (p 129, 147, 148, 150)
2. Vast populations and great wars (p 143, 148, 151)
3. The assertion that the hunter-gatherer lifestyle is lazy (143)
4. Native Americans are of Hebrew descent (entire book) (see also #4 on parallels list)
5. Native Americans observed the Law of Moses before Christianity was introduced

History teaches us that the hunter-gatherer lifestyle is the most primitive existence and leaves virtually zero idle time. It is only through cultivated crops, irrigation, domesticated animals, specialization, division of labor, and permanent settlements can civilizations support people with idle time. Therefore, I count both <u>A View of the Hebrews</u> and <u>The Book of Mormon</u> as inaccurate on this point, which may seem too subtle to be counted to many readers. I submit that I know of no other books that portray hunter-gatherers as idlers.

Weaker clues for plagiarism are common ideas. The shared ideas or parallels (that I could perceive) are as follows (BH Roberts lists 18 and can be viewed at <u>http://home.comcast.net/~zarahemla/BOM/parallel.html</u>:

1. Both books begin with the destruction of Jerusalem and banishment of Israel.
2. Use of the words "remnant" and "Gathering of the dispersed of Judah" in the introductions.
3. Use of the literal gathering of Israel as a theme.
4. Native Americans are of Hebrew origin, also a shared inaccuracy.
5. Stick of Judah, stick of Joseph, Ezekial 37 prophecy fulfilled (pg 34)
6. The people were of one color skin originally (p 114, 157)
7. Savage hunting tribes annihilated the more civilized tribes (pp 130-131, 143)
8. Ancient works, forts, mounds, vast enclosures, skill in fortifications (p 130-131)
9. Advanced metal working of all kinds (p 144)
10. Breastplate description (p 149)

11. Burying records in boxes (p 168-169)
12. Use of the phrase "Bring them to a knowledge of the gospel" (p 177)
13. Allegory of the olive tree and the House of Israel
14. Sacred records being handed down from generation to generation and then buried in a hill
15. Even though the migrating peoples were Hebrew, somehow Egyptian languages are involved
16. Both books use the terms "Zion" and "Mt. Zion" to designate restoration/gathering places.
17. Both books call upon the American people to preach the gospel to the Native Americans
18. Both books predict the eventual conversion of the "remnants" and that they will become white before the burning of the world. Smith uses the phrase "white and delightsome".

Anticipating that readers would have doubts about his book, Ethan Smith said:

Ye friends of God in the land addressed; can you read this prophetic direction of the ancient prophet Isaiah, without having your hearts burn within you?

Compare to <u>The Book of Mormon</u> promise:

And when ye shall receive these things, I would exhort you that ye would ask God, the Eternal Father, in the name of Christ if these things are not true; and if ye shall ask with a sincere heart, and with real intent, having faith in Christ, he will manifest the truth unto you, by the power of the Holy Ghost.

It is also interesting that Ethan Smith quotes the 11th chapter of Isaiah in his book. Joseph claimed the angel Moroni quoted the exact same chapter to him in his bedroom on September 12, 1828. Also interesting is the similarity of the name "Ether" to "Ethan". It could easily be coincidence, or it could have been Joseph Smith's sense of humor kicking in, a sort of inside joke that only he was privy to. Ideas for metal plate records may have come from long-winded descriptions of metal working (p 144, 146, 149). Joseph Smith would have definitely felt he was on solid ground asserting that the native Americans were of Hebrew descent after reading <u>A View of the Hebrews</u> based on 11 "proven" points (p 59), all of which have since been shown to be complete folly.

Bottom line: I agree with BH Roberts. The average reader will get the impression of plagiarism when comparing the two works. Could Joseph Smith have written the The Book of Mormon with this and other books as source material, an active imagination**, a background of Biblical study, keen intellect, a flair for writing or blessed with automatic writing skills, and some good sermon ideas from local pastors, popular doctrinal questions***, and poignant family life experiences (faith and seed, Tree of Life, Iron rod, etc.)? Not outside the realm of possibility in my mind. Twenty years ago I would have said NO WAY! After twenty more years of reading fiction, I have to admit that it is possible. If Edgar Rice Burroughs can create a fictional world on Mars and write 33 complex books with hordes of names and personalities to grip the reader, others with that creative talent can do likewise. I cannot bring myself to ignore this axiom: "WHAT ONE MAN CAN DO, ANOTHER MAN CAN DO."

* The incident of B.H. Roberts briefing the First Presidency and the Quorum of the Twelve in 1922 is classic and deserves special mention. Roberts spent several hours outlining for the brethren all of the 'problems' with <u>The Book of Mormon</u> as compared to historical and scientific evidence (domesticated animals, steel, plants, language, etc.). He then went on to describe the book <u>View of the Hebrews</u> and discussed the many parallels. He records in his diary that several members of the Twelve were visibly shaken by this information. Roberts, known today as 'The Defender of the Faith', was seeking guidance and direction, hoping the brethren could shed some light on his quandary and help him in the defense of the faith, and allow him to address the issues in an open format for the benefit of all church members. Roberts could foresee the day that this information would present itself to his descendants and was hoping for logical explanations he could provide to his progeny. He was gravely disappointed. All he got from around the table was testimony bearing (last bastion of the unreasonable fanatic), and a consensus opinion that for the church to openly address these issues would not benefit the cause and should therefore be squelched. Some months later, BH Roberts received a call to the eastern states mission. Thus began the pattern of hide, deny, duck, dodge, and misdirect that continues today.

**Regarding Josephs' vivid imagination, Joseph's mother Lucy wrote: "During our evening conversations, Joseph would occasionally give us some of the most amusing recitals that could be imagined. He would describe the ancient inhabitants of this continent, their dress, their mode of traveling, and animals upon which they rode; their cities, their buildings, with every particular; their mode of warfare; and also their religious worship. This he would do with much ease.... as if he had spent his whole life with them."

Excerpt from the journal of Joseph Smith Sr. (Note similarities to the dream of Lehi)

I was traveling in an open desolate field, which appeared to be very barren. As I was this traveling, the thought suddenly came into my mind that I had better stop and reflect upon what I was doing, before I went any farther. So I asked myself, what motive can I have for traveling here and what place can this be? My guide who was by my side, as before, said, "This is the desolate world; but travel on". The road was so broad and barren, that I wondered why I should travel in it; for I said to myself, "Broad is the road and wide is the gate that leads to death, and many there be that walk therein; but narrow is the way and straight is the gate that leads to everlasting life, and few there be that go in thereat." Traveling a short distance further I came to a narrow path. This path I entered, and, when I had traveled a little way in it, I beheld a beautiful stream of water which ran from the East to the West. Of this stream I could see neither the source nor yet the termination; but as far as my eyes could extend I could see a rope running along the bank of it, about as high as a man could reach, and beyond me, was a low, but very pleasant valley, in which stood a tree, such as I had never seen before. It was exceedingly handsome, insomuch that I looked upon it with wonder and admiration. Its beautiful branches spread themselves somewhat like an umbrella, and it bore a kind of fruit, in shape much like a chestnut bur, and as white as snow, or if possible, whiter. I gazed upon the same with considerable interest, and as I was doing so, the burs or shells commenced opening and shedding their particles or the fruit which they contained, which was of dazzling whiteness. I drew near, and began to eat of it, and I found it delicious beyond description. As I was eating, I said in my heart, "I cannot eat this alone. I must bring my wife and children, that they may partake with me. Accordingly I went and brought my family, which consisted of a wife and seven children and we all commenced eating, and praising God for this blessing. We were exceedingly happy insomuch that our joy could not easily be expressed. While this engaged, I beheld a spacious building standing opposite the valley which we were in, and it appeared to reach the very heavens. It was full of doors and windows, and they were all filled with people, who were very finely dressed. When these people observed us in the low valley, under the tree, they pointed the finger of scorn at us, and treated us with all manner of disrespect and contempt. But their contumely we utterly disregarded. I presently turned to my guide, and inquired of him the meaning of the fruit that was so delicious. He told me it was the pure love of God, shed abroad in the hearts of all those who love him, and keep his commandments.... I asked my guide what was the meaning of the spacious building which I saw. He replied, "It is Babylon, it is Babylon, and it must fall. The people in the doors and windows are the inhabitants thereof, who scorn and despise the Saints of God, because of their humility." – Joseph Smith Sr.

*** Alexander Campbell, one of Joseph Smith's contemporary critics, points out that:

This prophet Smith, through his stone spectacles, wrote on the plates of Nephi, in his Book of Mormon, every error and almost every truth discussed in N. York for the last ten years. He decides all the great controversies – infant baptism, ordination, the trinity, regeneration, repentance, justification, the fall of man, the atonement, transubstantiation, fasting, penance, church government, religious experience, the call to the ministry, the general resurrection, eternal punishment, who may baptize, and even the question of freemasonry, republican government, and the rights of man. All these topics are repeatedly referred to. (Millenial Harbinger, February 7, 1831)

I would add that he also provided explanations for the origin of the American Indian, gives a partial accounting for the lost ten tribes of Israel, and expounds on why skin colors differ among human races, all important issues of Smith's era.

APPENDIX F
DISCIPLINARY COUNCIL
TRANSCRIPT

<u>**Transcript, Excommunication of Lyndon Lamborn August 19, 2007,**</u>
<u>**Mesa AZ Salt River Stake, President R. James Molina Presiding**</u>

Stake Pres:
Brethren, I would like to introduce Lyndon Lamborn to you of the
Thunder Mountain Ward. Lyndon, I don't know if you know of every-
one here, but if you would look around, and..

Lyndon Lamborn (LL):
Just about.

Stake Pres:
as you look around, are you OK with everyone who is on this council
this morning?

LL:
I count all of you as my friend, yes. I am very comfortable with that,
President, thank you.

Stake Pres:
We would like to begin with a prayer and I will ask Brother P...
[prayer cut out for brevity]
Amen.

Stake Pres:
Lyndon, you and I have had the chance to speak several times, I don't
know if you and I have talked about how this generally is executed – I
may just expound on that a little bit more. I will talk briefly and just give
an overview and ask you if you agree with that overview of what I say to
everyone here. And will give you an opportunity to express your feelings

on it. Then we will have a chance to ask a few questions and deliberate a time and then come back together.

The overview that I would give that you and I talked about last time as we sat in council based on talks with you that you not only no longer believe in the teachings of the church......But also have taken some of your personal beliefs and findings and tried to persuade some members of the church into believing the same things or that you would maybe be opening their eyes to some of the facts that you had found and to me that is where the real issue lies. It is one thing for you to believe you are certainly welcome to believe what you would like, but when you start to take those things to other members of the church and persuade them not to follow the commands of the prophets, requires church discipline.

Is that a, a true overview?

LL:
That is quite an accurate overview, President.

Stake Pres:
Now we wanted to give you an opportunity to express your feelings on it now as you have a right to do. I would ask you not to try to use this as a forum to share what your findings and views that are important to you with these brethren here but in any way you would feel that you wanted to express something that would defend what you have been doing or why you have been doing it. Um, certain things you feel that have led to why your testimony has diminished you certainly have permission to come forward and relate and cover the real things. And you are welcome to share those things.

LL:
Do I have a time limit?

Stake Pres:
No, just take a few minutes.

LL:

If it is OK, I would like to stand...

First of all, I'd like to express my love to each of you - I esteem all of you highly. And regardless of what happens today I count you all as my friends, and will ever count you as my friends. I have no ill feelings toward anybody in this room, nor to any member of the church. I think the most important thing in life is how we treat other people. And I hope the words that I speak to you today will be of use to you and will help you in your perspective, and in the future, because I hope life is long for all of you and I think that you'll have many life experiences ahead. And perhaps my life experience and my journey will help you under- stand, and soften your heart to people who are like me - maybe some of your family members will tread the path that I have trod. And you'll be able to look upon that with a love that transcends any belief that you might have. And to that end, let me begin my journey. And I think it's important that you hear this.

About two years ago, a woman at work, her name is [removed] came to me with this book, and it was called <u>Under the Banner of Heaven</u>, by Jon Krakauer.

And I had read a book by Krakauer, called <u>Into Thin Air</u>, about an as- sault on Mt. Everest.

I highly esteemed him as an author, I loved his writing style. And she said, "This book, Under the Banner of Heaven, discusses Joseph Smith, and his wives, and uh.... What can you tell me about this? I can't believe that such a highly respected religion like Mormonism would have this kind of skeleton in the closet."

And I said, "Well, I didn't know that Joseph Smith had other wives in this life, other than Emma. I was taught that he had Emma, and then later [after he died] he was sealed to other women. But I'll research it, and I'll get back to you."

Here I am, a four-year graduate of seminary, I've served a mission for the church, I've attended my church meetings faithfully since I was a boy, loved the gospel teachings, and have been an Elder's Quorum president four times, not to mention all the other callings I've had.

I said, "I'll get back to you." So I read the book. It seemed to have some good facts. I thought, 'Well, I'm not going trust one book,' so I went to Deseret Book, and located a book called Mormon Enigma, by Tippets and some other authors [Linda King Newell & Valeen Tippetts Avery], and I read that book.

And in that book it details Joseph's polygamy, and also polyandry, of course, which is taking another man's wife to have a sexual relationship with her...

What struck me most about [this book]... I can buy into polygamy, but what struck me about this book was the secrecy, first of all. That he kept all these liaisons from Emma, and that he used the story... [and this is] the second thing that struck me is he used - and six women all documented this same thing - he used the story that an angel with a sword appeared to him, and told him that he was supposed to propose marriage to a particular individual.

I ask you, brethren: How would you feel if President Hinckley proposed marriage to your wife, and asked your wife not to divulge any of this information to you?

To me, that was a defining moment. I realized at that moment that I don't think I want to believe in a God who would send an angel with a sword and threaten death to his prophet because he wouldn't take another man's wife to be his.

And at that point, I thought, 'The church has obscured this from my vision. For some reason. How many other things are out there that the church may have obscured?'

And that set me on a path. The last two years, I've spent almost all my free time researching this information. I've found that this was just the tip of the iceberg. And I was so sad, I was torn apart, as you can imagine.

I went through every emotion you can think of. And again, it was the tip of the iceberg.

I'd like to talk to you about suppression of information. Because that's what we're talking about.

Stake Pres:
I don't think that has a place in here – A discussion of suppression of information. I don't know – that is your perspective.

LL:
Well, I think it is the perspective of the founding fathers. If somebody has some information, whether it be truth or propaganda, if it's denied my view, if I'm kept from seeing that information... If the information is true and the facts are accurate, then I have lost the opportunity to exchange a misconception I may have had with truth - that's bad.

Stake Pres:
Well, …

LL:
If - Let me finish, please. If the information is brought to me as propaganda, and is error - it's entirely possible - then I can review that information, that propaganda, that error, compare it with what I [already] know, and I gain a deeper understanding of the truth I already had in its collision with error. Either way, blocking that information does damage to me. That's why we have free speech. That's why we should share information freely.

The church, I hate to say this, but it appears to me that the church suppresses information.

And the real question here is not my membership, it's that if the church suppresses information, take for example financial information. The church does not divulge their full financials. Has not for the last thirty years. And [the church] does everything they can to not disclose their financials. And that's a telltale sign. The question here is not my membership, I think. The real question here is - if this is an organization that suppresses information, then, why are we all here? We should be not just walking away, we should be running away from any organization that suppresses information.

I'm sorry to have to say that, but that is my perspective.

And, you probably want me finish up, I know, but our basis of - you probably want me to finish up, I know, but.

Stake Pres:
Lyndon, I would ask you to be respectful from the standpoint of allowing you to express feelings that pertain as to why we are here.

Now you, just now, have, have went on in a manner that, in speaking of suppression of information – I mean that argument could hold, could hold true anywhere, in any organization, because of the information, not knowing where it comes from, one might look at it as suppressed information, and where another would not. So it is open to our own interpretation as to what information has been suppressed and what is freely given. The scriptures are laid before us, I've never heard the church teach anything but the scriptures, your own revelation, your own inspiration, praying to find out if things are true or not. I mean to me, that is an invitation to everyone, young and old, to find anything out for themselves.

As far as the other information you mentioned of a book that would be condemning of the prophet Joseph Smith that was published by Deseret Book. Who owns Deseret Book?
[laugh]

There are plenty of books published by Deseret Book that do not smile upon the church, yet the church allows those things to be published.

You could verify that that information, is, is, that free speech I could say is able to be, ah, be utilized if people so choose. Wouldn't you think that if they were interested in suppressing information they would not have these type of books published?

LL: I think, yes, that's true. But since then they have taken it off the shelves of Deseret Book.

Stake Pres:
There are plenty of books at Deseret Book that follow the same line. But again, that is not the point here.

LL
Yeah, the point is that when we go to church week to week, we're told one side of the story, and 7/10's of the information that's available on various aspects of the church, whether it's the martyrdom, the Joseph Smith story, The Book of Mormon, the origins of The Book of Mormon, what we hear at church is not the full picture.

And that has been a - that **is** a problem for me. That that information was not described to me as I was a youngster, and growing up. And made me to look somewhat foolish in front of people outside the church.

Here was a woman that I worked with who knew more about Joseph Smith's personal life than I did, a lifelong church member.

Isn't that not embarrassing? Isn't that not a [a problem?] To me that was a problem.

And the upshot here is that it did not work for me. And I hope there is something that you can take back [to church authorities] along those lines.

The other thing that I've expressed to you before, president, and I think that it's important to these brothers here, is [regarding] our basis of testimony as promised in Moroni, essentially. Study things out in your heart, pray, and receive a spiritual witness. Which I have felt, I have felt that emotional witness, that burning, that tingling in my spine... Whatever, however it happens to you, I'm sure it happens to you, I have no doubt about it.

However, I've found that particular stimulus to be unreliable. I felt that same stimulus when I listened to Paul H. Dunn as a young boy, and his experiences in the trenches in the Philippines, I had that same feeling. Yet now we know that those stories were contrived. I get the same feeling sometimes, when I hear a song by Nickelback, or read a patriotic story about a soldier, I get those same feelings - Not a bad feeling at all. However, it's unreliable [as an indicator of truth].

And if we had a man come to your door, with a bag of crack cocaine, with instructions on how to use it, say, "Okay, use [the crack cocaine] like this, and if this feels good and works good for you and your family, then you should buy crack cocaine from me for the rest of your life."

You would say, I'm not going to trust the drug dealer on the instructions on how to use that bag of cocaine, because he stands to profit from it. Then why would you trust the writer of a book, and the truth test, and [a method for how to] discern truth? It's a circular reasoning problem.

Stake Pres:
What you are saying though, is that, what we define as a spiritual witness which I wouldn't say is the same as an exciting rush of adrenaline, what you are saying is there is no way for us to have a spiritual witness.

LL:
I am saying that the spiritual witness as proposed in <u>The Book of Mormon</u> is unreliable [as the ultimate truth test]. Some people have even gone so far as to describe it as a recipe for self-deception. That may be a little over the top.

Stake Pres:
Tell us what a spiritual witness is, then. How would you describe a spiritual witness?

LL:
I would say, something, a feeling, deep in your soul, that enlightens you. That helps you believe, or trust something to be good and worthwhile.

Stake Pres:
Do you not believe <u>The Book of Mormon</u> to be good and worthwhile? What do you read in <u>The Book of Mormon</u> that would lead you to believe it is evil and not worthwhile?

LL:
I think it is a very worthwhile book, don't get me wrong. The historicity of <u>The Book of Mormon</u> is the problem. The church proposes that the book is historically accurate.

That [Book of Mormon people] are real characters, living in real places, in this world, that had the animals, and the crops, the cattle, the sheep, the cureloms and cunoms that Timo and I were talking about last week, the barley and the wheat, [that were not present] here on this continent.

...<u>The Book of Mormon</u> is full of wonderful things, President. I have no problem with that. but the idea that [the events of <u>The Book of Mormon</u>] actually transpired is really not a debate for me anymore. There are too many problems with <u>The Book of Mormon</u>. For example: Language. How could a people in 400 A.D. – all be speaking the same language and then have so many languages present here when the Europeans arrived?

How could Nephi have a steel bow in 620 B.C., when steel hadn't been invented yet? Or the processing for steel [necessary to construct a steel bow] hadn't been invented - it was still 2000 years away, at least. Everything around us we owe to the development of steel, the history of steel is well-known. It just didn't exist in 600 B.C. I'm sorry. And steel is very difficult to eradicate the signs of fabrication. Once you make steel you leave telltale signs a long, long time.

How did the brother Jared know about [clear] glass, and the properties of glass when he was building the barges, 2000 years before glass was invented?

I could go on for a half an hour about the historicity problems with <u>The Book of Mormon</u>.

Stake Pres:
You are telling us things here Lyndon, that really don't apply.

LL:
The problem here, President, is when everybody in the room testifies of <u>The Book of Mormon</u>, based on that spiritual witness. To me, by my standard, you would have the answers to all these questions, how all these things were possible, when in fact, I don't think you do. I don't think you have those answers. To me that's bearing false witness. And I think all of us in this room need to take accounting and be careful not to bear false witness.

If you look at - pick up an Ensign from general conference issue, and read how the brethren bear testimony, they bear testimony in such a way that they are not [asserting], in general, the historicity of <u>The Book of Mormon</u> or the divinity of the prophet Joseph Smith. Look at their words carefully, see if I'm wrong. But the reason I think they do that is because they fear God. And they fear the consequence for bearing false witness. And I want you, brethren, not to be guilty of bearing false witness.

There are plenty of things [of which] you can bear witness to <u>The Book of Mormon</u>. It's got wonderful teachings in it. By all means bear testimony to how you felt when you read them, how they affect your family. These are all wonderful things.

But bearing testimony to the historicity of <u>The Book of Mormon</u> without knowing these facts is a combination of ignorance and false pride - I'm sorry. And I would urge you to take heed to these words.

Now I'll close, and I'll sit down, President, you've given me ample time. I just wanted to say that I think there's plenty of room in my heart for the Church, but my training as a missionary, however, prevents me from being quiet.

It's just part of my makeup, I guess. That I tend to share things that I've learned, and I'm sure of, and I don't think I can agree to any kind of a restriction about praying or speaking up in church... I think it's really a question of, you can welcome me as a brother, or you can get a court order and have me not come to church. It's kind of those - Those are the two options that I think that are available to you.

I would invite any of you, if at any point in your life, you desire to know, about the things I've spoken... If your desire to know the truth – the real truth - about the history of the church, and how we've gotten to where we are today, becomes greater than your desire for the warm fuzzy feelings and illusion of security that's found in the church, I will buy you dinner. And I would be glad to talk to you about it. And at any point, you are welcome at my campfire. And I love all of you, and hold you all in high esteem, and as my friends.

Stake Pres:
Thank you Lyndon, we would like to invite you to go out for a few minutes while we deliberate and invite you back here.

LL:
OK, brethren. [leaves the room, closes the door].

So let the deliberations begin!
[a few minutes later]

(LL re-enters the room)

Stake Pres:
Lyndon, it is the decision of the council, this morning, that you are excommunicated from the Church of Jesus Christ of Latter-Day Saints. And with that, advise you of a letter you will receive that will describe all that takes place as part of excommunication, that, of course, you are no longer a member of the church you are certainly, in the same vein that you have expressed love and friendship to us... to participate, in that same love and friendship, and invite you to attend church and would ask that you would respect the environment that you are in and those you talk to let them to worship how, where, and what they may, by you.

In the same way I would go sit in on another congregation of another faith if you hear someone teaching and trying to worship. If you are willing to be with us in those circumstances we would like to have you with us and continue a bond of friendship. Is there anything you would like to say in closing?

LL:
No, just thank you all for your service, and your dedication, and the great people that you are, and I just want to let you know that I love all of you, and wish to remain your friend. Okay. And, uh, since my, especially my wife and son still are attending and enjoying being members of the church, I'll plan to attend. And I'll try to remain as positive as I can, and I think it'll be very positive... Well I should have a positive on the ones around me, because I like to treat other people with respect, and respect their beliefs, too. So I will do my best.

Stake Pres:
I appreciate that.

LL:
'OK – thank you all brethren... I have an original work of mine, a time-line here. If anyone would like one, I'm going to leave a stack here. Just as food for thought. If anybody would like one. I'm kind of proud of it, I guess, is all I'm saying. Take care, have a nice Sabbath.

LL leaves building… (speaking to the recorder in the parking lot)
So that was it, August 19th, 2007, 7am... It's over. I am no longer... Well, after the paperwork's all signed and delivered, I'm no longer a member of the church. The feeling is... Quite exhilarating. No longer will I have to say I'm a member of the church when asked, which is something I think I really wanted, deep down.

So, that ends it!

APPENDIX 6
EXCOMMUNICATION APPEAL

President James Molina 11 September 2007 (Patriot Day)

<u>Salt River Stake</u>

Dear President Molina,

I am in receipt of your letter dated September 2nd 2007. I was disappointed to hear the description of the planned course of action.

As you recall, in our final private discussion, you described the course of events to have my records removed:

1. I was to receive some papers in the mail, which I could sign and forward to Salt Lake City. Rather, I received the summons to the disciplinary council.
2. You assured me that nobody would find out about my research and conclusions, at least not through you. That assurance of confidentiality has apparently evaporated since the disciplinary council.

I was never offered any explanation why there was a departure from this original plan, I only assumed that it was what you wanted to do or were directed to do. [I was happy to discuss my situation with the High Council, and share with them the greatest of all gifts, the gift of knowledge.]

The finding of guilty for apostasy was the assessment of the council, based on the councils' definition of apostasy, not my definition. The main charge and tenet was distribution of materials that ran contrary to accepted church orthodox belief. I would counter that I distributed nothing but facts, and clearly stated when I was offering an opinion. Are we not all entitled to an opinion? Are distribution and discussion of facts considered apostasy? If so, I am guilty as charged.

I personally hope that Church leaders will eventually face the realities surrounding the origins of the Church, the RLDS (Community of Christ) has already made this leap and faced the music. Who is to say that in 10 or 20 years, the LDS Church will not follow suit? The day may not be far off that the entire church membership may actually agree with my conclusions regarding the historicity of The Book of Mormon (for example). I believe this scenario to be not only possible, but somewhat likely. Today the Church formally apologized, for the first time, for the role played by Church leaders in the Mountain Meadow Massacre. This was a huge step in the right direction. 25 years ago, nobody would have dreamt this to be possible, yet today it is reality.

Joseph Smith himself wrote that he did not like the concept of a creed, which a man must believe or be asked out of the Church. *"I want the liberty of believing as I please, it feels good not to be trammelled. It don't prove that a man is not a good man, because he errs in doctrine."* Joseph also was quoted as saying: *"The most prominent difference in sentiment between the Latter-day Saints and sectarians was that the latter were all circumscribed by some peculiar creed, which deprived its members of the privilege of believing anything not contained therein, whereas the Latter-day Saints have no creed, but are ready to believe all true principles that exist."*

Similarly, President Joseph F. Smith testified before the Congress of the United States that Latter-day Saints *"are given the largest possible latitude of their convictions, and if a man rejects a message that I may give to him but is still moral and believes in the main principles of the gospel and desires to continue in his membership in the Church, he is permitted to remain."* At the same time, he added,

Members of the Mormon Church are not all united on every principle. Every man is entitled to his own opinion and his own views and his own conceptions of right and wrong so long as they do not come in conflict with the standard principles of the Church. If a man assumes to deny God and to become an infidel we withdraw fellowship from him. But so long as a man believes in God and has a little faith in the Church organization, we nurture and aid that person to continue faithfully as a member of the Church though he may not believe all that is revealed."

I still believe in God and have good confidence in the Church organization. Therefore, by the standards of President Joseph F. Smith, church membership should not be withdrawn from me.

From my viewpoint, my education and indoctrination through a life-long membership was insufficient to prepare me for the real facts regarding the origins of the Church. I have turned away from conspiring to hide the facts and the truth. I am resolved to champion the truth and discuss all facts and reality. If this is considered apostasy, then I am guilty. If the Church cannot withstand scrutiny of the facts, that is not my problem.

LDS church pews are filled with closet doubters. I am come forward with my doubts, and have been open and honest. In what way does this behavior merit a public announcement that defames my character and embarrasses my family? Since when is researching the facts and embracing all truth and knowledge considered apostasy?

Finally, the announcement to the wards in the stake serves no Christ-like purpose. Nobody is going to ask me to give a talk, that is a non-issue. Non-members are allowed and encouraged to pray, and are instructed that partaking of the sacrament is optional, since it holds no meaning for a non-member. At least these were the policies regarding non-members when I was in the mission field. Furthermore, I could move 1 mile away, be in another stake in 6 weeks, and the announcements would have served no purpose, except to pain and embarrass my family. In short, the announcement tactic is just plain cruelty, and is not something that will lead to any positive effect on anyone.

If you have any regard for me and my family, you will find a way to avoid the announcements to Melchizedek Priesthood and Relief Society groups. I hope and pray that you will soften your heart and avoid this impending catastrophe. Please feel free to forward this letter to the First Presidency as you see fit.

Sincerely,
Lyndon Lamborn

APPENDIX H
MESA EAST VALLEY TRIBUNE
ARTICLE 9/23/07

Mormon ousted as an apostate

Being excommunicated for apostasy by the Mormon church is one thing, but Lyndon Lamborn is livid that his stake president has ordered bishops in eight Mesa wards to take the rare step of announcing disciplinary action against him to church members today.

"I thought if he could go public, so can I," said Lamborn, a lifelong member of the Church of Jesus Christ of Latter-day Saints, who said his research into church history gave him "thousands of reasons the church can't be what it claims to be."

Stake President R. James Molina acknowledged Friday he intends to have Lamborn's excommunication announced to the wards at men's priesthood meetings and womens Relief Society gatherings, even with Lamborn now taking his case public. Molina, as well as officials at church headquarters in Salt Lake City, call such a public warning about an ousted member extremely rare.

They say, however, church members must be protected from what discordant ex-followers may say to damage the church.

In a letter to Lamborn dated Sept. 2, Molina noted that a disciplinary council had been held Aug. 19 and excommunication was ordered. Lamborn, 49, a Mesa resident who has been a priesthood leader for 20 years, was informed he was no longer a church member, could not "enjoy any membership privileges, including the wearing of temple garments and the payment of tithes and offerings."

He could attend public meetings if his conduct is orderly, but would be denied giving any talks, offering prayers, partaking of the sacrament or voting.

"Because of the nature of your excommunication and your involvement with people in this area, an announcement will be delivered to the Melchizedek Priesthood quorums and Relief Society in each of the wards in our stake ... on Sunday, September 23, 2007, that you have been excommunicated for apostasy," Molina wrote.

"We need to let people know if there is a danger to them, such as him teaching doctrine that is contrary to what is taught by the church," Molina said Friday.

Lamborn, a member of the Thunder Mountain Ward, said his Mormon roots go back generations, with a great-grandfather in the famed Mormon Battalion that trekked from Iowa to San Diego in 1846 and 1847.

Lamborn served a two-year Mormon mission in 1977-79 in Belgium, was elders quorum president four times and led a Mormon Boy Scout troop. Most recently, he said he was assigned to teach older men in his ward and held other roles.

But everything changed in early 2005. Lamborn, an engineer employed at Boeing in Mesa for nearly 25 years, was asked by a work colleague about the wives of church founder Joseph Smith. She had read "Under the Banner of Heaven: A Story of Violent Faith" by John Krakauer and asked Lamborn if what she had read was accurate.

Smith, the first LDS prophet and president, had at least 33 wives by many accounts.

"Well, I had no knowledge of multiple wives, so I did some research, including using the church's own genealogical Web site, familysearch.org," Lamborn said.

He found the information concurred with the book. "Nonmembers seemed to know more about the personal life of Joseph Smith than me," he said.

Lamborn conducted further research, which led him to question many church teachings. He said he went to Molina with his questions, but received no definitive answers.

Lamborn has been attending the three-hour ward meetings with his wife and 16-year-old son. His two daughters, 22 and 24, "are totally out of Mormonism."

He said he learned that his five brothers "were doing the same research and arriving at the same conclusions" and doubts, he said. The same was true for his best friend since childhood. In a meeting earlier this summer with Molina, Lamborn acknowledged that he wanted to give up his church membership.

"I was planning to leave the church quietly, but was denied that opportunity, presumably because I was speaking openly to other members about my findings and (was) writing things down," Lamborn said.

Lamborn has compiled his research into a lengthy testament called, "Search for Truth 6/07," in which he states: "There comes a time in the life of many church members when the desire to know the truth about the church becomes stronger than the desire to believe the church is true."

He said he intends to continue to accompany his wife, Nancy, to ward services.

"It is tough to go, tough to attend, but I enjoy the fellowship," he said.

He said he has no desire to join another church, adding that the Mormon faith has many merits, such as its strong family values and its internationally recognized welfare system to help those in need.

The public announcement of his excommunication will be toughest on his wife, Lamborn said. "There's the embarrassment," he said. "Friends won't know how to treat her. The awkwardness. It is going to be tougher on her than anybody."

Clark Hirschi, manager of the area relations division in Salt Lake City, said Friday he talked to Molina after the stake president was contacted by the Tribune.

"Despite the fact that he has told you this is going to happen, it is up to the priesthood leaders," Hirschi said. "There may be a letter read to some of the adult members this Sunday. It might be in a few weeks. It may not happen. That is going to be at the discretion and call of the stake president."

Hirschi said he has never been in a meeting in his own 20 years as a Mormon where a public announcement about an excommunication has been made. He said he had only heard of one being made in a neighboring stake.

APPENDIX I
THE WHISKEY ANALOGY
APPLIED TO CHRISTIANITY

Whenever I am asked my opinion about Christianity I am reminded of the response of Circuit Judge N.S. Sweat, Jr., of Corinth, Mississippi, when during a prohibition campaign he was asked where he stood on the whiskey question. He said:

> If when you say whiskey you mean the devil's brew, the poison scourge, the bloody monster that defiles innocence, dethrones reason, destroys the home, creates misery and poverty, yea, literally takes the bread from the mouths of little children, if you mean the evil drink that topples the Christian man and woman from the pinnacle of righteous, gracious living into the bottomless pit of degradation and despair, and shame and helplessness, and hopelessness, then certainly I am against it.

> But if when you say whiskey you mean the oil of conversation, the philosophic wine, the ale that puts a song in their hearts and laughter on their lips, and the warm glow of contentment in their eyes; if you mean Christmas cheer; if you mean the stimulating drink that puts the spring into the old gentleman's step on a frosty, crispy morning; if you mean the drink that enables a man to magnify his joy, and his happiness, and to forget, if only for a little while, life's great tragedies, and heartaches, and sorrows; if you mean that drink, the sale of which pours into our treasuries untold millions of dollars, which are used to provide tender care for our little crippled children, our blind, our deaf, our dumb, our pitiful aged and infirm, to build highways and hospitals and schools, then certainly I am for it. This is my stand. I will not retreat from it. I will not compromise.

That's sort of how I feel about Christianity. If when you say Christianity you mean the faith that asks its members to be honest, true, chaste, and treating all humans equally, that applied love and service is the path to happiness, that frowns on discrimination, elitism, and tribalism, that teaches its affiliates to reach out with compassion and substance to the poor, the homeless, the infirm, the widowed, the lonely, the elderly, that wholeheartedly endorses each mans privilege of experiencing spirituality how and when he chooses, and takes no pride in itself, is willing to embrace all truth and emerging knowledge openly, is willing to abandon outdated fables, embraces uncertainty regarding the historicity of its canon, and readily admits to error among its officials and is quick to correct injustices, then certainly I am for it and want to be counted in its ranks. I will not retreat from it. I will not compromise.

But if when you say Christianity you mean organizations that teach that man is in a fallen state and naturally chooses evil, that there is a capricious God who is compelled to punish those who choose what is taught is evil, an organization that values gullibility, sanctions discrimination and inhumanity found in its infallible canon, asks its members to surrender their free will, fears the imaginary and grants power to demons, abuses children with guilt and shame, teaches its affiliates that the promise of a reward in the afterlife is a prime motivation for choosing good in this life, that there is a God who expresses displeasure by visiting mankind with illness, disease, floods, and disasters; organizations that ban the reading of any religious material not approved by church leaders and denies public access to archives; if you mean organizations take money from their membership to build more buildings and pay their clergy, that teach that there is only one way to properly experience spirituality, and God's rewards will be withheld from non-Christians, that non-Christians are spiritually deficient and in need of conversion, if you mean the collective organizations that teach its members to obey without question everything their leaders ask, while purporting to know God's will, and refuse to admit wrong-doing, being rigidly opposed to dismissal of primitive legends found in its canon in light of emerging truths, then certainly I am against these organizations and do not want to be considered among their rank and file. This is my stand. I will not retreat from it. I will not compromise.